CLIMATE FINANCE

ECONOMIC TRANSFORMATIONS

Series Editors: Brett Christophers, Rebecca Lave, Jamie Peck, Marion Werner

Fundamental to the *Economic Transformations* series is the belief that "geography matters" in the diverse ways that economies work, for whom they work and to what ends. This series publishes books that evidence that conviction, creating a space for interdisciplinary contributions from political economists, economic geographers, feminists, political ecologists, economic sociologists, critical development theorists, economic anthropologists and their fellow travellers.

Published

Climate Finance: Taking a Position on Climate Futures
Gareth Bryant and Sophie Webber

The Doreen Massey Reader
Edited by Brett Christophers, Rebecca Lave, Jamie Peck and Marion Werner

Doreen Massey: Critical Dialogues
Edited by Marion Werner, Jamie Peck, Rebecca Lave and Brett Christophers

Exploring the Chinese Social Model: Beyond Market and State
Weidong Liu, Michael Dunford, Zhigao Liu and Zhenshan Yang

Farming as Financial Asset: Global Finance and the Making of Institutional Landscapes
Stefan Ouma

Labour Regimes and Global Production
Edited by Elena Baglioni, Liam Campling, Neil M. Coe and Adrian Smith

Market/Place: Exploring Spaces of Exchange
Edited by Christian Berndt, Jamie Peck and Norma M. Rantisi

CLIMATE FINANCE

Taking a Position on Climate Futures

GARETH BRYANT AND SOPHIE WEBBER

agenda
publishing

First published in 2024 by Agenda Publishing

Agenda Publishing Limited
PO Box 185
Newcastle upon Tyne
NE20 2DH
www.agendapub.com

ISBN 978-1-78821-462-9

British Library Cataloguing-in-Publication Data
A catalogue record for this book is available from the British Library

Typeset by Newgen Publishing UK
Printed and bound in the UK by 4edge

CONTENTS

ACRONYMS AND ABBREVIATIONS

AOC	Alexandria Ocasio-Cortez
CDM	Clean Development Mechanism
CDP	Carbon Disclosure Project
CEFC	Clean Energy Finance Corporation
CEO	Chief Executive Officer
CERs	Certified Emission Reductions
COP	Conference of the Parties
DAC	direct air capture
DICE	Dynamic Integrated Climate-Economy
ECB	European Central Bank
EPA	Environmental Protection Authority
ESG	environmental, social and governance
ETFs	exchange-traded funds
ETS	Emissions Trading Scheme
EU	European Union
EU ETS	European Union Emissions Trading System
FSB	Financial Stability Board
FUND	Framework for Uncertainty, Negotiation and Distribution
GCF	Green Climate Fund
GDP	gross domestic product
GEF	Global Environment Facility
GFANZ	Glasgow Financial Alliance for Net Zero
GGSW	Great Garuda Sea Wall
GND	Green New Deal
IAMs	integrated assessment models
ILS	insurance-linked securities
IMF	International Monetary Fund

IPCC	Intergovernmental Panel on Climate Change
IPG	International Partners Group
JETPs	Just Energy Transition Partnerships
JUFMP	Jakarta Urban Flood Mitigation Project
MMT	modern monetary theory
NCICD	National Capital Integrated Coastal Development
NGO	non-government organization
OECD	Organisation for Economic Cooperation and Development
PAGE	Policy Analysis of the Greenhouse Effect
PAYG	pay-as-you-go
PCRAFI	Pacific Catastrophe Risk Assessment and Financing Initiative
PPAs	power purchase agreements
PV	photovoltaic
QE	quantitative easing
TCFD	Task Force on Climate-Related Financial Disclosures
UN	United Nations
UNFCCC	United Nations Framework Convention on Climate Change
V20	Vulnerable 20 Group of Ministers of Finance of the Climate Vulnerable Forum

ACKNOWLEDGEMENTS

We acknowledge the Indigenous Traditional Owners of the Country on which we work and live: the Gadigal People of the Eora Nation. Sovereignty was never ceded. We pay our respects to Aboriginal and Torres Strait Islander Elders past and present and to Indigenous movements who struggle for self-determination and to protect Country. There is no climate justice without Indigenous justice.

This book was developed perhaps more remotely than its peers; its first ideas and concepts imagined amid the catastrophic bushfire smoke of late 2019, and in proposal form in uneasy meetings in February and March 2020. It then emerged from lockdowns and virtual encounters and survived several parental leaves and isolations. And still we are deeply indebted to co-thinkers, readers and listeners.

In particular, our thanks to Sarah Knuth and Brett Christophers for a deep and ongoing engagement with the book, to the Agenda editorial team led by Alison Howson and to series editors Rebecca Lave, Jamie Peck and Marion Werner. Thanks to Frank Stilwell and Michael Webber for reading the draft manuscript and posing insightful if challenging questions. Natasha Heenan, Luciano Carment and Ellen Wong provided superb research assistance.

More broadly, our ideas have developed in conference sessions, seminars and conversations, including at the annual conference of Institute of Australian Geographers, the annual meetings of the American Association of Geographers, the University of Sydney, University of Technology Sydney, Durham University, University of Manchester, University College London and City University of London, and through our wider research collaborations and communities. As such, we are grateful to discussions with Lisa Adkins, Wahyu Astuti, Tom Baker, Mike Beggs, Patrick Bigger, Naama Blatman, Sangeetha Chandrashekeran, Neil Coe, Dan Cohen, Joe Collins,

Linda Connor, Lisa Lumsden, Deanna D'Alessandro, Devleena Ghosh, James Goodman, Sandy Hager, Kate Harrison Brennan, Riikka Heikkinen, Elizabeth Humphrys, Kurt Iveson, Ryan Jones, Emma Johnston, Svenja Keele, Robert Kirsch, Martijn Konings, Paul Langley, Sophia Maalsen, Jon Marshall, Nate Millington, John Morris, Adam Morton, Tom Morton, Katja Müller, Sara Nelson, Peter Newell, Natalie Osborne, Mareike Pampus, Claire Parfitt, Susan Park, Matthew Paterson, Rebecca Pearse, Priya Pillai, Sage Ponder, Dallas Rogers, Emily Rosenman, Stuart Rosewarne, Amin Samman, David Schlosberg, Ben Spies-Butcher, Marc Stears, Amanda Tattersall, Blanche Verlie and Elissa Waters.

This book was supported financially and institutionally by the Australian Research Council Discovery Early Career Awards DE210101443 and DE210101175 and Discovery Project DP180101368, and the University of Sydney's Faculty of Science, Faculty of Arts and Social Sciences, Sydney Environment Institute, Sydney Policy Lab, Sydney Southeast Asia Centre, Research Portfolio and Sydney Research Accelerator (SOAR) prize.

Our most profound thanks to our families. Our loving partners, Kara Hill and Andrew Higgins have embarked with each of us on our biggest projects: August, Max and Hugo. We dedicate this book to them, and the climate futures they will demand, and produce.

CHAPTER 1

INTRODUCTION: FINANCE FEELS THE HEAT

In contemporary global capitalism, both finance and climate change reach into every aspect of our lives. These two phenomena are increasingly coupled together as "climate finance". Finance is core to calculating and resourcing decarbonization and climate repair. Climate change is also now central to the way money flows across governments, businesses and households. Financial instability and crisis are, moreover, interlinked with multiplying climate impacts and tipping points. Climate finance has, in short, become integral to the political economy and economic geography of climate change. As finance has been positioned as the solution to climate change, different actors have engaged with climate finance to take competing positions on what the future of climate change and capitalism might look like. The different tools of climate finance that have emerged both reflect struggles over climate change and are actively shaping climate transition pathways. The politics of climate change is now being fought on the terrain of climate finance.

The Copenhagen 2009 and Paris 2015 Conferences of the Parties (COPs) to the United Nations Framework Convention on Climate Change (UNFCCC) were both monumental meetings for international climate politics and climate finance. As the global agreement among almost all countries to attempt to avoid "dangerous" climate change, the UNFCCC makes decisions and seeks progress through its annual COP meetings. At the Copenhagen COP in 2009, one of the major advances was a commitment by rich countries – which under the Convention are called Annex I, or developed and industrialized countries – to fund mitigation and adaptation actions in poor countries – called non-Annex I, or developing countries. Initially, there was a commitment to provide US$30 billion per year of climate finance, and then up to US$100 billion per year by 2020. By the Paris COP in 2015, the Green Climate Fund (GCF), a newly established financial mechanism of the UNFCCC, was chosen to attract, distribute and programme this "climate finance". Since then, the GCF has disbursed funding to more than 200 projects in 130 countries that

1

seek to reduce emissions or facilitate adaptation, from increasing urban water supply to building solar photovoltaic (PV) power plants and much in between. Notwithstanding disagreements, including about governance and control and the balance between mitigation and adaptation projects, the GCF was widely celebrated as a step in the right direction towards recognizing the additional costs of climate change for poor countries.

By the Glasgow COP summit in late 2021, the US$100 billion pledge was again in the spotlight, this time for its numerous and systemic failures. Developed countries had fallen short of the annual US$100 billion target in climate finance: the Organisation for Economic Cooperation and Development (OECD), which tracks climate finance at the request of donor countries, found that only US$83 billion in climate finance was mobilized in 2020, building on approximately US$80 billion per year in 2018 and 2019 (OECD 2022a). Further, for critics, this figure is vastly inflated because it counts funding that is only barely related to climate change, is not additional to already committed development funding and it includes the value of loans that must be repaid. As a result, the international non-government organization (NGO) Oxfam argued that the climate finance mobilized was closer to US$20 billion per year (Carty, Kowalzig & Zagema 2020). There are also debates about the quality, character and benefit of the projects the GCF has supported. This failure in climate finance is a fundamental abrogation of responsibility from those who have caused climate change to those who will experience its impacts most acutely.

The GCF and other similar pledges have dominated public debate about climate finance. In this frame, climate finance references finance that goes from developed countries to developing countries as a reflection of commitments to the Convention and the base injustices of climate change. The goal of this climate finance is to cover the costs of adapting to climate impacts and decarbonization in countries that might not otherwise be able to afford it. This climate finance ought to be "new and additional" to any rich country's existing development assistance to avoid double counting or greenwashing existing aid commitments. It is often assumed that climate finance is public, grant funding with no strings attached; however, the calculation of US$83 billion in climate finance mobilized in 2020 includes both loans and private sector "co-financing" for climate activities. Commonly, funding refers to resources such as grants or state allocations that are not repaid, whereas co-financing suggests financial terms around the repayment of debt, usually with interest, or ownership equity, to capture returns.

But let us put the US$83 billion in perspective. The UNFCCC defines "climate finance" as all public, private and alternative financing that supports mitigation and adaptation. Global flows of finance with some kind of climate goal well exceed the COP targets for international climate finance. As the non-profit research organization, the Climate Policy Initiative, shows in its oft-cited Global Landscape report, climate-related investments reached an estimated US$850–940 billion in 2020–21 (Climate Policy Initiative 2022). Both of these figures, in turn, fall well short of the costs of avoiding dangerous climate change. The Intergovernmental Panel on Climate Change (IPCC), the organization that assembles the latest scientific information on climate change for policymakers, estimates that keeping within 1.5°C of warming will cost an average of US$3.5 trillion per year (de Coninck *et al.* 2018). Then, add to that the costs of adapting to the climate impacts already baked into the climate system and compensation owed for loss and damage. In other words, the politics of climate finance as conventionally understood represent just a fraction of existing and necessary future investment flows and institutional configurations related to climate finance.

At the same time as the failings of the Copenhagen climate finance pledge were being tallied, other seismic transformations in finance linked to climate change were emerging. These transformations expanded the sphere of climate finance beyond political negotiations at UNFCCC meetings to the centres of the global financial system. In a speech to the 2019 Climate Action Summit at the United Nations (UN) General Assembly in New York, the former Governor of the Bank of England and UN Special Envoy for Climate Action and Finance, Mark Carney, announced that "a new, sustainable financial system is being built" (Carney 2019). Carney outlined three pillars of this emerging system: comprehensive disclosure of climate-related financial risks by companies, such as fossil fuel corporations; new and improved forms of climate risk management both by private sector financial institutions, such as banks, insurers and asset managers, and by financial governance institutions, including central banks and financial regulators; and sustainable investment that not only excludes fossil fuels but embraces the opportunities presented by supporting the transition to a climate-friendly economy.

A few months later in January 2020, Larry Fink, the Chief Executive Officer (CEO) of BlackRock, took up Mark Carney's arguments. BlackRock is the world's largest asset manager, controlling over US$8 trillion in assets. It is a shareholder in most major companies around the world. In his annual and widely read letter to CEOs, Fink wrote that he believed "we are on the edge of a fundamental reshaping of finance" (Fink 2020). Referring to the potential financial impacts of climate change on everything from municipal bonds to home mortgages and inflation rates, Fink stated that "investors are increasingly reckoning with these questions and recognizing that climate risk is investment risk". Fink pledged to bring Carney's pillars for a sustainable financial system into BlackRock's operations, including integrating "environmental, social and governance" (ESG) measures into its investment portfolio, divesting from coal-focused companies, launching new "sustainable"

3

investment funds and voting against company managers and directors for failing to disclose and act on climate risks.

These announcements were not conjured up out of thin air. Divestment activists had coordinated a sustained programme of action against BlackRock and other financial institutions. These groups – from direct action environmental movement Extinction Rebellion to mainstream environmental NGOs such as Friends of the Earth – have piled pressure on BlackRock over recent years, compelling it to tackle climate change by "stopping the money pipeline" (Yearwood & McKibben 2020). Activists have highlighted the astonishing size of the fossil fuel assets under management at BlackRock and have lobbied for stock-market heavyweights to divest. In doing so, activists have made causal and global connections, linking BlackRock's investment decisions to ecological destruction and dispossession, such as deforestation in the Amazon and the violation of Indigenous peoples' rights.

The interventions from Carney, Fink and divestment activists are significant for the approach and argument developed in this book. First, they signal that climate finance is something that is embedded in and reshaping the core institutions of capitalism in a way that encompasses but far exceeds climate-related development finance, such as that of the US$100 billion climate finance pledge. The global geography of climate finance is not only one of fiscal transfers from the Global North to the Global South, but of investment and divestment. The ecological and economic effects of this emerging climate finance reverberate around the world through the capillaries of financial systems and commodity chains. In contrast, the billions of dollars that flow as climate-related development finance – while undoubtedly critical for the possibility of climate justice, for lives and ecologies in the Global South and the future course of global climate change – are dwarfed by the trillions in assets globally that are being made subject to climate change considerations. As Carney stated in his speech, although the shift to a new, sustainable financial system is not occurring fast enough to reach climate goals, climate change "will prompt reassessments of the values of virtually every financial asset" that will trigger a major reallocation of capital (Carney 2019). In divestment and environmental activist Bill McKibben's description, Fink's announcement may have caused a physical tremble in Manhattan, with the "sheer heft of ... money starting to shift" (McKibben 2020).

Second, these comments and actions signal which *kinds* of climate finance – in the broader sense – are becoming dominant, as climate change becomes increasingly central to capitalist finance. The focus on carbon disclosure, risk management and sustainable investing adds up to a vision for climate finance that privileges market-oriented climate action that is heavily influenced by conventional economic thinking. Private actors simply need better information to identify climate-friendly investments and reallocate capital accordingly. The role of state institutions is not to directly fund climate actions, but to create the architecture for markets to deliver efficient outcomes, to take on risks on behalf of the private sector to unleash the full potential of private investment. Carbon pricing may play a role, but this economic ecosystem comprises many, many more climate-mediated markets and financial tools. According to the dominant ideas and actors of climate finance, with these elements in place, climate change can be addressed and be highly profitable. As Fink bullishly outlined, "our investment conviction is that sustainability- and climate-integrated portfolios can provide better risk-adjusted returns to investors" (Fink 2020).

Third, while Carney and Fink represent the dominant version of climate finance, their visions and agendas have been heavily contested by climate movements. BlackRock's shift – at least at the level of discourse and policy – has faced scrutiny from environmental organizations and activists. BlackRock retains significant fossil fuel investments and has a record of voting against climate resolutions at company annual general meetings. A few months after Fink's 2020 letter, protesters gathered outside BlackRock's annual general meeting with banners reading "BlackRock: Hot Air on Climate" and "BlackRock: Stop Stealing our Future" (Corbet 2020). Carney too has felt the heat from climate activists. At the same climate summit that recognized the broken US$100 billion climate finance promise, COP26 in Glasgow in 2021, climate striker Greta Thunberg with activists from Greenpeace and the Indigenous Environment Network, walked out of an event hosted by Carney launching a taskforce aimed at scaling up voluntary carbon offset markets, shouting "no more greenwashing" and calling offsetting a "get out of jail for free card" (Shankleman & Ainger 2021). Significantly, pressure on finance has not only come from pro-climate action progressive activists. BlackRock's climate rhetoric has come under fire from Republican politicians in the US who have threatened to divest funds under their control or outright ban climate-conscious investing.

Political contestation over climate finance often occurs on the terms of the finance sector. Divestment activists argue that fossil fuels are bad investments with unacceptable financial risks. Right-wing politicians argue that finance should not be politicized and should seek only to maximize returns. Financial institutions such as BlackRock are careful to position their statements in line with their fiduciary duties. Nonetheless, the emerging politics of climate finance has real impacts on financial markets and climate change itself. The structural decline of coal assets, for example, while a market phenomenon, cannot be separated from political heat applied over coal investments.

In this book, we follow these developments to take climate finance beyond the sphere of technocratic policy debates that seek to measure the size of financing "gaps" and categorize what is and is not "new and additional". We do not treat climate finance as a discrete – albeit major – component of international climate politics. Instead, we develop a political economy and economic geography account of climate finance that spans international climate finance, such as that represented by the GCF and its failed US$100 billion target, and climate-induced transformations in public finance, financial statecraft and financial markets. By examining these developments within the same analytical frame, we seek to bring climate finance into the realm of the political economy and geography of capitalist finance.

We argue that climate finance is an indicator and mediator of climate futures. In doing so, we follow a real shift taking place in global capitalism: climate change is becoming increasingly central to the operation of finance. Simultaneously, finance is becoming increasingly central to climate change. We trace a wide range of climate finance developments from the creation of new climate asset classes, climate disclosure, carbon pricing, climate tech start-ups, green monetary policy, and claims for repayment of climate debts. Across these and many other examples, we show how different configurations of climate finance are being positioned as the solution to climate change and how climate politics is taking place on and through the terrain of finance.

Thus, we grapple with both the opportunities and constraints that emerge by imagining and operationalizing climate futures through the lens of climate finance. The book introduces the political economy of climate finance through six "positions": climate capital, climate risk, precision markets, speculative markets, big green states and climate justice finance. These positions are financial, geographical and political and act to configure different possible climate futures. Before we develop this argument and approach, let us first introduce in more detail how we got to this point.

INTERNATIONAL CLIMATE POLITICS AND FINANCE: BEYOND "GAP TALK"

The international climate policy architecture is now three decades old, with scientific advances, negotiations and deliberations proceeding for many years before that still. Over this period, the form of the UNFCCC has changed, as have the actors and institutions involved, the mechanisms drawn upon in response to climate change and the key debates and contests. Despite these changes, the problem of finance has remained central to climate policy throughout. Climate targets have become financial commitments. Accordingly, different responses to climate change are examined in financial terms: how will we pay for adaptation to climate impacts or just and sustainable transitions away from fossil fuels? What kinds of financial tools will we use to incentivize this action and where will this money come from? And thus, a bigger question for our analysis: how did it become a common-sense policy and political formulation to equate the state of the climate to the size of financial flows mobilized in its name?

Major scientific and diplomatic conferences and summits on climate change occurred throughout the 1970s and 1980s, with achievements including the creation of peak science-policy aggregator the IPCC in 1988. It was not until the early 1990s, however, that the global climate policy architecture was consolidated through the UNFCCC, which took effect in 1994. This phase in global climate policy history was one of "regime creation", during which goals, key principles, actors and rules were agreed (Schroeder 2010). Accordingly, key institutions were established, including that the overarching goal is to avoid "dangerous" climate change, that responsibility for action to address climate change is "common but differentiated" and that the flexibility and efficiency of market mechanisms is paramount. Whereas the specifics of legally binding targets were debated for years to come in and beyond the COPs, these tenets remain in place today.

The global climate policy arena has subsequently evolved through numerous summits and new agreements. Since the original UNFCCC Treaty, followed by the 1997 Kyoto Protocol, climate change has gained momentum as a public policy and public concern, just as experienced and anticipated impacts have mounted. Political contestation over how to respond to climate change, however, has only intensified. As a result, the 2015 Paris Agreement no longer seeks formal commitments from states – which proved too high a hurdle for recalcitrant signatories. Rather, the Agreement allows signatory states to choose their own emissions reductions targets: their self-declared and assessed nationally determined contributions. As with previous agreements, the nationally determined contributions of the Paris Agreement fall short of emissions reductions that might avoid "dangerous" climate change. During this period, debates about the role and form of climate finance have remained central, while financial tools and actors have grown in prominence. These debates include those about the role of markets, transfers of money to poor and vulnerable states and the prominence of non-state actors.

Market mechanisms for achieving greenhouse gas emissions reductions have been core to the international climate architecture for decades. The Kyoto Protocol included several market tools for reducing greenhouse gas emissions. Called "flexibility" mechanisms, these included the Clean Development Mechanism (CDM), Joint Implementation and Emissions Trading. Reflecting neoliberal common sense, markets for carbon (and carbon equivalents) were claimed to be the most efficient means of delivering emissions reductions. Market tools were the most politically acceptable option for North American proponents in particular, although the centre of gravity for carbon markets shifted to Europe in the years following the Kyoto agreement. These market mechanisms operate under the assumption that greenhouse gas emissions reductions are globally equivalent. As such, the mechanisms facilitated flexibility and least cost, by allowing countries to meet their emissions target through projects that reduced emissions in another, cheaper country.

Political economists and economic geographers of climate change have called the financial activity generated by the market mechanisms of the Kyoto Protocol – as well as regional and national carbon prices, trading schemes and voluntary offset markets – the "new carbon economy" (Boyd, Boykoff & Newell 2011; Boykoff *et al.* 2009). The critical research about this new carbon economy has revealed its uneven geographies; while the flexibility mechanisms operate with a kind of flat earth assumption about the interchangeability of emissions and reductions across space, the production, trade and benefits of markets in bundles of carbon are unevenly distributed (Pearse & Böhm 2014). Despite their long-standing, carbon markets remain patchy and volatile, subject to political whims of nation states and international agreements and policies (Bulkeley & Newell 2015). Perhaps most importantly, these market mechanisms have rarely delivered on their goals of inducing emissions reductions (Bryant 2019).

A second contestation over the international architecture relates to funding and finance for developing and vulnerable countries, including for adaptation, climate-resilient development and, more recently, loss and damage. As an arena for climate governance, adaptation was resisted or sidelined through the early stages of the UNFCCC process (Schipper 2006). This started to change throughout the 2000s, with recognition that future climate impacts were inevitable and some were beginning to be felt; this shift emerged with advocacy about vulnerability in developing countries, including by the Alliance of Small Island States. The first steps towards funding adaptation activities were taken in 1995, when the Global Environment Facility (GEF), the financial mechanism for the UNFCCC housed within the World Bank, was drawn upon to fund adaptation planning. Although the years that followed saw limited financial and project-based activity, the 2001 Marrakesh Accords established three funds to support adaptation: the Special Climate Change Fund for adaptation and other activities; the Least Developed Countries Fund to support adaptation actions and the production of national adaptation plans of action in least-developed countries; and the Adaptation Fund, which would receive funding through the CDM. The GEF is the trustee for these funds. These advances culminated in the US$100 billion pledge to fund adaptation and mitigation activities in developing countries agreed at the Copenhagen COP in 2009 – the target that was ultimately missed.

The politics of this adaptation funding and finance are lively. One area of disagreement relates to the balance of activities and funding for mitigation, adaptation and loss and damage. Mitigation and adaptation are often seen as opposing policy domains, the former related to attempts to reduce greenhouse gas emissions and the latter related to managing the impacts of climate change. Loss and damage is more vague, without an official definition under the UNFCCC. It is often used to refer to the consequences of climate change that are "leftover" after mitigation and adaptation actions and can include both intangible losses as well as quantifiable costs.

As developing and vulnerable countries have lobbied for, the GCF is supposed to equally allocate its funding and finance to adaptation and mitigation. However, it and other sources of climate finance continually and overwhelmingly prioritize mitigation projects, meaning that adaptation in vulnerable countries remains under-resourced. The frameworks for obligations to pay for adaptation also differ, with states supporting either principles of responsibility, capability, polluter pays, doing no harm, or payments for damage (Khan & Roberts 2013). Another area of contestation relates to counting and accounting for adaptation funding. On the one hand, in the words of the Paris Agreement, adaptation moneys should work towards "climate-resilient development" in combination with official development assistance. On the other hand, the UNFCCC declares consistently that funding for adaptation must be "new and additional" to development funding of any sort. Accounting systems for ensuring this is the case do not exist (Weikmans & Roberts 2019). Integrating adaptation funding and finance within the existing architecture of development assistance gives a lot of power to multilateral development banks and foreign aid agencies (Webber 2016). As a result, many vulnerable recipient countries have difficulty accessing funding, meeting administrative and bureaucratic requirements and achieving country-led adaptation.

A final trend and point of contestation in the international climate regime is the growing role of non-nation-state actors, in particular private finance. Since the early climate conventions, which centred nation-state actors, the sites and scales of climate governance have proliferated to include the citizen, urban, regional and intergovernmental level (Bulkeley & Newell 2015). Private financial actors, including industry, banks, institutional investors, asset managers and financial service providers, have become increasingly prominent over time. Where the lofty promises of various financial solutions to climate change have failed, state negotiators have typically sought to overcome these issues through greater involvement of private finance and investors (Bigger & Webber 2021). Funding adaptation and mitigation activities within the UNFCCC and its agreements is now a world of loans and investment underwritten by states but delivered by private finance (Gabor 2021b). Private finance sources and financialized tools have become solutions to both funding crises and political roadblocks within the international regime.

Debates about these different climate finance tools – markets, adaptation funding and the role of private finance – reflect a common mode of analysis of climate finance: "gap talk". Gap talk seeks to organize climate finance into formal categories that describe its source (e.g. public or private), aim (e.g. mitigation or adaptation) or tool (e.g. grant or loan). The Global Landscape of Climate Finance reports from the California-based non-profit research organization, the Climate Policy Initiative, are indicative. These widely shared and cited reports diagram climate-related financial flows and investments (e.g. Climate Policy Initiative 2022). They show the overall size and trends in climate-related investments: year on year increases that nonetheless fall short of investment needs; the growing role of private finance; and, despite rapid increases, limited investment in adaptation. The overarching purposes of this gap talk are to calculate gaps between current flows of climate finance, according to different categories, and the estimated financial cost of responding to climate change.

Within this gap talk framework, the successes of adaptation and mitigation are measured explicitly in terms of financial throughput or mobilization. Rather than focusing on policy goals and project achievements, gap talk centres pledges and targets. Climate politics becomes a question of what can be counted as climate finance and how more can be mobilized. In this sense, gap talk is "prefigurative", gesturing towards future climate finance flows to be "unlocked" or "tapped" and reorganizing state and inter-state action towards this task (Knuth 2015). Gap talk and its associated reports and analyses tell us a great deal about climate finance flows across space and time, including trends in the actors and financial tools involved. Importantly, the enormous quantity of monetary resources needed to fill financing gaps communicates the urgency and scale of action that is required. However, it tells us less about the political economy of climate finance, or the climate futures that different forms of climate finance might produce.

CAPITALISM AND THE RISE OF FINANCE

The dominance of gap talk reflects the the that way finance has been positioned at the centre of climate politics and policy. This "financialization" of climate change has its roots in the broader, extraordinary rise of finance in the contemporary capitalist economy. In this book we refer to the particular kind of economy we are in as *capitalism*: an economic system based on a set of social relations dominated by privately owned production for profit, in which most officially valued work is done by workers for a wage (Stanford 2015). As an economic system, capitalism is embedded in four key social, political and cultural institutions: private enterprise, market exchange (including for labour), the money and credit system and the state (Ingham 2008) – all of which are punctuated by gendered, racialized and other inequalities, exclusions and oppressions. Importantly, capitalism is variegated across space, with different geographical "models" of capitalism and geographical unevenness within global capitalism (Block 2019). Capitalism is also variegated across time, with distinct periods of capitalism with their own financial histories, that intersect in important ways with climate change.

The second half of the twentieth century saw the creation of a global financial architecture designed to support economic growth. Post-war growth drove what scientists of the Anthropocene describe as the Great Acceleration in human impacts on Earth systems, including the climate system (Steffen *et al.* 2015). Political economists instead trace the social and economic roots of climate change to the transition to capitalism itself – a phenomenon described as the Capitalocene (Moore 2016). Nonetheless, it was during post-war capitalism and its crisis-led restructuring that many of the institutional drivers of, and dominant solutions to, climate change were set in motion. Following the capitalist crisis period of the 1970s, neoliberal reforms elevated financial expansion as a goal in its own right. Widespread awareness of climate change and pressure for climate politics and policy emerged at the height of this neoliberal reform period that placed finance on the ascendency – a historical coalescence described by Naomi Klein (2014) as "bad timing". From this conjuncture, it is no surprise that finance became positioned as the essential solution to climate change.

The post-war financial order established national and international institutions that could manage the economy in the interests of its architects in the Global North (Panitch & Gindin 2012). Nationally, its genesis was in the eventual "New Deal" response by the US Government to the Great Depression of the 1930s. The US New Deal developed systems of financial regulation that sought to restrict and separate different financial activities and institutions; due to its coupling with public infrastructure investment, this approach has provided inspiration for more radical climate finance proposals for a Green New Deal (GND). In 1944, the Bretton Woods conference established an international financial and monetary system aiming to support post-war growth and financial stability, with the US at the helm. The Bretton Woods agreements established an international monetary regime in which currencies were fixed to the US dollar, in turn convertible to gold. The International Monetary Fund (IMF) and the World Bank Group were created to oversee post-war reconstruction and promote international economic cooperation. Governments developed their capacities to control the flows of investment and credit across national borders, enabling emerging economies to try to build national financial and economic capacity through state-led import substitution industrialization strategies.

Together, these financial arrangements underpinned what is often called the "golden age" of capitalism. High growth rates sustained a long boom across the advanced capitalist world, although with socially uneven effects both between and within borders. However, the Bretton Woods system came under strain in the 1970s as a stagflation crisis of increasing unemployment and inflation shook the global economy. Oil shocks, declining profits and productivity, financial imbalances and increasing labour conflict stressed the Bretton Woods system. In 1971, the US ended coverability of US dollars to gold, ushering in the system of flexible or floating exchange rates. A third-world debt crisis subsequently spread from Latin America across the developing world.

This crisis created the political-economic conditions for the neoliberal transformation of the global economy (Cahill & Konings 2017). Constraints on finance were liberalized, as the neoliberal state shifted towards its role as a facilitator of the expansion of private finance and financial "innovation". In the US, the New Deal era Glass–Steagall Act, which had separated commercial and investment banking practices, was circumvented and then repealed. The capital controls that were a hallmark of Bretton Woods were dismantled, enabling the globalization of finance. A new monetary regime saw central banks prioritize inflation targeting over goals such as full employment. Fiscal austerity rules of budget discipline constrained traditional channels of public investment, opening new avenues for states to instead subsidize private investment. The reregulation of organized labour engineered historic defeats for workers who were faced with decades of wage stagnation. Bretton Woods-era international financial institutions moved away from their original mandates and instead sought to enforce Washington Consensus policies of fiscal and monetary discipline and financial liberalization, opening up economies in the Global South to global markets. These policies were implemented as conditions for receiving debt restructuring or concessional loans and functioned to unevenly integrate developing countries into global trade, production and financial networks.

The neoliberal policy toolkit, in turn, created the conditions for the rise of finance and the "financialization" of the economy (Mann 2013). Finance, broadly speaking, consists of the institutions, actors, relations and logics that organize flows of money through the economy. Finance can take many different forms, including credit and debt instruments, the ownership of equities and other assets, the trading of derivatives and other "innovative" financial securities, insurance products, government grants and subsidies, cooperative enterprise and payments for damages. These types of finance span private, public and household finance – sectors that are increasingly hybridized – and institutions such as banks, insurers, ratings agencies, central banks, international financial institutions, treasury departments and financial regulators. The "financialization" of capitalism describes the growth of the finance sector, both in terms of the relative share of the financial sector in the economy and the shift of non-financial corporations and actors towards financial avenues of realizing profits (Krippner 2005). More than this, financialization describes the growing prevalence of financial logics and structures across the ostensibly non-market realms of politics, society and the environment (Martin 2002). The central position occupied by climate finance in climate politics is indicative of this shift, as debate over different possible climate futures are mediated by financial instruments and institutions.

The convergence of the rise of finance and scientific consensus about deepening climate change has coupled a volatile financial system with a volatile climate as two forces that will co-determine the course of the twenty-first century. Across developed and developing worlds, recurrent bouts of financial crisis and instability are increasingly intertwined with mounting climate impacts and tipping points (Alami, Copley & Moraitis 2023). In this context, a political economy and geographical approach to climate finance is necessary to comprehend not only the positioning of finance as the solution to climate change, but also how climate change and its politics are reshaping the financial structures and logics that dominate contemporary global capitalism.

THE POLITICAL ECONOMY OF CLIMATE FINANCE

The simultaneous rise of finance and climate change has made climate finance central to political-economic pathways for capitalism in the climate crisis. In this book, we argue that climate finance is a window into different possible climate futures as both an indicator and mediator of the political economy of climate change. We show that climate finance is not a singular, technical or politically neutral means towards achieving a shared end goal of a safer climate. Climate finance is the product of political contestation between actors and institutions with different visions of and interests in climate policy, operating within and through the financial structures and spatiotemporal financial relations of contemporary capitalism.

Different forms of climate finance and their relative significance are *indicators* of the balance of political-economic ideas and forces that make some responses to climate change possible while foreclosing others. Climate finance is also now deeply entangled in the broader structural dynamics and geographies of capitalism. Through the actors and institutions that are enrolled in its design, construction and operation, climate finance is a powerful *mediator* of how responses to climate change reshape, or potentially transform, capitalism. Contests over climate finance show that existing

13

ways of doing finance are being challenged, and these changes will both have a major bearing on and provide a crucial window into our climate and (post-) capitalist futures.

To achieve the aims of the book, we develop a critical and expansive definition of "climate finance" as *strategies that mobilize financial ideas, instruments and institutions to reshape the relationship between capitalist economies and climate change.* This definition has several advantages compared with other more restrictive definitions of climate finance that tend to focus on funding and finance mobilized through the UNFCCC and bilateral and multilateral grants and lending. First, it situates climate finance within the political economy of the existing financial system. In the current context, all financial processes have implications for climate change, from household mortgages to sovereign debts. Thus, all finance is, in a sense, climate finance. Although it is not possible to fully capture all the climate impacts of the entire financial system in this book, we argue that climate finance cannot be fetishized as separate from this broader system. Thus, we consider financial strategies that both address and drive the production of, and vulnerability to, climate change, including those not conventionally defined as climate finance. Second, climate change is reshaping finance in capitalist economies. Our definition of climate finance refers not only to the role of finance in addressing (or not) climate change, but how climate change has created pressures for change within the financial system itself. Third, our definition of climate finance brings together adaptation and mitigation. Rather than viewing them as particular spheres of investment or specific financial products, we integrate adaptation and mitigation as a reflection of their growing integration in policy domains and financial tools and institutions. Adaptation and mitigation are increasingly conjoined elements and outcomes of climate finance, which are together co-constitutive of climate pathways.

Our approach goes beyond critiques of dominant forms of climate finance as "greenwashing". Greenwashing refers to the situation in which climate finance actors, tools and institutions are making misleading or unsubstantiated claims about their environmental and climate benefits as a form of self-promotion. This mode of critique is common in media reporting and exposés about climate finance. Such reporting has uncovered important scandals about issues such as "junk" carbon offsets or investment funds that are "mis-sold" as sustainable (Fletcher & Oliver 2022; Rathi, White & Green 2022). Charges of greenwashing have proven politically potent and have even seen financial regulators launch investigations and seek to tighten rules in their jurisdictions. However, the framing of greenwashing can be limiting when it pre-supposes the existence of uncontested and objective measures of "greenness" that can be achieved with stronger regulation or better motives.

Existing political economy accounts of "green capitalism" have instead focused on the structural limits of green finance. For instance, Adrienne Buller's (2022: 277) excellent examination of the "illusions" of green capitalism concludes that "green capitalist solutions are a deadly distraction from the urgent task of actually slowing, reversing, and adapting to climate and ecological crisis; at worst, they are actively undermining our ability to do so". This conclusion crystallizes from an approach steeped in economic geography, political economy and their affiliated disciplines by analysing the mechanisms, claims and outcomes of financial tools that seek to respond to the climate challenge. Rather than finding that green financial tools have fallen short due to technical difficulties or errors, this research demonstrates the inherent limits of many of the central instruments of climate finance such as carbon markets, disaster insurance and climate risk disclosure. These financial mechanisms, despite their innovation and evolution over decades, have manifestly failed to curb greenhouse gas emissions or prompt robust adaptation decisions at the scale required, often while multiplying socio-spatial inequalities and undermining climate democracy.

In this book we both cover examples of outright greenwashing and draw extensively on the critical literature emphasizing the structural limits of green finance. However, our ultimate goal is not to propose reforms to reduce greenwashing or insist that green capitalism is inherently unreformable, although both are valuable projects. If, as we argue, climate finance is a powerful mediator and indicator of the political economy of climate change, then existing limitations reflect the current relationship between capitalist economies and climate change, and the balance of political contestation over that relationship. The fact that finance is positioning itself as a climate saviour is an outcome of climate politics and the pressure this has put on finance. Climate finance is continuing to be shaped by political action, which, as with all politics, is constrained by inequalities of power. Our book is intended as a critical guide to the "plural" character of climate finance (Bridge *et al.* 2020), as actors negotiate the financial subsumption of climate change, or use climate change to contest systems of finance. We do so by outlining six "positions" of climate finance as windows into different possible climate futures.

SIX "POSITIONS" OF CLIMATE FINANCE

We analyse climate finance by identifying six "positions": climate capital, climate risk, precision markets, speculative markets, big green states and climate justice finance. As finance has been increasingly positioned as the solution to climate change, a range of different financial positions have begun to emerge. Each of these are ways of taking a financial position on climate change – and we mean this in several senses.

In the world of financial trading, a *financial position* is a strategy of owning and selling securities and assets. Taking a financial position indicates a particular orientation to the direction of a market, whether bullish (a positive expectation) or bearish (a negative expectation), and denotes a strategy of speculation or risk mitigation. The six climate finance positions identified here each take an active position on the financial opportunities and risks associated with climate change and orient their financial action in response. We take an *analytical position* on these configurations of climate finance within the political economy of climate change, examining how they each see climate change as a problem, what the goals of climate finance should be and how its outcomes might be evaluated. Furthermore, we insist on climate finance being *positioned geographically*. Climate finance plays out atop productive, existing geographies of uneven development, racialized and gendered inequalities and colonial financial regimes. It also creates new geographies.

Finally, different climate finance strategies take a *political position*. Climate finance is not, or is not only, a technical arena focused on correcting information asymmetries or modelling prices for carbon. Instead, it is contested by different actors, coalitions and movements that take different political and financial positions on climate finance and the futures it imagines and programmes. Analysing climate finance requires attending to these contestations as well as the political possibilities they offer. Taking a position on climate finance cannot be passive. In financial terms, this means climate finance is not an observer of the climatic or financial world around, but an active producer of climate futures. Similarly, taking an analytical position on climate finance requires engagement beyond dismissal to enliven the political propositions. To stretch the financial lingo, we are interested in unwinding these climate finance positions and leveraging others towards more socio-ecologically democratic and just ends.

These six positions are coexisting and overlapping elements of climate finance that combine to configure different pathways for climate change and capitalism, or "climate-changing capitalism" (Bryant 2019). Each is associated with different actors and interests and involves different financial mechanisms and relations. Some of these are complementary and others are in tension. How they combine – with some positions dominating others over time and across space – to create different modes of climate finance is contested. None is predetermined in its social, economic and environmental outcomes. However, as we argue, some positions offer greater scope for rapid, fair and democratic action on climate change than others.

Our notion of positions of climate finance differs from other scenario-based approaches to future climate pathways. Scenario-based approaches have become increasingly ubiquitous as climate change reshapes time horizons and demands future planning (Anderson 2010; Chakrabarty 2009). They have come from a range of actors – from businesses and communities to social and climate scientists – and use different methods. In general, scenarios identify a set of variables and use these to present different possible pathways and futures. Examples include the IPCC's Shared Socioeconomic Pathways that are based on future trends for things such as population, technology and economic growth as baselines combined with climate models to consider required mitigation and adaptation polices. Another prominent example is the scenarios regularly produced by multinational oil and gas company Shell, which pioneered corporate scenario planning from the 1970s as a tool for investment decisions. These scenarios, unsurprisingly, focus on the place of energy within different "plausible" – from Shell's perspective – futures.

From quite different perspectives, scenarios have also been embraced by more critical thinkers. Mann and Wainwright's (2018) *Climate Leviathan* draws on political economy and political theory to imagine four potential social formations that could emerge across binaries of (non-)capitalism and (anti-)planetary sovereignty. Similarly, Frase's (2016) *Four Futures* combines the tools of social science with speculative fiction to envisage futures scenarios according to the axes of equality-hierarchy and abundance-scarcity.

Scenario-building exercises are heterogenous. Yet, as Rickards *et al.* (2014: 595) argue, scenarios both open and close the future, "simultaneously bound[ing] and releas[ing] our future imaginary, organizing and categorizing". Macro-level scenarios are usually presented as "ideal types" with qualifiers about the complexity of real-world processes. Instead, our positions attempt to create a meso-level framework that enables systemic analysis of climate finance in a way that can navigate the complex political economies of climate change and thus be of practical use for those grappling with questions of climate finance in the real world. The topic of our analysis – climate finance – sits on a scale below that imagined by climate scenarios. But our contention is that climate finance will be crucial to those larger scenarios and that studying climate finance is a useful way to understand their trajectory. Rather than variables in a formula, our positions reveal key points of inflection for climate finance and, therefore, the future of climate change and capitalism itself. Importantly, this makes space for geographical variegation and contingency as different forms of climate finance, constituted by different confirmations of and tendencies within our six positions, are implemented spatially, temporally and relationally.

CHAPTER OUTLINE

The book is structured through six chapters, each of which describes one of the positions of climate finance that will configure political-economic pathways through and beyond climate change. These positions are competing but often coexistent possibilities that will shape different climate and socio-ecological futures. Each position differs in terms of how seriously they commit to responding to climate change, the power of state and other regulatory actors, their democratic and redistributive ambitions, the liberties afforded to financial and other commercial actors and the prominence of accumulation strategies compared with other goals. To untangle the six positions and how they relate to each other, we ask: How do they define the problem of climate change? What are their visions and goals? Who are the actors and what are their interests? What financial mechanisms are involved? What are their climate, social and political-economic possibilities? In considering these questions, each chapter incorporates prominent illustrative examples that span public and private, Global North and South, and adaptation and mitigation.

The first position we examine, in Chapter 2, is "climate capital". This is a position of climate finance that sees climate change as an opportunity for capitalist growth. Climate capital shapes climate futures by its pursuit of profitable investment opportunities and centring of private finance institutions such as banks and investment funds. As such, we argue that the creation of climate change-related assets – property that can be owned, controlled and traded – is increasingly important to both capital markets and climate finance itself in mitigation and adaptation policy spheres. We introduce two financial institutions and instruments that create climate-related asset classes (sustainable investment funds and green bonds) and then examine some of the assets into which this climate capital is mobilized: urban resilience and renewable energy infrastructure. The basic claim of climate capital is that there is no necessary trade-off between making profits and acting on the climate. Our chapter puts this claim to the test, finding an uneven geography of investability, climate risk, public costs and private benefits.

The second position of climate finance is "climate risk". If climate capital seeks to harness the financial upside of climate change, climate risk uses existing financial risk management practices to manage its downsides for profits, asset values and the stability of the financial system as a whole. Accordingly, climate risk sees a climate future where the risks of climate change *to finance* are governed by financial markets. In Chapter 3, we examine the two key, closely related, risk management strategies of finance: climate risk disclosure and ESG integration. Within these two strategies, financial actors and systems themselves solve their climate and self-image problem in

pursuit of securing a stable transition for finance under climate change; reducing the risks of climate changes produced by finance through its investments
is often secondary. Nonetheless, we show how taking a climate risk position
also opens up "risky politics" through which divestment movements engage
with climate risk to make fossil fuel investments riskier. The politics of climate risk often revolve around whether climate change is a risk to finance or
whether climate change can be made a financially material risk.

Next, in Chapter 4, we examine "precision markets" – a climate finance
position seeking to make climate mitigation and adaptation economic and
efficient. Precision markets seek to price climate change and climate responses
in order to identify "least-cost" responses to climate change. Pricing different
scenarios allows comparisons of costs and benefits, and risks and opportunities, of different climate pathways. The goal is to find the right balance of
climate change impacts and climate policy decisions: precision markets serve
both an information and incentive purpose. We examine three kinds of precision markets: social costs of carbon calculations, carbon markets and disaster insurance. As its name suggests, precision markets promise to facilitate
calculations related to different climate pathways, enabling decisions towards
optimal climate and cost outcomes. However, each of the cases shows that,
beneath this promise of objectivity, precision markets orient towards a climate future that centres calculations of profitability.

In contrast to the search for predictive accuracy in precision markets,
Chapter 5 examines a position of climate finance that takes a particularly
speculative position on the future. In "speculative markets", actors and industries seek to produce the technological and financial climate solutions of the
future. These are inherently imprecise markets that focus not on stability
and incrementality, but embrace the chaos of climate solutions that produce
spectacular wins and losses. We examine speculative markets through three
cases: Elon Musk and his class of green billionaires, climate engineering technologies and the off-grid solar industry. These might seem wildly different
cases, but each works at the edges of clean tech and fintech, and each is
constantly working to overcome their limited profitability and associated
liquidity constraints. Speculative climate solutions propose to "disrupt"
existing practices and relations. However, each of the speculative techno and
financial fixes we examine here are underwritten by state investment and
tethered to ongoing resource extraction. In other words, speculative markets
tend to leave capitalism's existing power and socio-ecological relations intact.

Our fifth position examines how "big green states" can take a position
on climate change via state financing powers. Although states are essential regulators, subsidisers, bankers and de-riskers in all the climate finance
positions in the book, in Chapter 6 we explore the role of states actively
using public finance to shape future climate pathways in line with climate

policy goals. Big green states have two main ways to govern the distribution of resources in an economy: monetary policy and fiscal policy. We explore both of these in this chapter, focusing on central banking and a variety of fiscal tools and institutions, including carbon taxation and state investment banks. The possibilities of public finance for climate change remain somewhat open, across a spectrum of state action spanning from the greening of existing monetary and fiscal methods to state coordination of green investment. Each reflects different mixes of big green carrots, where public finance is used to expand climate investment, and big green sticks, where states seek to penalize fossil finance or constrain the role of private climate finance. Underpinning these possibilities is contestation over whether big green states create space for public participation in the direction of public climate finance.

Whereas each of the preceding positions are oriented around a particular configuration of finance, ideas, instruments and institutions, our final position considers how climate finance has been used to advance "climate justice". Climate justice finance places climate change in the context of historical and contemporary inequalities and works towards climate futures based on equality, freedoms and democracy. In Chapter 7, we explore claims, movements and strategies towards climate justice through international public climate finance, climate debt and reparations, and GNDs and degrowth. The range of social and climate outcomes embedded in claims for climate justice finance vary widely. Nonetheless, these proposals begin to chart the path towards justice through climate finance and potentially embed climate justice within finance itself. Rather than representing celebrated progressive experiments that explicitly contrast with the positions explored previously, climate justice finance is contested, shaping contingent climate futures. Realizing climate justice finance will depend on building the political power of these movements.

CHAPTER 2

CLIMATE CAPITAL

In early 2021, the business and economics newspaper *Financial Times* announced it was creating a new dedicated section on climate change called "Climate Capital". That the *Financial Times*, one of the major media sources for the finance sector, has elevated climate change in this way, illustrates the extent to which managing climate change is understood as a financial issue. The name "Climate Capital" also indicates a particular orientation towards climate change, as an opportunity for capitalist growth. Our first position of climate finance, and the subject of this chapter, examines climate capital as the exemplary form of capitalist climate finance. Climate capital describes initiatives that promote accumulation and growth through climate action. When climate finance is positioned as climate capital, it shapes climate futures through the pursuit of profitable investment opportunities.

The idea that climate change does not simply threaten people and their environments, but also creates opportunities for businesses and capitalism more generally is not new. Political economists Peter Newell and Matthew Paterson (2010) describe this phenomenon as "climate capitalism", where the growth and profit imperatives of capitalism are met through the transition away from fossil fuel-based industrial development. For Newell and Paterson, the foundation of climate capitalism was carbon markets, among other emerging initiatives such as climate risk disclosure. Our focus on climate *capital* in this chapter is indicative of shifts in the political economy of climate finance since the publication of Newell and Paterson's book. Climate finance in the mould of climate capitalism is now constituted by a highly variegated constellation of strategies and instruments beyond carbon markets. Carbon markets remain significant, and we explore their history, operation and record in Chapter 4 on precision markets. However, climate change is reshaping the capital markets that create and allocate debt and equity, and state action is increasingly oriented towards leveraging and de-risking climate investment. In this chapter, we analyse climate capital with a focus on the creation of climate change-related *assets*. Climate-related assets encompass both the "greening" of conventional asset classes, such as bonds and investment funds, and the creation of novel climate assets. Increasingly, climate transitions themselves – encompassing both mitigation and adaptation goals – are being rendered as asset classes. This chapter therefore explores the establishment of investment markets in resilience alongside green technologies.

Assets, as Birch and Muniesa (2020: 7) describe, are "capitalized property", oriented towards future earnings. Climate capital, as we understand it in this chapter, describes climate finance strategies that turn climate futures into capitalized property by creating different kinds of climate-related financial assets. An asset is property that can be owned, controlled and usually traded. Assets produce future income streams that the owner has rights to. Assets store value, and the valuation of assets has conventionally been based on expectations of future income, although increasingly asset values have become detached from earnings. Investment in assets is shaped, among other things, by expectations of returns and capital gains. Assets sit on the balance sheets of businesses, states and households, and can be used to leverage further investment.

The extent to which climate policy is geared towards the creation of new financial assets is indicative of the rise of asset-based capitalism. While wealth and the asset form have always been central to capitalism, Adkins, Cooper & Konings (2020: 12) argue that contemporary financialized capitalism is "dominated by the logic of assets". This calls for a focus on the processes through which things are turned into assets, analysis of the various actors and institutions involved and, especially where an asset involves monopoly control, struggles over the creation and distribution of rents (Birch & Ward 2022; Ouma 2020). As a corollary, Bridge *et al.* (2020) have made a case for a shift in research focus from "carbon-as-commodity", which has animated carbon market studies in particular, to "carbon-as-asset", as a means of understanding how climate change becomes "investable" (Ouma, Johnson & Bigger 2018).

As our first position on climate finance, climate capital illustrates how climate finance is an indicator and mediator of climate futures. The climate-related asset classes we discuss are the means through which private finance takes positions on, while reshaping, the path of climate change. Climate capital centres private financial actors, such as banks and investment funds, as an indicator of contemporary political-economic conditions that confront climate change. The claim that private finance is needed to overcome the gap between the big costs of responding to climate change, and limited capacity of states to fund these costs publicly, is repeated often and widely. This condition is both historically contingent and reflective of real but politically imposed constraints. As we will show, climate capital nonetheless maintains an important role for the state. Rather than directly investing in and owning climate infrastructure, international organizations and national, regional and local governments are leveraging, subsidizing and guaranteeing the values and returns of private capital (Gabor 2021b).

Climate capital is shot through with possibilities and risks. To meet climate goals, there is an urgent need to "switch" large amounts of capital into low-carbon, climate-friendly infrastructure. But, as geographers Castree and Christophers (2015: 379) argue, the finance sector can act like an "unelected government" in making decisions over what is and is not "investable" based on assessments of future returns, with potentially negative socio-ecological-political outcomes. A common refrain in the world of climate capital is the pursuit of "doing well by doing good" – that there is no necessary contradiction between making profits ("doing well") and acting on climate ("doing good"). In this chapter, we critically analyse these claims by exploring what kinds of investments are financed, who benefits from them and whether political contestation can reshape climate capital for better outcomes. We are also careful to situate climate capital in the context of capital markets more generally, to ensure perspective on the scale of climate capital vis-à-vis global financial markets (Dempsey & Suarez 2016).

To explore these themes, this chapter is structured in four sections. Our first two sections focus on the rise of "sustainable" investment funds and green bonds as financial institutions and instruments that have created the most prominent climate-related asset classes for investors. Our second two sections focus on two of the infrastructures that climate capital is being mobilized to invest in: urban "resilience" and renewable energy assets. We show how this position on climate finance constructs a future constrained by the requirements of capital for climate change to become an investable and bankable asset. We demonstrate how this generates pressures to design climate infrastructure to perform financially for investors and creditors, and the role of government bodies in "de-risking" investments by locking in future income streams. We also analyse climate capital as a site of contestation, focusing on the troubling inequalities faced by those on the ground that are being reshaped in the image of climate capital and controversies over defining the "greenness" of climate assets.

"SUSTAINABLE" INVESTMENT

The rise of "sustainable" investment is part of a long history of capital seeking to provide solutions to prevailing social concerns. This history spans from early examples of negatively screening investments with connections to slavery or alcohol based on political and moral concerns, to the rise of the "responsible" corporation in the post-war period in the context of threats of regulation from the growing welfare state and the labour movement. The idea of corporate social responsibility was attacked by neoliberal thinkers such as Milton Friedman (1970), who famously argued that "the social responsibility of business is to increase its profits", although he did leave open the possibility that in some cases "goodwill" may prove to be a useful "cloak" for pursuing profits. Responsible investing has since grown rapidly, moving from a defensive posture against the threats of state regulation, or an added extra for corporations, to an accumulation strategy in its own right (Parfitt 2024). As the mantra of "doing well by doing good" indicates, it is commonplace for investors to argue that there is no longer a contradiction between social responsibility and profits; addressing issues from poverty to climate change is instead viewed by many investors as an opportunity for business.

Today, investing for climate purposes is a subset of a significant "sustainable", "responsible", "ethical" or "ESG" investment industry (Kölbel *et al.* 2020). This industry not only seeks to avoid harmful activities, such as negatively screening tobacco or fossil fuels (which we will cover in Chapter 3's analysis of divestment), but also make investments to fix social and environment problems while maintaining capitalist modes of accumulation (Cohen & Rosenman 2020). One of the main such proponents is high-profile venture-capitalist-turned-impact-investor Sir Ronald Cohen, who argues for a "triple-helix of risk-return-impact" that adds measures of "impact" on to conventional risk-return considerations in investment. How impact is measured is both crucial and a source of controversy, ranging from very specific social or environmental outcomes, as in social or environmental impact bonds (Christophers 2018a; Langley 2020), to a more general "positive consequences that business activity and investment have on our planet" (Cohen 2020: 11). In this section, we focus on one example of this: the rapidly growing investment funds that are rendering climate change an asset class for equity investors. However, the scope and ambiguous outcomes of sustainable invest funds suggest they are not leading to systematic reallocations of capital. Moreover, a focus on bankability in investment disadvantages certain kinds of necessary climate responses.

Climate change has been gradually recast by investors from threat to opportunity. In the 1980s and 1990s, corporations in fossil fuels and other heavily emitting industries funded organizations to cast doubt over the science of climate change and lobby against domestic and international climate policies (Oreskes & Conway 2010). This response gradually gave way to more pro-climate action stances from some businesses, such as renewable energy companies wanting to grow their market share, oil companies wanting to rebrand as "green", insurance companies exposed to the risks of climate change, or manufacturing companies wanting to avoid government regulation (Newell & Paterson 2010: 43–4). In the lead up to the

Copenhagen COP in 2009, 950 corporations and businesses around the world called for an outcome that would "unlock the potential of business to do what it does best: to invest profitably, to innovate, and make affordable low-carbon products and services to billions of consumers around the world" (Corporate Leaders Group on Climate Change 2009). By 2020, Bank of America's investment bank division declared in its analysis of the "climate solutions market" that "the 2020s are shaping up to be the decade of climate opportunity" (BofA Global Research 2020). These optimistic assessments of the economic opportunities from sustainable investing also developed as a promising avenue for investors with access to cheap money who were desperately searching for yield in the context of economic stagnation.

Building sustainable investment funds

Investment funds, managed by various kinds of financial institutions, pool money and invest it into company shares and other kinds of assets. Sustainability-labelled investment funds internalize the notion of climate change as investment opportunity. One of the early sustainable investment funds was Generation Investment Management, founded in 2004 by former US vice-president and star of the documentary *An Inconvenient Truth*, Al Gore, together with David Blood, former head of Goldman Sachs Asset Management. The fund, which had US$36 billion in assets under management by mid-2022, seeks to "mainstream" what it calls "sustainable capitalism" (Generation Investment Management 2012). Such funds have been growing rapidly. The financial ratings company Morningstar (2022) tracks the world of sustainable investment funds, which it defines as those that do more than negatively screen controversial sectors such as coal or tobacco, or merely consider ESG issues, and instead have binding sustainability objectives and criteria. At the end of 2021, sustainable investment funds managed US$3 trillion in assets globally. This represented a tripling in the two years since the onset of the Covid-19 pandemic, before post-pandemic interest rate increases saw the value of sustainable investment funds decline alongside general declines in global asset prices. These funds are concentrated in Europe, where around 5,000 funds account for over 80 per cent of sustainable-labelled assets, with around 500 US-based funds accounting for most of the remainder.

Sustainable investment funds are rendering sustainability in general, and climate change in particular, an asset class for investors. Beneath this lies a range of different approaches to what constitutes a "sustainable" asset- or a climate-"themed" investment strategy. Sustainable funds pool capital from multiple sources, whether institutional or retail (individuals), to invest across a portfolio of different assets. These funds have different structures, such as open-ended "mutual funds" or "exchange-traded funds" (ETFs). They may follow "active" trading strategies enacted by fund managers, or take a "passive" approach that follows a set index of assets. Reflecting financial markets more generally, passive sustainable funds have been steadily increasing their share of the market. Sustainable investment funds primarily invest in equities (shares in companies), but there are a minority of funds that invest in bonds, including green bonds for fixed-income returns, directly into "alternative" physical assets such as green infrastructure, or a combination of these (Christophers 2023; Morningstar 2022). Most of these funds include climate change alongside other ESG criteria, but climate change nonetheless dominates. For example, some funds, such as BlackRock's iShares Global Clean Energy ETF, are invested specifically in the low-carbon sector, including renewable energy, electric vehicle and green hydrogen companies. Other investment funds, such as Lyxor's S&P Global Developed Paris-Aligned Climate ETF, track an index of companies deemed to be collectively compatible with less than 1.5°C of global warming – literally turning a climate agreement into an asset class.

How sustainable is sustainable investing?

The growth of sustainable investing is significant, but still needs to be considered in the context of the overall investment landscape. The value of sustainable investment funds represented 6 per cent of the total value of assets under management in investment funds globally at the end of 2022 (OECD 2023: 12–13). This limited scale has led to efforts to "integrate" ESG factors into all investment decisions beyond specialist funds (see Chapter 3 on climate risk). Despite these efforts, their current scale suggests that sustainable investment funds have limited capacity to effect a systemic reallocation of capital from polluting to green industries.

Sustainable investment funds have also come under criticism for "greenwashing" – using sustainability discourse as cover for unstainable practices – raising questions about how "sustainable" they really are. Indeed, most "sustainable" funds are not free of fossil fuel investments. Only 20 per cent of US-based sustainable funds have zero or close to zero (less than 1 per cent of assets) exposure to thermal coal mining and electricity generation, or gas and oil production (Morningstar 2021). Sustainable investment funds are not necessarily focused on investing in typical "green" industries such as renewable energy either, with tech, finance and real estate investments dominating many sustainable-labelled funds (Buller 2020). Al Gore's Generation Investment Management, for example, is heavily invested in tech companies Google, Amazon, Microsoft and Alibaba (Generation Investment Management 2021).

Investment decisions depend on the various ways "sustainable" is defined in the ESG rules of the funds. Greenwashing scandals and inconsistences between different ways of measuring "green" are leading to efforts to create common and harmonized sustainability accounting standards, both through international standards bodies and government-sponsored green taxonomies (Parfitt 2022). Historically, there has been little oversight of which funds can be labelled sustainable, but these voluntary and regulatory moves have led to some funds losing their sustainability status (Klasa 2022). We pick this issue back up in Chapter 3, focusing on the role played by assessments of which sustainability concerns do, and do not, constitute financially material risks.

More fundamentally, the "climate capital" position on climate change taken by sustainable investment funds, as "unelected government" (Castree & Christophers 2015), is ultimately mediated by the drive for profits and capital gains. This is evident in Generation Investment Management's contention that "sustainable capitalism ... does not represent a trade-off with profit maximisation but instead actually fosters superior long-term value creation" (2012). Indeed, "sustainable" investment strategies have tended to outperform conventional strategies (Friede, Busch & Bassen 2015). Generation Investment Management itself claims its global equity fund has significantly outperformed equity markets as a whole (Walker 2018). These financial results raise questions about what kinds of "good" are and are *not* being pursued in order to "do well".

The asset managers that manage sustainable investment funds are not neutral poolers of capital. Asset managers have incentives to maximize income streams and ultimately capital gains from their investments (as well as their own fees), which can reduce levels of capital expenditure and increase turnover in ownership. The structure of funds themselves have implications for their capacity to provide a long-term source of sustainable capital, even when the source of capital is institutional investors with long time horizons like pension funds. This is because funds may be close-end investment vehicles that wind up after a pre-defined time period, such as 10 years (Christophers 2023).

Are all climate solutions profitable, and should they be? Maintaining a focus on returns – which investment funds are obliged to do as a fiduciary duty – discounts much-needed investments that may not satisfy these criteria. Poorer countries most exposed to climate risk may not be assessed by sustainable investment funds, which are geographically concentrated in the North Atlantic, as providing financially attractive sustainable investment opportunities. Alternatively, requirement for returns biases the construction of privatized climate infrastructures, such as renewable energy assets, that produce income streams for investors, potentially entrenching climate inequalities in poorer and wealthier countries alike. The growth of sustainable investment funds is nonetheless indicative of an increasingly significant debate about the "greening" of the core structures of global finance – a debate that extends to debt instruments, or "bonds", which we consider now.

GREEN BONDS

Green bonds are one of the paradigmatic tools of climate capital. As the most significant portion of the broader sustainable debt market, green bonds promise to treat "our ecological deficit with debt" (Jones *et al.* 2020: 50). The first green bond was issued in 2007 by the European Investment Bank for US$0.8 billion. The Climate Bonds Initiative (2022), a non-profit advocacy organization that also produces a certification scheme for green bonds, calculates the subsequent annual growth rate to be around 95 per cent, with total issuance reaching more than US$1.5 trillion by the end of 2021. Even with this growth, green bonds are purportedly three times oversubscribed, indicative of the extent to which the market is driven by investors seeking new climate asset classes and the financial (and publicity) rewards of green investments.

A green bond operates in much the same way as a "vanilla" bond – as a mechanism for public or private actors to borrow money. Accordingly, a borrower issues a bond and sells it to an investor, who effectively loans money to the issuer in return for regular interest payments and repayment of the bond principal at maturity. For both issuers and investors, bonds are, as fixed-income assets, relatively secure and reliable – or "boring" (Bigger & Millington 2020: 607) – offering steady and secure returns for investors who own a liquid (tradeable) asset, and often cheaper capital or otherwise more favourable terms than bank loans for issuers. Green bonds are structured in the same way, except that their capital is intended for projects with environmental and climate credentials. The majority of green bonds are "use of proceeds" bonds, which, as their title suggests, use their proceeds for specifically green projects, or collectives of projects. Under different bond types, however, borrowers have recourse to either the issuer's entire balance sheet, to specific revenue streams or particular project assets.

As with rules around what constitutes a "sustainable" investment fund, assuring the green outcomes of the projects is a point of contention in the green bonds market. To date, assurances are only provided through voluntary frameworks – such as the Green Bond Principles or the Climate Bond Standard – which prescribe eligible sectors, alignment with the goals of the Paris Agreement and reporting requirements. A broader asset class than green bonds has emerged: sustainability-linked bonds. These bonds allow issuers to spend their money however they like, subject to agreement with the investors on higher-level sustainability goals, rather than on specific projects as with green bonds.

Global geographies of green bonds

Almost half of the value of total green bonds issued is from Europe, with another quarter concentrated in North America. China has also become a major player, driving growth since 2015. This rapid growth is closely linked to a booming debt-financing market in China more broadly, in turn connected to big infrastructure portfolios in the country. Chinese issuance is subject to its own regulatory frameworks and criteria; according to these, for instance, green bonds can be used to finance "clean coal" (Chen & Li 2021).

There has also been a shift in who is issuing green bonds: originally the market was driven by multilateral development banks, but over time they have principally become investors in green bonds issued by other actors. The green bond issuance market is now driven by financial and non-financial corporates, with sovereign (state) issuers growing over time. However, both in terms of financial and environmental benefit, the Global South remains locked out of the green bond market. Even as sovereign issuers have recently come to include countries such as Fiji, projects in Asia (excluding China) and Africa account for only 6.5 per cent of the green bond market (Banga 2019). While there is potential for green bonds to attract much-needed finance and climate benefits to vulnerable countries, there remain institutional and market barriers. For instance, the "minimum size" of the green bond – the size required for the bond to be attractive to investors – is typically cited as around US$200–250 million. This size is rarely reached in the Global South. Not only are small projects in the Global South unfavourable in terms of liquidity, but their small size implies relatively higher transaction costs from certification, perhaps exacerbated by more extensive creditworthiness checks. As with vanilla bonds, effective borrowing costs for sovereign issuers of green bonds in the Global South face higher interest costs (Volz 2022). Thus, while green bonds promise to unlock finance to address climate change, there remain large swathes of the most vulnerable parts of the world that are yet to benefit. Indeed, as an interviewee describes in a study of Cape Town's green bond, "if you don't need the money, you can get it. If you need it, you can't" (Bigger & Millington 2020: 602).

Green bond issuers are usually established borrowers from the private and public sectors that do not currently have difficulty raising capital from other sources (reflected in the Cape Town quote above). The direct implication is that green bonds are not providing any additional financing to address climate change or environmental damage. In Mexico City, for example, green bonds were simply used to refinance existing projects and debts, without environmental or climate impact (Hilbrandt & Grubbauer 2020). The additionality promise of green bonds, according to advocates, rests in the capacity of green bonds to offer a lower cost of capital, or "greenium". There is some evidence that, in the green bond market as a whole, yields tend to be fractionally lower than vanilla bonds. In theory, the greenium should reflect the lower climate and other ESG risks in green bonds. In practice, however, the greenium has been driven by demand for green assets from sustainable investors, pushing green bond prices up and, thus, yields down (Liberati & Marinelli 2021). Indeed, the cost of capital for green bonds remains anchored in the borrower rather than the green projects the capital is being mobilized for. As a result, green bond markets reproduce the inequalities of vanilla bond markets.

Green bond inequalities

Patterns of socio-spatial inequality are repeated within projects that are funded by green bonds. Although there are relatively few granular studies of the expansive impacts of projects funded by green bonds, case studies demonstrate unequal distribution of risk between investors, issuers, the publics to which government issuers are ultimately responsible and the environment. Geographers Patrick Bigger and Nate Millington (2020) have studied the use of municipal green bonds to finance repairs to the New York City transit system following Superstorm Sandy in 2012 and to refinance water supply infrastructure in Cape Town in the midst of its severe drought from 2016 to 2018. In both instances, the financial risks of responsibility for repayments of the green bond, and the environmental risks of climate change and its disruption of essential urban goods and services, were largely distributed along historically produced racialized and class lines. Bigger and Millington show that financing through green bonds facilitated a perverse reverse subsidy from the poor to the wealthy through the increased taxes and user fees required to repay the bonds. The use of green bonds as part of the refinancing, restructuring and redesign of essential sewer and stormwater upgrades in Washington DC created similar issues, as citizens ultimately paid more for green than vanilla debt products (Christophers 2018a). The water utility, DC Water, and ultimately its constituents who service its debt through taxes and fees, carried the financial risk of the green bond product. These examples highlight the importance of the financial terms of green bonds – often bespoke products – and the distribution of costs for constructing and administering their particular requirements.

In addition to reproducing rather than redressing socio-spatial inequalities, the extent of environmental benefits from green bonds is in question. As with sustainable investing and ESG, one set of problems revolves around a lack of metrics for "green-ness" (Bigger 2017). There are no compulsory standards or assessment mechanisms for green bonds, such that certification – while common – is voluntary. The green bond market, as a result, has serious integrity issues, potentially allowing the greenwashing of environmentally damaging projects or "green default", where there is environmental "non-performance" in an already financed project. There is limited legal recourse, or the pricing of risk, for these integrity issues. Some of these integrity issues could be addressed through taxation incentives, regulatory changes or cultural change within the financial industry. However, reckoning with the socio-spatial inequalities produced by bad green bonds, and badly distributed green bonds, is much more challenging, particularly in the context of concentrated power – amid credit ratings agencies, bond underwriters and the creditors themselves – of climate capital. For now, these actors are "doing well" turning "public goods into private income" (Jones *et al.* 2020: 56), while the evidence for "doing good" is far more ambiguous.

RESILIENT INFRASTRUCTURE

"Resilient" infrastructure is another example of climate capital, where climate and other environmental stresses are being used to redefine physical infrastructure as an asset class. Sustainable investing and green bonds are primarily concerned with the source of capital in climate capital. Resilient infrastructure offers a prominent case through which to understand not only how climate capital is being mobilized, but also where it is being directed. There are close connections between these kinds of climate capital. Many sustainable investment funds invest in resilient infrastructure, and the structure of green bonds, where they provide long-term sources of funding with steady returns, is well suited to capital-intensive infrastructure investment.

Infrastructure encompasses the assets and systems (physical and social) that allow essential goods and services to flow in and between cities. Resilient infrastructure is a sub-component of these systems that promises to produce resilience through being specifically able to withstand the shocks and stresses of climate change (Hallegatte *et al.* 2019). For instance, electricity and water and sanitation systems are key infrastructures; for these to be resilient infrastructures they should be built, maintained and operated in such a way as to withstand the anticipated impacts of climate change, as well as to enable people, communities and economies to themselves build "resilience" in the face of climate change. In reality, many cities and countries currently face extensive infrastructural failures. In the US, the American Society of Civil Engineers assesses that water systems are leaking up to 8 trillion litres of water a year, facing the failure of over 2,000 dams, and a mere 30cm of sea level rise will place dozens of wastewater treatment facilities at risk (Cousins & Hill 2021). Fixing this infrastructure in the face of climate change will be costly.

Like much of the climate finance universe (see Introduction), climate capitalists have been engaged in "gap talk" about infrastructure generally and resilient infrastructure in particular. The OECD (2017b) states that the built infrastructure of energy, transport, water and buildings will be central to any low-carbon, climate-resilient transition. But, increasing demands on infrastructure driven by processes such as rapid urbanization and climate change, and the current era of "bad timing" fiscal constraints, mean that there is an "infrastructural financing gap". The World Bank and other key climate capital institutions estimate this resilient infrastructure financing gap to be in the order of several trillions of dollars per year (Lu 2020). Climate capitalists seek to close this gap by producing resilient infrastructure as an asset class: an investment proposition characterized by predictable cash flows and returns, natural monopolies and longevity.

The challenges of financing resilient infrastructure are particularly apparent in the Global South, where governments face difficulty accessing debt to finance assets that assure the circulation of essential goods and services in the context of urbanization and climate change (Bigger & Webber 2021). For proponents, climate capital for resilient infrastructure, particularly in cities, offers a promising fix for this confluence of challenges. The World Bank suggests that investing in resilient infrastructure will address the impacts of climate change while fuelling economic development through growth and productivity gains. Indeed, World Bank economists calculate that investing $1 in infrastructure produces net benefits of $4 (Hallegatte *et al.* 2019).

However, while climate capitalists are thought to be willing to invest in "illiquid [resilient] infrastructure assets in frontier emerging markets as a means of enhancing otherwise poor returns" (World Bank 2015: 58), gap talkers bemoan that very little of the hundreds of trillions of dollars available on capital markets is currently invested in this asset class. Limits to unlocking this climate capital, according to the World Bank, include the risk aversion of the investors themselves, a lack of financial and strategic governance to plan suitable resilient infrastructure investments in vulnerable cities and, as with green bonds more generally, ratings, standards, metrics and benchmarking systems against which prices, risks and returns can be indexed. Currently, "markets lack guidance on what constitutes a climate resilient investment", according to the World Bank (2019: 16). They suggest addressing these challenges requires public funding to offset risks, produce price signals about nonmonetary benefits and thereby leverage climate capital. The public sector, including the likes of the World Bank, is therefore acting as a "herald of capital markets", leveraging its multilateral finance to "crowd in" private capital. This reflects what political economist Daniela Gabor (2021a: 430–1) has described as the de-risking paradigm in which the role of the state is to "to 'escort' financial capital into de-risked asset classes". This discourse and associated set of financial practices is indicative of the public subsidy and market-based regulatory architecture that undergirds climate capital's investment in resilient infrastructure, by guaranteeing returns and facilitating market access for private capital.

Financializing flood protection in Jakarta

As the cases in previous sections detail, green bonds can be invested as project-based finance in a variety of resilient infrastructures. Often, through the architecture the World Bank and its partner institutions have established, resilient infrastructures are to be financed through technologies of public-private partnerships and land value capture (and associated tradeable development rights). Public-private partnerships are a broad collective of financing and construction strategies that share risk, reward and responsibility between the public and private sectors to finance, build, own and operate big, capital-intensive projects that produce essential goods and services. They typically vary based on the extent to which the private party takes on risks, with more risk meaning a more expensive contract. Land value capture is a financing strategy that claims future incomes from the increased value of land following infrastructure (or urban development) investment through tools such as taxes, fees or incentives. These are ultimately strategies to turn fixed infrastructure into a liquid asset. By (financially) engineering infrastructure to deliver an income stream, rights to those returns can be assetized, making "climate resilience", if not the physical infrastructure itself, a tradeable and bankable asset.

These financing techniques have been proposed to build resilient infrastructure to protect Jakarta from the increasing devastation wrought by flooding from the city's rivers and coast. Two coastal and flood protection infrastructures – infrastructures that seek to be both resilient themselves as well as induce resilience for the city more generally – are exemplary: the Jakarta Urban Flood Mitigation Project (JUFMP) and the National Capital Integrated Coastal Development/Great Garuda Sea Wall (NCICD/GGSW). These two projects seek to fortify the city against floods by channelizing and dredging rivers (JUFMP) and building expansive sea walls (NCICD/GGSW). As with the green bonds cases noted above, the social implications of these projects are troubling: both projects have led to the large-scale dispossession of marginalized kampung communities and the destruction of livelihoods throughout the capital city (Leitner, Sheppard & Colven 2017).

The JUFMP was financed through the World Bank with a US$140 million loan (restructured to US$90 million due to the devaluation of the Indonesian rupiah). Following World Bank economics, the loan would be easily repaid given the anticipated savings from reduced flood water levels, duration of flooding and flooding area achieved by the infrastructure investment. Indeed, the calculated economic internal rate of return of 29 per cent and benefit:cost ratio of five on a ten-year flood cycle (Independent Evaluation Group 2020) suggests the project would be viable for large-scale capital investment. This accounting seeks to construct "resilience" through reduced flooding and flood impact as an asset that can deliver long-term returns for private capital that exceed upfront costs. Capturing those returns, however, requires market restructuring to local institutions resembling Green Structural Adjustment – a climate twist on the infamous structural adjustment programmes imposed on poor countries by international financial institutions in the 1980s and 1990s. Moving beyond public funding for the JUFMP, which project personnel maintain could easily "pay for itself" through land value capture or tradeable development rights, demands reform to put "systems to capture that rent" in place (Bigger & Webber 2021).

These cases demonstrate that impulses towards creating "resilient" infrastructure as an investable and bankable asset class reshapes climate-affected communities around the need to create "resilient" income streams for investors and their creditors. Diverse activists have responded to these financialized infrastructures, reimagining resilience to climate change as emerging from social and collective relations (Colven & Tri Irawaty 2019). In doing so, they have resisted evictions and flood protection infrastructure, alongside battling with the impacts of flooding. Achievements have been won through networks of NGOs, activists, organizers and kampung communities, who through their campaigning, have made investments in resilient infrastructure "risky" (see Chapter 3) and pressured the Jakarta provincial government to upgrade kampungs and pay for a modest seawall along the coast. Resilient infrastructure, like other forms of climate finance, are contested. In this case, pressure not only came from progressive climate and community activists, but opposition to the sea wall was supported financially by conservative religious groups (Wilson 2016). For now, kampungs communities can stay put, but rising seas and the allure of financialized infrastructure may soon win out (Webber *et al.* 2022).

Despite sustained investment in preparatory work to try to "fix" climate capital in essential urban infrastructure in cities of the Global South, it remains a niche but profitable opportunity for a small class of investors. Even with its public subsidies, and public guarantees of substantial returns, resilient infrastructure remains a distinctly illiquid asset class. Meanwhile, tensions are emerging between the promise of resilience for communities and the financial structure and institutional reforms needed to guarantee resilient returns and asset prices for investors.

RENEWABLE ENERGY ASSET FINANCE

In quantitative terms, climate finance is dominated by flows of capital towards renewable energy. Globally, approximately half of climate finance is directed towards renewable energy infrastructure (Baysa *et al.* 2021: 20). In 2022, global investment in renewable energy reached US$499 billion – significantly more than investment in fossil fuel-based electricity generation, but less than what flowed to oil and gas mining and transport infrastructures such as pipelines and export terminals. East Asia – in particular China, as well as India and Vietnam – is the largest destination for finance to install renewable energy, followed by the US and Europe. Most finance flows towards utility and distributed (e.g. household) scale solar PV technologies, followed by utility-scale onshore and offshore wind (IRENA & CPI 2023: 11, 13, 54).

Like other areas of climate finance, the problem of transitioning to a renewable energy system has been translated into an issue of bridging a financing "gap". Although significant, the US$499 billion investment figure for 2022 remained below the $1.2 trillion per year estimated by the International Energy Agency to be needed to meet net zero by 2050 (Baysa *et al.* 2021: 20). Private finance is being relied upon to close this gap such that between 2013 and 2020, three-quarters of renewable energy finance was classified as coming from private sources (IRENA & CPI 2023: 18).

The significant role of private finance in the renewable energy sector results from the intersection of "climate capital" and the restructuring of electricity markets, where liberalization policies opened up an electricity sector in transition to private investment. According to the International Energy Agency, only 4 per cent of renewable energy assets in advanced economies are state-owned, compared to 21 per cent of fossil fuel generation assets. In developing economies, 28 per cent of renewable energy assets are state-owned, compared to 59 per cent for fossil fuel power (International Energy Agency 2020: 18). Transitions to renewable energy have often simultaneously privatized ownership over electricity, as new privately owned renewable energy assets replace previously state-owned fossil fuel assets.

As climate capital, renewable energy finance is structured around making renewable energy into a distinct and investable asset class for private capital. The falling costs of new wind and solar, which are now below the costs of new coal-fired power, means that renewable energy can more than compete with fossil energy on price. But the uptake of renewable energy by the private sector does not automatically flow from cost competitiveness, and instead requires decisions and restructuring to invest in renewable energy as a profitable asset (Christophers 2021a). The creation of renewable energy assets depends on regulatory and market classifications of low-carbon energy (Behrsin, Knuth & Levenda 2022) and, as Bridge *et al.* (2020: 733) show, "assembling assets that qualify against these criteria – i.e. forms of capitalized property which yield an income stream, and which are sufficient to bear debt". The combination of asset finance used by renewable energy developments to access credit, and public and private arrangements to guarantee future projects from these projects, is what makes these assets "bankable".

There are two main forms of "asset finance" that owners of utility-scale renewable energy projects use to gain access to credit: balance sheet and project finance (Baker 2022b; Bridge *et al.* 2020; Knuth 2021). Balance sheet finance makes up 65 per cent of asset finance for renewable energy projects (Ajadi *et al.* 2020: 35). With balance sheet finance, it is the company that owns, for example, the solar park, that raises the capital, for example by issuing (green) bonds. This tends to be done by larger power utilities that use the full suite of assets on their balance sheet, which may include both renewable and fossil fuel-based generation, as well as assets in other sectors of the economy, as security for the debt. Most of the remainder of renewable energy asset finance is project finance. Here, the renewable energy project is established as a special purpose vehicle that is legally separate from its owners, which are often independent power producers. This means that the renewable energy asset itself (e.g. the wind farm) is effectively the sole bearer of the debt, operating similarly to a non-recourse mortgage. In both cases, there is pressure to ensure that the asset "performs" as an investment by producing income streams so that it becomes "bankable".

Owners and managers of private renewable energy projects seek to make their projects bankable using various strategies to lock in future income and reduce the risk for creditors. Power purchase agreements (PPAs) to forward sell electricity are an important way of doing this. PPAs are contracts made between generators and electricity retailers or large energy users that specify an amount of electricity to be bought at a certain price over a period of time. PPAs therefore lock in income streams for renewable energy projects, often for long periods, sometimes more than 20 years, reducing market risks. Corporate PPAs have grown rapidly, particularly in the US, driven by PPAs signed by tech companies such Google, Facebook and Amazon to cover the enormous amount of electricity used by their servers. PPAs not only enable renewable energy asset finance, but also underpin corporate accumulation strategies elsewhere in the economy, such as the data-driven business models of big tech (Christophers 2022).

Governments have nonetheless played important roles in making renewable energy assets "bankable". Rather than direct state ownership, governments have tended to implement policies that help guarantee income streams for projects (see Chapter 6). As renewable energy has become more cost competitive with fossil fuels, these policies have shifted from feed-in tariffs, which guaranteed a premium price for renewable energy in energy markets, to tendering. Over 100 countries globally were using tendering mechanisms by 2019 (REN21 2020: 19). Often termed "reverse auctions", tendering processes involve renewable energy generators placing bids for long-term contracts to sell and/or receive a guaranteed price for electricity at the lowest price possible. This market-based policy mechanism is informed by mainstream economics thinking focused on finding efficient or "least-cost" solutions to climate change, and is an example of a "precision market" (Chapter 4).

Both PPAs and government-tendered contracts underpin the construction of renewable energy-as-asset by guaranteeing future income streams needed to service debt obligations. By "de-risking" the future, PPAs and government-tendered contracts make renewable energy assets bankable. The almost risk-free public finance provided by government contracts is particularly useful for lowering the cost of credit. Both corporate PPAs and tendering processes enforce competition between renewable energy projects to provide large amounts of power cheaply. This is formalized through reverse auction processes that force renewable energy assets to compete with each other on price. Competition based on price has systematically favoured larger-scale corporate renewable energy projects over smaller or community-owned alternatives because they are in a better position to negotiate or bid for contracts. Lucy Baker (2022b: 1758), in her study of renewable energy investment in Mexico and South Africa, characterizes this as a movement towards "big technology, big infrastructure and big capital".

However, narrow terms of government tendering processes for PPAs are being challenged, and governments are experimenting with allocating renewable energy contracts not just on the basis of least cost, but alongside other goals such as the quality, quantity and location of jobs. Union campaigning successfully saw the New York state government design its PPAs for offshore wind with conditions including public sector wage levels, local employment, national procurement and union agreements (Climate Jobs NY 2021). In doing so, the state government is leveraging its position as a large purchaser of renewable energy, rather than simply de-risking the private sector.

Renewable energy is being constructed not only as particular company or project assets, but as a standardized asset class for global investors. As fixed capital that promises to deliver reliable income streams over a long period of time, with government backing as part of energy transition and electrification policies, renewable energy is becoming an asset class that sits alongside established classes of (often polluting) infrastructure assets such as tollways. Indeed, returns from renewable energy have proven to be relatively stable in the face of economic volatility, such as the Covid-19 crisis, and uncorrelated with other classes in equity, debt and real estate markets due to the regulatory and market dynamics of the energy transition (BlackRock 2020). This alternative risk profile of climate finance is attractive to investors looking to diversify risks (see Chapter 3). It has also facilitated a range of secondary market financial products – asset-based securities – that are derived from income streams from credit and leasing arrangements for both utility- and household-scale renewable energy systems (International Energy Agency 2020: 168).

However, the dynamics of constructing renewables as assets creates contradictions between what Baker (2022b: 1757) identifies as the competing objectives of renewable energy "as a predictable, long-term revenue stream for investors, and as a mechanism for socio-economic development and community empowerment". The latter is a crucial part of proposals from international development organizations through to grassroots climate and labour movement activists, who focus on the potential benefits of renewable energy for employment, regional economic development and community empowerment at the centre of plans for "just transitions" (Newell & Mulvaney 2013). But there is evidence that efforts to secure contracts from governments and corporations, and access debt, are undermining socio-ecological benefits. In Mexico and South Africa, the focus on reducing prices and de-risking investments has reduced potential for community benefits such as ownership, revenue sharing and employment, and has led to conflict over and dispossession of land (Baker 2022b). Similar dynamics have been identified in Indonesia, where the risk-return calculations of renewable energy capital has directed financial benefits to global investors and concentrated investment in regions least in need of electrification (Kennedy 2018). These findings are echoed in a growing number of studies showing how renewable energy capital has appropriated or displaced land and livelihoods, particularly in the Global South (Pearse & Bryant 2022).

The case of the Pavagada solar park in Karnataka, South India, illustrates how climate capital structures the socio-ecological-economic outcomes of renewable energy. The 2050MW solar park – the biggest in the world when it was completed in 2019 – is divided into eight plots that are operated by Indian and foreign multinational corporations. The state attracted these investors by auctioning off PPA contracts that guarantee income streams for 25 years. It also brokered access to land by entering into 28-year leases with local landholders and subleasing this land to the renewable energy companies. The spread between payments to the state for land and payments to renewable energy companies for electricity is set to guarantee long-term profits for investors. However, bankability was secured by displacing costs on to local landless labourers, who have lost livelihoods as the agricultural land they previously worked on became a site of energy production (Ghosh, Bryant & Pillai 2022). The case demonstrates that the benefits of climate capital tend to be narrowly shared by asset holders and parties to its associated contracts. As with union campaigning for union-friendly PPAs in New York state, community members actively demanded reforms that would see the

Pavagada project facilitate revenue sharing, co-management of land across energy generation and agriculture and more employment and training opportunities. However, these demands were largely blocked on the basis that they represent unacceptable investment risks.

CONCLUSION

Gap talk makes a compelling case for the need to mobilize capital for climate investments across sectors, scales and sites. Climate capital seeks to address this gap by creating bankable asset classes: an asset and financial arrangement that is able to guarantee future incomes and future green outcomes. In the cases we have explored in this chapter, bankability is secured at the interface of physical assets (e.g. flood protection or renewable energy infrastructure) and financial assets (e.g. sustainable investment funds and green bonds). While climate capital often justifies its existence and operation with reference to the failures of the state under austerity, future income streams from and valuations of climate-related assets are often secured through public finance through leveraging and de-risking, as in both the case of resilient infrastructure and renewable energy assets. The asset classes being developed in the image of climate capital is premised on a climate potentiality: some agreement between buyer and seller that the asset class will have a positive, or at least non-negative, climate impact (Langley *et al.* 2021). And yet, across the different cases we have discussed here, the climate potentiality is vague or undefined. There remain fossil fuels investments in sustainable investment funds or there are only voluntary commitments in the case of green bonds. Climate capitalists recognize the problems with the existing lack of metrics and benchmarks within the industry. One way to redress this is under the rubric of climate risk, to which we turn in Chapter 3. In the meantime, the financial and contractual relations of climate-related asset classes are producing decidedly mixed outcomes.

In each of the financial arrangements and assets explored in this chapter, the trade-offs between and relative successes of financial and climate outcomes remains in question. On the one hand, climate capital is producing good returns for investors, often outperforming non-sustainable forms of investment, and proving to be particularly resilient to other economic shocks and stresses. Nonetheless, and despite these returns, climate capital is yet to witness or induce a structural shift in financial markets to fill this climate "gap": even in the most secure, liquid and scaled of climate asset classes, renewable energy, the scale of investment falls short of what is needed to support a climate transition. The gap between existing and required levels of investment to meet climate goals continues to grow. On the other hand, the green credentials of climate capital are contested, as each of the cases in the chapter show. Worse still are the distributional and socio-spatial outcomes. While the dominant discourse of climate capital is that their investments are integral to address state limits, instead these instruments appear to produce a large-scale transfer from different, often marginalized, publics to financial privates, reproducing socio-spatial inequalities. Moreover, climate capital seems structurally incapable of meeting the financial needs of the most vulnerable sites and citizens. Climate capital remains geographically concentrated in the Global North, both in terms of the sources and destinations of finance. It is the "unelected government" (Castree & Christophers 2015) of private finance who ultimately determine which narrowly prescribed – yet abundantly subsidized – forms of climate capital proceed.

What is the role of climate capital in the context of the very real, if contingent, conjuncture of the climate finance gap? If climate capital is to really do good while doing well, there remain some key sites that must be contended with. Despite the climate capital rhetoric, states are clearly essential for securing climate capital as bankable asset classes (see Chapter 6). There is considerable scope, therefore, for state regulation and intervention as to which climate solutions become investable, with what outcomes and for whom. This requires confronting two key problems of capital in a climate context: its short-term horizons and its structural bias towards maximizing returns over other goals. Further, with existing metrics, the definitional politics of what counts as green remains open. Achieving climate outcomes will require an expansion of currently narrow approaches to measuring impacts to include attention to socio-spatial and distributional impacts that themselves produce climate risk. Ultimately, for climate capital to work for the climate on its own terms, it needs to replace and challenge, not simply be added on top of, the carbon capital of the fossil economy. The next chapter's position on "climate risk" explores private and public efforts not only to profit from climate change, but to use financial instruments, logics and institutions to manage the risks of fossil fuels and climate change.

CHAPTER 3

CLIMATE RISK

Risk is the prominent metric of both contemporary finance and climate change. At its simplest, risk computes the probability of an unexpected or unwanted event occurring. As a function of the severity of an event and its probability, high risk could imply either a more drastic event or greater chance of occurrence, or indeed both. Finance is premised on investment return being a reward for speculating on these risks – with higher yields expected from higher risks, and the inverse. Financial modelling, in turn, is replete with methodologies intended to predict and manage risks, with the ultimate goal of maximizing returns. The basis of these models is that an uncertain future can be navigated – bet on or against – for financial gain, whether by looking back or guessing forward. For both insiders and critics, however, emerging forms, scales and distributions of climate risk trouble this form of risk management. In short, climate change produces risks that not only create existential instability for the financial system, but also for the planet on which finance, and life itself, depends.

In his industry-leading and oft-cited "Tragedy of the Horizon" speech to insurance and reinsurance marketplace Lloyd's of London 2015, then-Governor of the Bank of England, Mark Carney (2015), predicted that the next big financial crisis would be caused by climate change. For Carney and his co-thinkers, climate risk is translated to financial risk in two ways: as physical risk, those direct risks from the impacts of climate change; and as transition risk, or risks associated with societal responses to climate change. While all climate risks might be a financial risk in the general sense that they might have financial impacts, they pose risks to financial stability, and thereby to the financial system, when they are highly interconnected, correlated, large and sudden (Zenghelis & Stern 2016). The US economist, Frank Knight made an influential distinction between uncertainty and risk: the former is classified as "unknowable unknowns" and the latter as knowable, or probabilistic unknowns. Where finance is premised on taking advantage of, or

41

profiting from, these probabilistic risks through hedging, speculation and arbitrage, it is up for debate whether the uncertainties of climate change can be managed in this way.

The politics of climate change has long been one of uncertainty – from manipulations of confidence in scientific projections of climate changes into the future, to changing forecasts of anticipated outcomes and severity. Part of this uncertainty relates to the simple fact that climate change science projects into the future at various spatial and temporal scales; while climate projections describe trends, they are not predictions for specific future events (Dessai *et al.* 2009). Methodologies for measuring and communicating these uncertainties in climate science have evolved over time to both identify and reduce uncertainties, but also to assess how best to communicate uncertainties to diverse publics to facilitate understanding and effective responses. For the IPCC, one necessary shift in nomenclature has been to embrace risk as a communication tool. As described in its first report to adopt a climate risk frame, the Fifth Assessment Report, this focus "evaluate[s] how patterns of risks and potential benefits are shifting due to climate change" (IPCC 2014: 3), and how these might be managed through strategies of adaptation and mitigation. With this turn towards climate risk, the IPCC recognizes the contingent, experiential and dynamic nature of climate changes and its responses. Risk sits alongside resilience in reorienting the "proper" analytical, policy and even individual response to climate change (Derickson 2018). Compared to more static and clunky concepts, risk and resilience are entrepreneurial governance strategies emphasizing management through crisis.

The position of climate finance on climate change examined in this chapter is that taken by financial actors who believe climate change is amenable to prevailing financial risk management practices. Climate risk, as a position on climate change, envisages a climate future that manages, or at least accurately prices, the risks of climate change to profits, asset values and the financial system as a whole. The risks that these financiers are primarily seeking to manage are the risks of climate change to finance, rather than the risks finance produces through its contributions to climate change. This chapter focuses on finance sector initiatives that seek to self-govern climate risk. In Chapter 6 we explore how central banks are adopting a climate risk position in their monetary policy and financial governance activities.

This chapter explores three key tools and practices for managing climate change as financial risk: climate risk disclosure, ESG integration, and divestment. Considering each in turn, the chapter describes the emergence and evolution of the tools, their assumptions and operationalization and their outcomes and implications for climate futures. The politics of climate risk disclosure and ESG integration relate to the cultivation of a more "sustainable" capitalism through which financial actors and systems are left to solve their own problems – both material and in the public image. These tools have become unlikely sites of struggle as divestment campaigners embrace "risky politics" to further their climate goals. Climate risk as financial risk is conceived in industry terms as neoliberal voluntary disclosure and integration strategies through which investment can be subject to objective measures of value and risk that are enforced by market discipline. However, divestment campaigns highlight, and leverage, the inherently political nature of climate risk, by actively risk*ing* fossil fuels to force a reallocation of capital.

CLIMATE RISK DISCLOSURE

As debates and policy about climate change have coalesced around the notion of climate risk, disclosure has emerged as one of the main pillars of climate finance. Companies have various requirements to disclose relevant information to investors and other stakeholders. This information is usually things that may materially impact future prices and values in a positive or negative way. Disclosure requirements aim to provide information to markets so that they can price risks and allocate capital accordingly. Climate disclosure initiatives have sought to extend disclosure regimes to the issue of climate change, primarily through voluntary frameworks. These frameworks have, in turn, shaped understandings of climate risk itself. Like other corporate disclosure frameworks, they rely on economic assumptions of market rationality and the power of market discipline to generate a market response to climate change.

The Carbon Disclosure Project, or CDP, was one of the early climate-focused disclosure organizations. The CDP itself built off the wider move towards sustainability reporting, best represented by the Global Reporting Initiative. The CDP is an NGO that operates by bringing together large investors and major buyers in global supply chains to request disclosures on things such as carbon emissions and climate targets from companies, as well as city and regional governments. This information is self-reported by companies using the CDP's questionnaires, which form the basis of assessments and rankings by the CDP and other organizations. By 2021, the CDP reported that 590 investor members with US$110 trillion in assets, and over 9,600 companies, representing about half of global market capitalization, were disclosing through their system (CDP 2021). Initially, the CDP placed emphasis on the disclosure of emissions in an environment where carbon accounting information of that kind was not otherwise available. Over time, the CDP has come to focus more squarely on the disclosure of emissions and other climate-related information as climate *risks*.

Disclosure was placed at the top of the Mark Carney's agenda in his "Tragedy of the Horizon" speech (Carney 2015). Climate risk disclosure is founded on the principle, as he articulated "that which can be measured, can be managed". Seeking to avoid the scale and suddenness of co-varying climate risks that pose stability threats to financial systems, disclosure asks companies to provide information "to the market" about their exposures to climate risks – whether physical or transition risks. In the speech, Carney announced the establishment of the Task Force on Climate-Related Financial Disclosures (TCFD). The aim of the TCFD would be to coordinate a consistent, comparable, reliable, clear and efficient framework for climate disclosures in response to a fragmented excess of hundreds of different disclosure initiatives, such as the CDP.

Physical risks and transition risks

The TCFD was formed in 2015 by the Financial Stability Board (FSB), an international organization made up of central bank governors and finance ministers from G20 countries, of which Carney was then the chair. The disclosure framework it has developed has been influential in shaping how climate risk is understood and managed. The TCFD is comprised of 32 members, mostly from major companies with a role in climate risk disclosure, including major financial institutions that use climate risk data in their investment decisions, big polluting industrial companies, as well as other actors that analyse climate risk data, such as big accounting firms. In 2017 it released recommendations for climate disclosures to become part of the disclosures already made in mainstream public and annual financial filings. It set out four areas of climate disclosure: the governance of climate risks, actual or potential impacts of climate risk on business strategy, the management of climate risks, and the metrics and targets used to assess risk (TCFD 2017: 14).

The TCFD identifies two broad areas of climate-related risk: physical risks and transition risks. Crucially, these are both understood as *financial* risks, rather than risks of climate change in a more general sense. Physical risks are financial risks that are directly related to the physical basis of climate change. They include both the "acute" risks of extreme climate change-induced events, such as fires and floods, and "chronic" risks of longer-term climatic shifts, such as sea level rises. The TCFD gives examples of the financial impacts of the physical risks of climate change, including disruption to production, increased operating costs, damage to assets and increased insurance premiums. These will appear to be the most obvious climate-related risks to many, but it is transition risk that is becoming more significant in debates about the financial risks of climate change.

Transition risks are the financial implications of the "extensive policy, legal, technology, and market changes to address mitigation and adaptation requirements related to climate change" (TCFD 2017: 5). These are the "socio-political *feedbacks*" of climate change as societies respond to the physical risks of climate change in different ways (Goodman & Anderson 2020) – or what the UN Principles for Responsible Investment call "the inevitable policy response" to climate change. The TCFD breaks this up into four different kinds of transition risk: "policy and legal" risks are the risks from climate policies such as carbon pricing, as well as the risks of litigation for climate damages or breaches of policy; "technology" risk is the risk from shifts towards more climate-friendly technologies such as renewable energy; "market" risks are risks from broader shifts in markets, such as changing prices for raw materials, or changes in consumer preferences; and "reputation" risks are the risks associated with perception of a company's actions in relation to climate change, such as the stigmatization of fossil fuels (TCFD 2017: 5–6, 10). Transition risk and physical risk are clearly related. A well-managed transition should reduce physical risks, or at least the financial costs of the physical impacts of climate change, and increasing physical risks may have socio-political feedbacks to transition risk via public demands for climate action. But it is transition risk that Carney and the TCFD contend represents the biggest risk to asset values, company profits and the stability of the financial system.

Information, efficiency and neoliberal governance

The role of the FSB in establishing the TCFD indicates its origins in post-global financial crisis institutional thinking. The FSB was established in 2009, soon after the 2008 financial crisis with a task of addressing threats to financial stability and, in particular, to develop policy that can address the systemic risks that emerge from the financial risks of particular markets and market actors (Christophers 2017). One of the key areas of post-crisis reform has been to enhance disclosure requirements in the banking sectors, through both the FSB and the Basel III Accord on banking supervision (Financial Stability Board 2011). This reflects a diagnosis of the causes of the global financial crisis as inadequate information about the risks of the subprime mortgage-backed securities market in the US and its relationship to the stability of the finance sector as a whole.

As with subprime mortgages, climate risk disclosure links climate-related financial risks to the possibility of "systemic risk" (Özgöde 2021); that is, the risk that adverse events relating to certain sectors or institutions can be connected to the other sectors and institutions in a way that poses a threat to the broader financial system and economy. Systemic risks often become visible in the context of financial instability caused by what is termed a "Minsky moment", referring to the twentieth-century post-Keynesian economist Hyman Minsky's theory of the tendency of financial markets to take on too much risk during periods of growth, leading to an inevitable market collapse (Minsky 2015). Climate-related financial risks are said to represent systemic risks – a *climate* Minsky moment – if they trigger sudden and unexpected devaluations in fossil fuel or other climate-affected assets that have flow on effects for stability in financial markets exposed to these prices (Carney 2015). Thus, with disclosure climate change is viewed as another potential threat to the financial system, rather than the other way around (Dafermos, Gabor & Michell 2021). As we explore in Chapter 6, this framing of climate is increasingly influential in the way central banks are thinking about their price and financial stability mandates.

While the Minskian ideas that have linked the problem of climate risk to systemic risk have heterodox foundations in post-Keynesian macroeconomics, the rationale for disclosure is closely connected to neoclassical economic ideas of economic efficiency. The TCFD (2017: 42) outlines the logic of disclosure as a process of ensuring that climate "risks and opportunities will be more accurately priced, allowing for the more efficient allocation of capital". Disclosure is understood to do this because of the *information* it provides to the market. As the TCFD (2017: i) outlines, "without the right information, investors and others may incorrectly price or value assets, leading to a misallocation of capital". From a neoclassical economic perspective, efficient, competitive markets allocate scarce resources in an economically optimal way. For this to occur, rational market actors need to have perfect information to make decisions that will maximize their profits or "utility" (satisfaction). Climate disclosure is an attempt to provide financial markets with greater levels of information about climate risks, as a "market correcting strategy" so that market conditions more closely approximate the assumptions of neoclassical economics models (Chenet, Ryan-Collins & van Lerven 2021: 2). With better information, disclosure is intended to promote smoother and more predicable climate transition by adjusting prices to reflect that information. This understanding of the relationship between prices and information is sometimes called the "efficient markets hypothesis" because it assumes that market prices reflect all available information (Ameli *et al.* 2020).

The neoclassical economic rationale of disclosure underpins its status as a distinctly neoliberal form of climate finance governance, based on the claim that markets are processors of information and mediators of uncertainty. Economic geographer Brett Christophers (2017) describes disclosure as a "light-touch" strategy of market correction that relies on market discipline to respond to previously unavailable information about climate risks facing individual companies, investor portfolios and the economy in general. This can be contrasted with somewhat "heavier", although still market-oriented, strategies in which governments construct regulatory markets, such as emissions trading schemes, to more directly price carbon emissions (see Chapter 4), or actively "de-risk" private sector investment (see Chapters 2 and 6). By seeking to create market conditions that are more informed about climate change, rather than construct a market in climate change (e.g. by pricing carbon), disclosure reflects a neoliberal understanding of markets, following key neoliberal thinker Friedrich Hayek, as an omniscient "information processor" (Mirowski 2009).

Despite this expansive configuration of actors and institutions of climate risk, the disclosure of climate risk remains patchy. A report by the CDP (2020) found that only half of financial institutions, such as banks, analysed and disclosed the emissions created by the activities financed by their portfolios, even though these are over 700 times greater than their own direct operational emissions from things such as buildings and travel. The report argues that this is leading to an underestimation of the climate-related credit and market risks that make up the majority of value-at-risk to which financial institutions are exposed. However, even with a more comprehensive disclosure regime, questions would remain about whether perfect information on the uncertainties of climate change is possible and whether market actors would follow the economic theory underpinning disclosure and act rationally. To examine these issues further, we explore how climate risk information is entering into (or not) the decisions of investors through the rise of ESG.

ENVIRONMENTAL, SOCIAL AND GOVERNANCE (ESG) INTEGRATION

In practice, climate and other disclosures enter market decision-making through ESG "integration". At its most basic level, ESG is an approach to investment decision-making and corporate management that seeks to incorporate factors beyond conventional financial metrics. These include climate factors such as greenhouse gas emissions or fossil fuel intensity, other "environmental" factors including biodiversity impacts, as well as "social" factors such as labour conditions and human rights, and "governance" factors such as a business's compliance with regulation or corporate board diversity. Crucially, these factors are integrated into investment and management practices in a particular way: as *financial risks* (Parfitt 2020). Chapter 2 discussed the role of ESG in "sustainable investing" through sustainable-labelled funds. However, the ambition of ESG goes beyond particular sustainable investment strategies to encompass the assessment and management of climate and other risks into the operation of financial markets generally (Parfitt & Bryant 2021).

ESG both informs and processes the disclosure of climate and other risks by providing frameworks for what should be disclosed and by creating metrics that turn these disclosures into ratings. This is central to the neoliberal governance vision of disclosure because it represents a "private taxonomy for green/dirty finance" (Gabor 2021b: 15). ESG has enjoyed a rapid rise, with most institutional investors and publicly traded companies espousing their ESG credentials. With this rise has come a range of difficult questions surrounding what ESG criteria should be applied and how ESG performance should be measured. Political actors from both left and right have questioned the validity of ESG strategies. ESG also highlights the limits of risk as a position on climate finance, by elevating "financial materiality" as an arbiter of action over climate risk.

A politics of measure in ESG

ESG has become an industry in its own right. The voluntary, private sector-led movement towards disclosure and ESG integration has resulted in a proliferation of competing ESG frameworks. By 2018, there were already over 600 globally (Murray 2021). These include major stock market index providers such as S&P Dow Jones and FTSE Group, investment research and advisory firms MSCI and Morningstar, and other boutique ESG firms. Meanwhile, many investors have developed their own internal ESG frameworks, or developed shared benchmarks with other investors, such as the "asset-owner led" Transition Pathway Initiative.

Disclosure and ESG ratings are inconsistent and often contradictory. Even the most significant ESG ratings providers – MSCI, Morningstar, Moody's, S&P, FTSE and Refinitiv – demonstrate significant inconsistencies in how the same companies are rated (Berg, Kölbel & Rigobon 2020). Conflicting ESG ratings are the result of different methods employed by agencies. Differences in the scope of factors that are assessed between the E, the S and the G (e.g. climate versus labour rights) and the different weightings given to these factors lead to differing ratings. For instance, Tesla received a high ESG rating by MSCI due to the contribution of the electric cars it produces to reducing transport emissions, but a low ESG rating from FTSE due to the emissions from its factories and governance concerns, including the lack of climate disclosure (O'Mahony 2019). Different ways of measuring performance are also at play, because ratings can be based on absolute achievements towards, for example, actually reducing emissions, or relative emissions intensity compared with other firms in the same sector, or the strength of future emissions targets. Divergences in ESG ratings between agencies starkly contrast with the high correlations between credit ratings given by the same companies. Gabor (2021b: 17) argues that the existence of different and often contradictory private ESG ratings enables investors to game the system to their own advantage in a process of "green regulatory arbitrage" as investors pick and choose ESG ratings that suit them.

The issue of inconsistency is being met with a range of initiatives to harmonize standards (Parfitt 2022). As discussed above, the TCFD seeks to create a framework for consistent, comparable and objective disclosures on climate risk. Other initiatives aim to create a common set of rules for reporting, accounting for and rating information that is disclosed. NGOs have been established with the aim of standardizing ESG metrics through processes that mirror earlier efforts to standardize corporate accounting and financial reporting. The Social Accounting Standards Board developed ESG accounting standards for 77 industries in 2018. In 2021, the Board merged with the International Integrated Reporting Council, to create the Value Reporting Foundation, to further consolidate ESG accounting frameworks. In 2022, the latter then joined the International Financial Reporting Standards Foundation, the peak international corporate accounting and financial reporting body, which hosts the International Accounting Standards Board, as part of its project of developing an International Sustainability Standards Board that can act as an equivalent to the International Accounting Standards Board.

Other attempts to standardize ESG are coming from government authorities, the most advanced of which is the European Union's (EU's) "taxonomy" for sustainable activities. Initiatives such as this shift ESG from its roots as a form of private regulation, into greater levels of public control, political debate and contestation. For example, the development of the EU's taxonomy was heavily contested by governments, industry and environmental groups over issues such as how to classify natural gas and nuclear power (Khan 2021). As with levels of disclosure, while inconsistencies remain, the trend is towards greater levels of standardization. However, contestation over both public and private metrics show that there is no absolute or objective ethical basis of ESG (Parfitt 2020) – it is subject to politics and competing interests.

Contesting ESG

ESG has become heavily contested as a result of scandals over greenwashing. In a prominent example, the offices of German asset manager DWS, which is owned by Deutsche Bank, were raided by police following allegations by a whistleblower that it had made misleading statements about the high proportion of its assets being ESG-integrated, despite them being managed according to conventional methods (Tett 2022). This kind of green integrity issue is not limited to particular asset managers and investment funds. Shares of Adani, the controversial Indian company that has faced high-profile accusations of corporate misconduct relating to stock price manipulation, and that, as we discuss below, has been targeted by divestment activists for its coal operations, were found in over 500 ESG-labelled funds (White 2023). Mounting ESG scandals have led to investigations and legal proceedings by regulators in the US, UK, Europe and Australia over ESG claims. Authorities such as the US Securities and Exchange Commission have responded by announcing initiatives to strengthen their anti-greenwashing powers (Quinson 2021).

Scandals have left ESG exposed to progressive criticisms that it represents the latest phase of greenwashing. Simultaneously, ESG has become a significant terrain of contestation over climate finance led by right-wing politicians in the US. The right-wing anti-ESG backlash charges ESG as a "woke" agenda that, instead of providing green cover for business as usual, is leading to a wholesale rejection of fossil fuels. The ESG backlash has been driven by Republican-controlled states in the US, including Texas and Florida, which have sought to ban managers of state pension fund assets from considering ESG risks in their investments. BlackRock, along with Credit Suisse, BNP Paribas, UBS, Nordea and Danske Bank, were placed on an anti-ESG list of financial companies that "boycott" fossil fuels released by the Texas government (Texas Comptroller of Public Accounts 2022). The Governor of Florida, Ron DeSantis, said that ESG investing was being used to "impose an ideological agenda on the American people" based on "whimsical notions of a utopian tomorrow" (DeSantis 2022). This right-wing backlash against ESG has led to the formation of "anti-ESG" investment funds that either promise not to screen for ESG factors, are deliberately focused on fossil fuel investments, or even explicitly screen for companies that are aligned with the political right (Green 2021).

Financial institutions and US Democratic politicians have, in turn, defended ESG, stressing that ESG investing applies a strictly risk-based approach that is in line with, and indeed required by, fiduciary duty. In 2023, 270 banks, asset managers and institutional investors, including Californian and New York public sector pension funds, formed the "Freedom to Invest" alliance. Their founding statement read: "Our consideration of material environmental, social, and governance (ESG) factors is not political or ideological. Incorporating these issues into financial decision-making represents good corporate governance, prudent risk management, and smart investment practice consistent with fiduciary duty" (Freedom to Invest 2023). Democrats in the federal House of Representatives similarly formed a Sustainable Investment Caucus with the aim of promoting ESG in Congress, and Democrat-controlled states, such as Maryland and Illinois, have passed legislation requiring state pension funds to integrate ESG factors (Ropes & Gray 2023; Vargas 2023).

The limits of risk

Right-wing critiques of ESG demonstrate that climate finance is being contested across the political spectrum. However, they overstate the influence of ESG in financial markets. A study of investment managers, analysts and ESG or senior managers at institutional investors found limited evidence that climate risk was having a material impact on investment decisions (Christophers 2019). It found a range of reasons for this, including the largely advisory role of ESG positions, perceived clashes between ESG goals and fiduciary duties to maximize returns, and the growth of passive forms of investing, such as index investing.

This is further reflected in data on the pricing of climate risk in financial markets and continued significant exposure to fossil fuels despite disclosure and ESG commitments. Given that disclosure is supposed to enable the pricing of climate risk, investments that have greater levels of climate risk should carry a "risk premium" in the cost of capital compared with less risky assets. The evidence for this is mixed. Carbon risk premiums, compared with market averages, are mainly observable in the coal, but not oil and gas, industries, and only applied to direct, "scope 1" emissions, rather than the wider carbon footprint of firms (Zhao *et al.* 2021). The material impact of these interest rate spreads are, however, marginal. Even for the top 10 per cent of carbon-intensive companies, the average carbon risk premium adds only fractionally to the interest rate paid (Ehlers, Packer & de Greiff 2021). The relative costs of capital for solar and wind have, nonetheless, fallen significantly in the last decade as the investment risks of renewable energy have declined, with state support.

Many banks are opting to take on climate risk by continuing to lend to fossil fuel industries. Of the financial institutions listed by Texas as boycotting fossil fuels, none are in fact fossil free (Kirsch *et al.* 2022). Indeed, in the four years following the adoption of the Paris Agreement (2016–19), 35 of the largest global banks – many of which have made pledges and created policies around climate risk – provided $2.7 trillion worth of finance to the fossil fuel sector (Kirsch *et al.* 2020). ESG may also facilitate fossil fuel lending, when companies use ESG pledges, or non-climate ESG factors, to secure finance. For example, the Port of Newcastle, Australia, the world's biggest coal export terminal, secured a loan, after being previously denied by another lender, by agreeing to ESG conditions including reducing the port's direct emissions from its own energy use (scope 1 and 2), but not those who ultimately burn the coal it transports, which is the biggest climate impact of its activities. These climate impacts were also traded off against other "social" commitments, such as those around the prevention of modern slavery, in the loan conditions (Millington 2021).

There are also deeper questions about whether risk itself is an appropriate frame for addressing climate change in the context of radical uncertainty. For economists Hugues Chenet, Josh Ryan-Collins and Frank van Lerven (2021) climate risks are Knightian uncertainties, due to the complexity and multiplicity of climate change. From this perspective, there is a disjuncture between the models produced by climate science and the information required by finance to calculate physical risk (Fiedler *et al.* 2021). While advances in climate models will close this information gap, transition risk is even more uncertain because it is inherently political. This is the kind of uncertainty that has led environmental advocates to support a precautionary approach, which is cautious, rather than financially optimizing (Chenet, Ryan-Collins & van Lerven 2021). The risk framing also constrains the scale and kind of climate action that is undertaken. Framing climate change as risk may bias policy and decisions against transformative change, because transformative action is configured as too large of a policy risk (Gabor 2021b). At its worst, this bias against transformative change could work against the kinds of polices and political action needed to effect it.

A risk position does not prevent any activities absolutely, it simply shifts the financial terms on which market actors make their decision. As discussed above, if an investment has a higher climate risk, then this should be reflected in a higher cost of capital; this is intended to make some activities unviable if they are unable to service higher debt costs or deliver the increased profits required to access finance. But investing in activities with high climate risk will be immensely profitable for some actors, if the price is right. As one investor stated in relation to how they integrate climate risk: "It's not a question of invest or not. In terms of company valuation, it's a question of am I being paid sufficiently to accept the risk I have identified" (quoted in Christophers 2019). This even provides opportunity for speculation (see Chapter 5). As Tariq Fancy (2021), former Chief of Sustainable Investing at BlackRock turned public critic of ESG revealed, there exist "portfolio managers who actively mine ESG data to bet against environmentally responsible companies in the name of profit, a short-selling strategy". Climate risk presents an explicitly alternative framework compared to prohibition via command-and-control policies.

The risks captured by disclosure and ESG integration are partial. Disclosure and ESG integration largely aim to capture only *financially* material risks – only risks to investors and the financial system (Parfitt & Bryant 2021). The defence of ESG by the Freedom to Invest alliance was explicit about this limit to ESG in its statement, which proclaimed "we remain wholly committed to sustainability and addressing the financial impacts of climate change ... that have a *material impact* on our own operations and investments" (Freedom to Invest 2023, emphasis added). Social and environmental risks, both from the physical impacts of climate change and the transition to a lower carbon economy, that are not considered financially material are largely excluded. As Fancy (2021) puts it, "... risk managers are focused on protecting their investment portfolios from potential damages done by a worsening climate rather than helping prevent that damage from occurring in the first place". By limiting *whose* risks are considered, ESG configures a profit position by disregarding, or even shifting, risks to people and environments not deemed to be financially material (Parfitt 2020). There are efforts to push these limits: the EU taxonomy introduced the notion of "double materiality" to incorporate both financial risk to companies and socio-ecological risk (European Commission 2021). However, these moves have to contend with the inherent asymmetries contained within risk metrics between the financial and the non-financial.

DIVESTMENT

Progressive activists have responded to the hegemony of "risk" in debates about climate change and climate finance. Divestment movements take a climate risk position as a means to challenge fossil fuels – a "risky" politics that makes financial arguments against investment in fossil fuels on the basis that it represents an unacceptable climate risk. Divestment can form part of, but goes beyond, ESG investment. As demonstrated, ESG investment may positively or negatively screen certain kinds of investments or integrate assessments of ESG risk into wider investment decision processes. In contrast, fossil fuel divestment is about convincing an organization to sell investments or stop providing finance or financial services to fossil fuel-related activities.

Fossil fuel divestment has developed with reference to historical examples of divestment, such as Quaker divestment from slavery in the UK and US, and the international anti-South African apartheid movement in the 1970s and 80s. An article in *Rolling Stone* titled "Global Warming's Terrifying New Math", by founder of 350.org, Bill McKibben, was a key moment in the emergence of the global fossil fuel divestment movement (2012). In that article, McKibben quotes Archbishop Desmond Tutu on the importance of international divestment in ending apartheid. While noting that the global scale, financial importance and state backing of fossil fuel companies makes the industry "a tougher opponent", the article pointed towards university endowments and pension funds as potential strategic targets for fossil fuel divestment due to the political opportunity emerging from both industries' commitment to the future of their stakeholders, as graduates and retirees.

Stranded assets

The case for divestment is informed by high-profile studies on the necessary constraints on future carbon use and concentration of responsibility for emissions among a relatively small number of fossil fuel corporations (Heede 2013). Limiting warming to 2°C requires staying within a carbon budget, which means abandoning at least one-third of oil reserves, half of gas reserves, and 80 per cent of coal reserves between 2010 and 2050 (McGlade & Ekins 2015). Keeping these reserves grounded has also produced swathes of "unburnable carbon", "stranded assets" and potentially a financial "carbon bubble". The notion of "unburnable carbon" was propagated by the think tank Carbon Tracker which, in its influential 2011 report, found that "up to 80% of declared reserves owned by the world's largest listed coal, oil and gas companies and their investors would be subject to impairment as these assets become stranded" (Carbon Tracker 2011: 2). It was argued that this becomes a financial problem because a large proportion of the listed value of prominent stock exchanges comes from fossil fuel companies each with substantial assets at risk of becoming stranded. The report pointed out that one-third of the market capitalization of the FTSE100 index of the 100 biggest companies listed in the London Stock Exchange came from fossil fuel-intensive energy companies. Carbon Tracker described this problem as a "systemic risk" due to the "threat it pose[d] of a carbon bubble bursting" – an especially effective warning in the immediate aftermath of the 2008 financial crisis (Carbon Tracker 2011: 3).

The divestment campaign mobilized analysis of stranded assets to reframe carbon from asset to liability and thus a financial risk (Goodman & Anderson 2020; Knuth 2017). It sought to convince investors to respond to the spectre of stranded assets by divesting from fossil fuels in their investment portfolios. Initially, divestment campaigners targeted two kinds of institutions: those with an explicit social purpose more susceptible to moral arguments, such as universities and charities, and so-called "universal owners", long-term institutional investors with diversified portfolios that reach across all sectors of the economy (Hawley & Williams 2007). For example, Hampshire College, a small liberal arts college in Massachusetts USA, was the first to divest its endowment from fossil fuels in 2011, a move that has since been followed by over 1,000 institutions (Go Fossil Free/350.org 2021; Ross 2020). Institutional investors, such as sovereign wealth funds and pension funds, are thought to be more concerned about systemic risk than investors with more targeted investments because their diversified holding leaves them exposed to the performance of the financial system as a whole. The sovereign wealth funds of Norway and Ireland, and the pension funds of New York City's teachers and civil servants, have all divested accordingly.

The divestment campaign has used a range of different tactics to pressure institutions to divest, including traditional movement tactics such as direct protest and targeted petitioning, and, increasingly, financial tactics such as shareholder activism. UK-based ShareAction and US-based MajorityAction use shareholding power to put divestment and other climate resolutions up at company annual general meetings. These tactics are increasingly moving from initial "moral" targets, such as churches and universities, and targets that have some avenues for members or citizens to create democratic pressure, such as pension funds and sovereign wealth funds, to the mainstream of financial markets.

Divestment campaigns have targeted the institutions at the heart of "asset manager capitalism" (Braun 2021). The world's largest asset managers, BlackRock, Vanguard and State Street, own on average 20 per cent of all S&P 500 companies (Backus, Conlon & Sinkinson 2021). ShareAction and MajorityAction have criticized the poor record of BlackRock, Vanguard and State Street in voting against divestment and other climate shareholder resolutions, where their substantial voting rights would have provided enough votes to pass numerous resolutions (Majority Action 2020; ShareAction 2020). Similarly, the "BlackRock's Big Problem" campaign – a coalition of environmental organizations and financial activist organizations – has highlighted BlackRock's substantial fossil fuel investment portfolio and called for it to exclude "climate-harming" companies from its active funds (BlackRock's Big Problem 2021).

Climate litigation has also emerged as a tactic of divestment movements. In a landmark case, a Dutch court ordered the oil and gas major Shell to increase its climate targets in a lawsuit instigated by the Dutch wing of Friends of the Earth. In the judgement, the court found that Shell was "expected to take the necessary steps to remove or prevent the serious risks ensuing from the CO_2 emissions generated by them", meaning Shell would need to "forgo new investments in the extraction of fossil fuels and/or will limit its production of fossil resources" (*Milieudefensie et al. vs Royal Dutch Shell PLC* 2021). Such cases have had varying degrees of success in different jurisdictions, with around half of cases in Europe having favourable climate outcomes since 2000 (Setzer & Higham 2022). However, climate litigation, as a tactic of divestment, is not only about forcing outcomes by the company being sued, but to make the financial risks of climate change material by creating litigation risk across the fossil fuel industry.

To be, or not to be, a shareholder

The usefulness of divestment as a strategy to combat climate change is heavily debated. Critics of divestment argue that it makes little, if any, direct financial impact on fossil fuel companies and greenhouse gas emissions, because divested shares are simply bought by other investors. As these shares have already been issued, selling does not directly impact the working capital available to the company, even if it reduces share prices, for which the evidence is uncertain. This argument was articulated by Bill Gates, whose foundation came under pressure from divestment activists and *The Guardian* newspaper in 2015. In his book, Gates (2021: 9) declares:

> … as much as I appreciated the protesters' passion, I didn't see how divesting alone would stop climate change or help people in poor countries. It was one thing to divest from companies to fight apartheid, a political institution that would (and did) respond to economic pressure. It's another thing to transform the world's energy system—an industry worth roughly $5 trillion a year and the basis for the modern economy—just by selling the stocks of fossil-fuel companies.

Gates put it even more bluntly in a 2019 interview when he said "divestment, to date, probably has reduced about zero tonnes of emissions. It's not like you've capital-starved [the] people making steel and gasoline" (quoted in Edgecliffe-Johnson & Nauman 2019).

Advocates for divestment counter Gates's arguments. While divestment may not affect existing capital available to companies, advocates argue that it can reduce the capacity of fossil fuel companies to raise future capital by negatively impacting new rounds of share issuance. Divestment also now reaches beyond equity markets and the selling of shares to increasingly target debt markets by calling for banks to stop lending to fossil fuels, for investors to stop buying bonds used to finance fossil fuels or for insurers to provide insurance. As we will discuss shortly, this was a key strategy in the Stop Adani campaign in Australia. Divestment advocates acknowledge the limited direct economic impact of divestment, and instead highlight the stigmatization it brings to fossil fuels. Stigmatization, advocates contend, "poses the most far-reaching threat to fossil fuel companies and the vast energy value chain. Any direct impacts pale in comparison" (Ansar, Caldecott & Tilbury 2013: 13). By stigmatizing the fossil fuel industry, divestment aims to delegitimatize and damage the reputation of fossil fuels in a way that both creates uncertainty for investors and encourages governments to take policy action (Goodman & Anderson 2020).

Divestment is often contrasted with shareholder engagement, as a classic case of the choice between "exit" and "voice". For critics, by divesting from companies, investors give up their power to engage with companies as shareholders, which has been a crucial strategy beyond the divestment campaign. Shareholder engagement has delivered some important climate wins in fossil fuel companies. For example, in 2021 an activist hedge fund called Engine No. 1 orchestrated a shareholder vote that removed and replaced some of oil company Exxon Mobil's management board over lack of action on decarbonization. The hedge fund held just 0.002 per cent of shares, but used this position to gain majority support from major shareholders such as BlackRock, which had been previously criticized for a poor voting record on other such resolutions (Marsh & Kishan 2021).

There are, however, limits to "shareholder democracy" in publicly listed companies. Ownership of shares remains concentrated among the wealthy, and many companies are structured in ways that make it difficult for shareholder resolutions to pass. For example, the big conglomerate company Berkshire Hathaway successfully resisted shareholder resolutions about climate disclosure because billionaire Warren Buffet's A-Class stock gave him significantly more (10,000 times) voting power than institutional and retail investors that own B-Class stock (Platt 2021). Nonetheless, engagement strategies are not counterposed, and often go hand in hand with divestment. Many campaigns and organizations supporting divestment, such as "BlackRock's Big Problem", have engagement goals alongside divestment goals. Indeed, divestment can provide leverage for engagement: company managements that are sensitive to shareholder value and wish to attract and maintain institutional investment may seek to make changes to avoid threats of divestment.

There are, however, barriers to divestment arising from prevailing structures of fossil fuel ownership. Divestment discourse adopts a polarizing in or out narrative that may not quite match how investors think (Mangat, Dalby & Paterson 2018). Investors tend to think in terms of whether they are under or overweight in a certain asset class on the basis of risk and return calculations, rather than whether to invest or not (Christophers 2019). Divestment is also limited by the rise of passive investing, where investments track a pre-defined index of companies and other assets. Here divestment requires either movement from one index fund to another or the reworking of established indices.

The greatest challenge, though, comes from the declining role of publicly listed ownership in the oil, gas and coal sectors. An increasing proportion of oil, gas and coal assets and companies are owned either by private equity firms, such as Blackstone or KKR, or are state-owned companies, such as Saudi Aramco, PetroChina and Gazprom, with minimal public shareholders. In addition, publicly listed fossil fuel companies, such as the Western oil majors, are primarily financed through debt – "brown" bonds and bank loans – rather than shareholder equity. This shift creates challenges for disclosure initiatives and divestment movements alike, as their avenue for change, be it market discipline or political pressure, occurs via the mechanisms of public share-holding that are limited in private equity and state-owned companies. There has been a long-term decline in the proportion of market capitalization on major stock market indices, such as the UK's FTSE100, or the S&P500 in the US, represented by fossil fuel companies (Christophers 2021b: 247). On one hand, this reflects the long-term financial struggles of Western fossil majors that are still listed, which divestment activists can claim some credit for. On the other hand, it reflects a shift of fossil fuel production away from the main spheres of influence for divestment movements.

Risky politics

The Stop Adani campaign, targeted at the Adani Carmichael coal mine in Queensland, Australia, illustrates many debates about divestment. When first proposed in 2010 by Indian multinational company Adani, the Carmichael mine was planned to be one of the biggest coal mines in the world. It was immediately controversial in Australia and internationally due to the significant amount of greenhouse gases its coal would produce, and the fact that the bigger Galilee Basin of coal deposits could be further opened up by Adani's infrastructure to other miners. Critics of the mine also raised concerns about respecting land rights of Indigenous Traditional Owners, extirpation of endangered species and impacts on other industries such as agriculture and tourism from threats to groundwater and the Great Barrier Reef (Curran 2020).

A key plank of the Stop Adani campaign has been a campaign to "stop the money", alongside other campaign tactics such as direct action and climate litigation. Given state regulatory approval and fiscal support for the mine, which received significant loans, subsidies and tax credits from federal and state governments, activists turned to divestment tactics targeting banks considering financing the project, insurers considering providing insurance, engineering and construction contractors and investors in Adani's coal port. Across each of these categories, 140 major companies ruled out providing finance and services to Adani's Carmichael mine, including insurers AXA and Allianz and banks JPMorgan Chase and HSBC (Market Forces 2021). In appealing to these companies, the Stop Adani campaign primary highlighted the financial risk of Adani becoming a stranded asset, as well as the liability risks of future climate litigation. This pitch was helped by the decline of coal prices from 2010 to 2020, and growing recognition of the structural decline of coal.

The campaign against Adani shows the evolving dynamics of, and the possibilities and constraints facing, divestment campaigns. The campaign illustrates the repertoire of tactics that divestment has developed beyond divestment of share portfolios, including targeting debt and insurance markets as an avenue for responding to privately held companies based outside of Anglo-American capitalism. Yet, when Adani was not able to secure financing from any banks, its billionaire owner Gautam Adani announced the company would instead self-finance a smaller-scale project (Curran 2020). He later said "… if we realised there's so much objection, that so much resistance will come … we would have not done" the Carmichael mine. Divestment campaigners, therefore, mitigated the scale of the mine, and have signalled future risks to prospective developers of the vast coal reserves of the Galilee Basin, but were not able to stop it. Despite successfully stigmatizing the project, with two-thirds of Australians opposed to the mine, the campaign failed to stop the project, financially or politically (Massola 2018). This suggests that divestment alone needs to be coupled with other political tactics to further shift politics.

Where climate change is increasingly viewed and managed through the prism of risk, divestment is a form of "risky politics". While Gates's foundation eventually did divest, he justified this not as an economic decision but as an ethical one, in not wanting to profit from fossil fuels, stating, "I'd feel bad if I benefited from a delay in getting to zero" (Gates 2021: 10). For Gates, economic impact comes from investing in climate solutions (such as those in Chapter 1 on climate capital, or Chapter 4 on speculative markets), whereas divestment only works narrowly, in targeting particular institutions. But Gates misses how divestment aims to change politics through an explicitly financial strategy.

Rather than simply making arguments to reallocate capital as a response to climate risk, divestment aims to put fossil fuels "at risk" through its own actions, bringing future risk forward to today as a kind of political feedback from the climate crisis into the corporate and financial world (Goodman & Anderson 2020). Divestment tactics, from direct action to shareholder resolutions to climate litigations, *add* to the financial risk calculations of prospective fossil fuel investment decisions. That is, risky politics can increase levels of risk and uncertainty, particularly around government policy, or transition risk, to performatively induce asset-stranding. Climate risk is a domain of political contestation that is being actively produced and expanded by political movements.

CONCLUSION

The "climate risk" position on climate finance is the corollary of "climate capital". The latter looks for opportunities to profit from the financial opportunities of climate change through the creation of new climate-related assets.

The former seeks to manage the financial risks of climate change to avoid large shocks to existing asset prices. Together, climate capital and climate risk combine to form a singular strategy for the financial governance of climate change that is oriented towards securing profitable climate futures through an orderly transition. Disclosure and ESG represent the key tools for private sector governance of financial risk. They demonstrate a bias in the financial risk framing of climate change towards managing the risks of climate change to finance, rather than reducing the risks of climate change to people and environments that are being created by fossil fuel companies and the institutions that finance them.

Tools such as disclosure and ESG are grounded in neoclassical and neoliberal economic rationalities. However, contestation over these tools shows that climate risk is not a pure domain of objective financial analysis and rational market forces. The very concept of transition risk, which captures the financial risks created by future political responses to climate change and is at the heart of climate risk frameworks, is fundamentally political. Valuing an asset through this prism requires political judgements about factors such as the stringency of future emissions targets and the power of climate movements creating pressure on governments to act. Climate risk now includes the political risks of radical decarbonization alongside abrupt tipping points. Divestment movements are actively engaging in strategies that aim to shift risk calculations against fossil fuels. Climate litigation cases, or campaigns for institutions to divest their fossil fuel shareholdings, usually rest on an argument that firms or investors are inadequately pricing climate risk. But the strategy, in effect, is to *make* climate change a financially material risk. Ironically, the right-wing backlash against ESG demonstrates the extent to which climate politics is increasingly occurring through debates and negotiations over climate risk frameworks. The US Republicans seeking to ban ESG investing, and conservative-aligned "anti-ESG" investment funds, are no less participating in the risky politics of climate finance than the fossil fuel divestment activist aiming to make "stranded assets" a self-fulfilling prophesy. Both are actively constructing financial risk as a political battleground of climate change by placing different climate futures "at risk". Climate finance is now the central platform on which this "risky politics" of climate change is playing out.

CHAPTER 4

PRECISION MARKETS

Market environmentalism is premised on market-based tools being the most efficient methods for managing the allocation of environmental goods and services. This chapter explores what we call "precision markets": markets and market-based policies that seek to allocate responses to climate change by charting pathways towards an efficient level of adaptation and mitigation. Precision markets are the quintessential tools of climate finance envisaged by economists and actuaries (Keen 2021; Taylor 2023). The position on climate change taken by precision markets is based on precise predictions about the future, and the differentiated costs of those futures. Precision takes a variety of forms, but is reliant on models of the interaction between climate and economic systems across different possible scenarios.

In this chapter we explore three configurations of precision markets: attempts to estimate the social cost of carbon, the construction of carbon markets, and catastrophe insurance markets. Each involves projections of climate futures that seek to compare the costs and benefits of different forms of climate action and of climate change itself. As we show, precision market mechanisms do not attempt to avoid or minimize climate change to the greatest extent possible through technology or political action. Transformative adaptations spurred by insurance pricing or deep cuts to greenhouse gas emissions are usually viewed as violating goals of economic optimality due to inefficiently high economic costs. Rather, precision markets use calculative predictions and the price mechanism to find the right balance of action between current and future costs.

Precision markets are ways of making climate mitigation and adaptation economic. Michel Callon and his economic sociologist colleagues would call this *economization*: the contested and contingent processes of making things and subjects economic (Caliskan & Callon 2009). There are different mechanisms through which the allocation of carbon and catastrophe become economic: through accounting techniques such as cost-benefit analyses and through probabilistic assessments of future climate risks, climate action and the impacts of climate change are assigned a price. Following these calculations, different policy actions and individual choices can be compared, with decisions based on an adjudication of options according to monetary costs. Accordingly, precision markets serve both an information and incentive purpose.

Through economization, both climate policy and climate policy decision-making become a calculative exercise, with rational decisions and decision-makers expected to trade off current and future risks, costs and benefits. As a result, economization requires making market subjects – what Blok (2011) calls "Homo Carbonomicus" or the carbon-price-calculating-subject. Whether it is government agencies using calculations of the social cost of carbon to make decisions, polluting companies deciding whether to reduce or offset their emissions, or individual households and farmers taking out insurance policies, precision markets position new agents to account for climate risk. Creating market agents is always a distributional process, defining who is responsible for managing which climate risks (Collier, Elliott & Lehtonen 2021).

As climate governance in the post-Kyoto period has largely been left to market tools, new climate markets have proliferated. The making of markets for managing climate change is often studied through the framework of econo-mization, or the performativity of economics. In Callon's simple description, the performativity of economics describes how economics "performs, shapes and formats the economy, rather than observing how it functions" (1998: 2). This statement appears to suggest that markets are an almost automatic, tech-nical outcome of economic models and financial predictions, where politics are relegated to what theorists call overflowings and misfires (Callon 2010). But marketization, and economization more broadly, are only ever contin-gent achievements, subject to ongoing contestation over the distribution of and responsibility for calculation – or debates over "what is included, what is excluded, and what seems to defy calculation altogether" (Elliott 2021: 4).

This chapter explores the economization of climate finance via precision markets. The position of "precision markets" describes forms of climate finance that promise to facilitate precise calculations of the costs and benefits, or risks and opportunities, of different climate pathways. The first section debates the "social cost of carbon", where economists construct shadow markets to calculate the economically efficient level of climate change. The second section moves to carbon markets, which make different emissions reductions equivalent and tradeable, in search of the lowest cost climate miti-gation. The third and final section then considers insurance markets that calculate, make fungible and price exposures to future climate risk. We look beneath the veneer of precision in each of these markets and show how they contain a vision that organizes climate transition according to calculations of profitability.

SOCIAL COSTS OF CARBON

In his landmark report to the UK government, former World Bank Chief Economist Nicholas Stern (2007: i) famously described climate change as "the greatest and widest-ranging market failure ever seen". Stern's report on the economics of climate change diagnosed the cause of climate change as unpriced greenhouse gas emissions. These unpriced emissions are understood to create "externalities": social costs arising from things such as sea level rise, drought or vector-borne diseases that are not paid for by polluters. Climate change, as market failure, is viewed as a malfunctioning of the role of markets and prices in allocating resources efficiently.

The goal of climate change economics is not necessarily to reduce greenhouse gas emissions, and the impacts of climate change, to as close to zero as possible. Following the welfare economics tradition pioneered by Arthur Cecil Pigou, the aim is to "internalize" the externality by finding the economically optimal level of pollution and climate change (Pigou 1932). Yet, economists stress that there are trade-offs between the costs of climate change and the costs of acting on climate change. The goal, following Ronald Coase's new institutional economics critique of Pigou, is therefore to "avoid the most serious harm", meaning the cost of climate action should not outweigh the costs of climate change itself (Coase 1960: 2). Correcting climate change as a market failure becomes "a question of balance" (Nordhaus 2008).

Economists calculate the precise level of carbon mitigation and adaptation by measuring the "social cost of carbon". Social costs of carbon are estimates of the economic damage of each additional amount of carbon emissions released into the atmosphere, usually expressed in terms of US dollars per tonne of carbon dioxide-equivalent. In theory, the social cost of carbon is the precise monetary value of the externality caused by unpriced carbon emissions. Calculations of the social cost of carbon are powerful because they can be used to judge exactly how much climate action, and climate damage, is acceptable, by enabling cost-benefit analyses of climate change under different scenarios of future action or non-action. Higher social costs of carbon signal that future climate change will be more costly, making efforts to reduce emissions today "pay off". In contrast, low social costs of carbon signal that the economic benefits of today's pollution may be greater than the eventual costs of climate damages.

Integrated assessment models and the Nordhaus Nobel prize

The primary way of calculating social costs of carbon is through "integrated assessment models" (IAMs) focused on aggregating climate costs and benefits. IAMs are climate economics models that calculate social costs of carbon by "integrating" scientific models of climate change with economic models of growth to find the "optimal" levels of both (Pindyck 2013). There are three main IAMs: DICE (Dynamic Integrated Climate-Economy model), FUND (Framework for Uncertainty, Negotiation and Distribution model) and PAGE (Policy Analysis of the Greenhouse Effect model). The DICE model, developed in the 1990s by climate change economist William Nordhaus and since refined, has been the most influential of the three, although the Stern Review opted to use PAGE.

IAMs work by connecting climate science models of "climate sensitivity" (how much temperatures rise as a result of anthropogenic increases in atmospheric greenhouse gases) and "climate damages" (how much temperature rise will impact things such as property, industry or labour productivity) with economic models of growth, population and pollution. The models are integrated via a "damages function" that calculates the total loss to the level of economic output because of climate change. The social cost of carbon is then calculated in today's dollars by applying a "discount rate" to the future costs of climate change. "Discounting" attempts to enable decision-making over time by making the costs of climate action today comparable with the costs of future climate change in monetary terms, by reducing the value of future costs relative to today. The rate chosen has both drastic consequences for calculations of the social cost of carbon and profound ethical implications.

The IAM and social cost of carbon approach is influential and controversial. In 2018, William Nordhaus was awarded the Nobel Prize in Economics for his work "integrating climate change into long-run macroeconomic analysis". Critics of Nordhaus immediately labelled the decision the "Nobel Prize for Climate Catastrophe" and the "Nobel Prize in Climate Chaos" (Dale 2018; Hickel 2018). They pointed to Nordhaus's track record of applying his cost-benefit framework to downplay the costs of climate change and overstate the costs of climate action, to argue against large-scale emissions reduction. Nordhaus's (1991) early work on climate economics posed the question of whether "to slow or not to slow [climate change]?". His answer, paraphrased, was "not too much". A more recent iteration of Nordhaus's DICE model, outlined in his Nobel lecture, finds the economically optimal amount of global warming to be 3°C by 2100, well above that recommended in IPCC reports or the Paris Agreement (Nordhaus 2019). Nordhaus's Nobel speech argued that limiting warming to the 1.5–2°C goals of the Paris Agreement would entail suboptimally high costs that outweigh economic benefits. Coincidentally, Nordhaus's Nobel prize was announced on the very same day the IPCC's landmark 1.5°C report was released. These kinds of temperature goals, for Nordhaus, are "essentially infeasible" (Nordhaus 2019: 2002). However, the infeasibility of 1.5°C does not imply a practical impossibility, but rather, according to Nordhaus's calculations of the social costs of carbon, that it would result in unacceptable economic costs.

Nordhaus's optimal level of global warming is based on a social cost of carbon much lower than many other economists. His US$36 per tonne (in 2018 dollars; Nordhaus 2019) operates as a monetary benchmark for choosing between alternative climate pathways. If the cost of reducing greenhouse gas emissions is less than US$36 per tonne, then it makes economic sense to do so. If, however, the cost of abatement is more than US$36 per tonne, it makes economic sense to accept the additional climate damage. By contrast, the Stern Review, using the PAGE model, used a higher estimate of the social cost of carbon at US$85 (in 2000 prices, about $125 in 2018). As a result, Stern (2007: i) concluded that "the benefits of strong, early action on climate change outweigh the costs". Yet, Stern's optimal solution was still to stabilize atmospheric greenhouse gases at levels consistent with between 2 and 3°C of warming – well above UNFCCC-agreed and IPCC-recommended levels. Like Nordhaus, for Stern this amount of climate change represents not just a ceiling, but also a floor, as "anything lower would certainly impose very high adjustment costs in the near term for small gains" (Stern 2007: xvii). Beyond Nordhaus and Stern, there is an extremely wide range of estimates from economists of the social cost of carbon: from –US$13.36 to US$2,386.91 per tonne, with a mean value of US$54.70 (Wang *et al.* 2019).

Discounting an uncertain future

One factor has an outsized influence in different estimates of the social cost of carbon: the discount rate. Discount rates are a financial solution to the problem of comparing costs of climate policy and climate impacts that occur at different points in time. There are two key justifications for discounting the future. The first is about equalizing prices over time. Future costs and benefits are discounted to account for inflation that reduces the value of future prices and economic productivity that makes future societies richer than today. The economic productivity rationale is more controversial because it assumes that future societies will be in a relatively stronger position to deal with climate impacts. But this treats climate change as an external imposition on an otherwise normally functioning economy, downplaying the potential impacts of climate change on productivity itself. Economic growth might be less the solution to, and more the problem for, climate change. The second justification is even more controversial because it assumes that people discount the welfare of future generations compared to the present. The basis of this assumption is that people have a "pure time preference" to bring forward consumption, meaning they value consuming the same thing today more than in the future.

Seemingly small differences in discount rates make large differences in how the costs and benefits of different climate pathways are calculated over relatively short time horizons. Nordhaus adopts a relatively high discount rate of around 4.25 per cent, whereas the Stern Review adopted a lower-than-average discount rate of 1.4 per cent. These figures mean that, each year, the value of future climate costs and benefits, measured in today's dollars, are reduced by either 4.25 or 1.4 per cent. Due to compounding effects, small changes in discount rates cause big changes in the social cost of carbon: adopting a 3 per cent rate in Nordhaus's own DICE model yields a social cost of carbon of US$93 per tonne; for a 1 per cent discount rate, it is US$497 per tonne (Nordhaus 2019: 2006). Implicit in Stern's discount rate of 1.4 per cent is that the welfare of people in 50 years is worth about half that of people today. Nordhaus's 4.25 per cent discount rate reduces this figure to one-eighth (Mann 2022).

Discount rates reflect economic and ethical justifications. Nordhaus's rate is based on observations from capital markets, assuming that spending on climate change mitigation should be able to compete with standard returns on investment. Stern, in contrast, devoted many pages of his report to considering an ethically justifiable way to value future generations. Yet, given the compounding effects of even low discount rates, others argue that the only way ensure equal rights for future generations is to assume a zero real discount rate (Spash 2007). Small differences in the assumed discount rates indicate vastly different scales of necessary policy response. Using a lower discount rate in Nordhaus's model would justify bringing forward deeper and more costly forms of climate action. This reveals a substantive politics of discount rates that is hidden behind the calculus of economic reasoning.

The precision of social cost of carbon calculations is challenged by the uncertainties of climate change. Indeed, Nicholas Stern, with colleagues, has argued that IAMs are "inadequate to capture deep uncertainty and extreme risk" (Stern, Stiglitz & Taylor 2022: 183). This uncertainty about climate sensitivity, damage and discount rates make precise calculations of climate futures difficult. Climate uncertainties create a "fat" or "long" tail of climate risk, due to those catastrophic climate damages that are unlikely but not impossible. Such risks have near infinite costs that do not fit well with standard cost-benefit frameworks, because any cost today is justifiable to avoid infinite costs in the future. As geographer Geoff Mann (2022) puts it, "cost-benefit analyses hardly seem appropriate when we are considering the possibility of human extinction".

Wagner and Weitzman call this the "Dismal Dilemma". Although precise calculations are based on the average scenario modelled by IAMs, there is no guarantee that the climate scenario that eventuates will not be a more serious, outlier scenario. Given there is only one planet, the stakes of such bets on the future are high. They conclude:

> Focusing on getting precise estimates of the damages associated with eventual global average warming of 4°C (7°F), 5°C (9°F), or 6°C (11°F) misses the point. The appropriate price on carbon is one that will make us comfortable enough to know that we will never get to anything close to 6°C (11°F) and certain eventual catastrophe. (Wagner & Weitzman 2016: 78)

The risk of climate catastrophe, while perhaps less likely than the averaged modelled scenario, is nonetheless higher than many ordinary people would consider acceptable. Both the scientific uncertainties, and politics, of climate change resist – or overflow from, in Callon's terms – precision market logics.

Manipulating social costs of carbon

Alongside the intellectual politics of its assumptions, the social costs of carbon have also become targets of political contestation between forces with different visions for climate policy. The US example illustrates this. In the absence of national carbon pricing, the US Environmental Protection Authority (EPA) has used social costs of carbon as a shadow carbon pricing system since the Obama administration ordered it to do so in 2009. The EPA averaged out the results of the three main IAMs, using discount rates of 2.5–5 per cent, to come to an average social cost of carbon of US$37 in 2013 (Shelanski 2013). This cost of carbon would be used to apply "cost effectiveness" criteria to EPA policy proposals, such as regulations of carbon intensity in the power sector; interestingly, this approach can be traced to the economically rationalist agenda of Republican President Ronald Reagan in the early 1980s (Howard & Schwartz 2016).

Social costs of carbon became a political target for the Trump administration, which sought to roll back regulation on fossil fuel industries. In 2017, the Trump administration reduced the social cost of carbon to a range of only US$1–7, so that it was too low to support ambitious climate policy. To reach this goal, the geographical scope of the costs of climate impacts were restricted to within the national borders of the US, despite the fact that climate impacts are both globally and unequally distributed. The Trump administration also adopted a much higher discount rate of 3–7 per cent (Wagner et al. 2021). In 2021, the Biden administration reversed the Trump changes and reset the social cost of carbon to inflation-adjusted Obama levels of US$51, pending a review by the EPA, which released new estimates of the social cost of carbon at US$120–390 in 2020 dollars (Environmental Protection Authority 2022).

While the social costs of carbon projects the precision of the costing methodology for adjudicating cost effecting futures, the calculative approach is no neutral technology. Indeed, calculating a social cost of carbon takes an explicit position on how we value the future, its inhabitants and socio-ecologies, by applying discount rates and averaging out future long-tail climate risks. More than anything, the explicit contestation over the social cost of carbon in the US underscores the point that climate costing projections "create a perception of knowledge and precision, but that perception is illusory and misleading" (Pindyck 2013). The precision market impulse nonetheless remains strong, particularly in the ideal and idealized regulatory tool of carbon markets.

CARBON MARKETS

The quest for calculating the social cost of carbon is not limited to the spreadsheets of economists and the shadow markets of regulatory agencies. Carbon pricing attempts to translate nominal social costs of carbon into real economic costs for greenhouse gas emissions. This occurs either through taxation, where governments put a price directly on carbon emissions, or trading, where the polluters set the carbon price through the buying and selling of emissions permits. Carbon trading, which is the focus of this section, is a precision market par excellence because, by commodifying carbon, it aims to make different emissions reductions infinitely comparable and substitutable. In the idealized construction of carbon markets, it is the market itself, rather than state regulators, that precisely determines the efficient climate pathway (Ervine 2018).

Carbon pricing is often viewed as the crucial piece of the climate finance puzzle by policy elites. The International Monetary Fund (2019: 3) describes carbon pricing as "the single most powerful and efficient tool" for reducing greenhouse gas emissions. The appeal lies not only in economic theory, but also the potential for carbon markets to cohere a coalition of states, industry and environmental organizations in favour of a regime of "accumulation by decarbonisation" (Bumpus & Liverman 2008). Yet, the carbon pricing project has been constantly unsettled by arguments and protests that the equivalences of carbon markets are a "fantasy" (Watt 2021) that represents a "dangerous distraction" for climate policy (Bullock, Childs & Picken 2009).

Carbon markets were established as a central pillar of the international climate policy regime following the negotiation of three "flexibility" mechanisms in the 1997 Kyoto Protocol, which enabled parties to meet their emissions targets by trading emissions reductions. The successor agreement to the Kyoto Protocol, the 2015 Paris Agreement, again established a framework for carbon markets in Article 6, which envisages a system of "internationally transferred mitigation outcomes". International carbon markets have given impetus for a wide range of carbon pricing instruments at the national, regional and city level, with significant variation in design, coverage and force. According to the World Bank, by 2022, 23 per cent of global greenhouse gas emissions were covered by 68 such carbon pricing instruments (World Bank 2022: 9, 15). Of these, about half were carbon taxes and the other half carbon markets. We focus here on the two main kinds of carbon markets: emissions trading and carbon offsets (see Chapter 6 on carbon taxes).

Cap-and-trade markets

Emissions trading schemes are usually constructed as "cap-and-trade" markets. As suggested by the name, governments as regulators set a total cap on emissions, which should, in theory, be consistent with the economically optimal level of climate change. They then distribute a quantity of permits equal to the total cap. In effect, these permits represent "rights to pollute", because they are underpinned by compliance rules that require polluters to surrender a quantity of permits equal to their level of pollution over a given time period, usually a year. Crucially, these permits are tradeable, which means that polluters with either deficits or surpluses of permits can buy or sell permits with other polluters, respectively. The economic logic of emissions trading is that different companies, industries and countries have differing "abatement costs", meaning some are able to reduce their pollution more cheaply than others. Trading is said to allow polluters to find "least-cost" emissions reductions – achieving what is understood to be the same climate outcome with the least economic impact.

The most established and, until recently, the largest cap-and-trade scheme in the world is the European Union Emissions Trading System (EU ETS). The EU ETS, which commenced in 2005, is described by the EU as the "cornerstone" of its climate policy. It encompasses about 11,000 polluting "installations" – mostly coal- and gas- fired power plants and manufacturing facilities – spanning the electricity, oil refining, iron and steel, aluminium, cement, ceramics, paper, chemicals and aviation sectors. The proportion of global emissions covered by emissions trading schemes received a big boost with the implementation of China's national scheme in 2021. Starting from 2013, China had implemented pilot ETS schemes in seven cities, provinces and a special economic zone. Upon commencement, China's national carbon trading scheme immediately became the largest in the world by emissions volume, despite initially being limited to the energy sector. The scheme is a "hybrid" in that it does not have an absolute "cap" on emissions, but rather ties permits to industry benchmarks for emissions intensity (Bigger 2018; Liu 2021).

Beyond Europe and China, the spread of emissions trading has been uneven. Carbon pricing policy failures in the US and Australia are indicative of the contestation that continues to follow technocratic market-based policy frameworks. The Obama administration attempted to legislate a US-wide cap-and-trade system in the form of the Waxman-Markey Bill of 2009. While it was passed by the House, it failed to progress to the Senate (Meckling 2011: 61–2), creating the impetus for the EPA to rely more heavily on shadow carbon pricing (see above). However, several US states have implemented cap-and-trade systems, including the 11 north-east states that formed the Regional Greenhouse Gas Initiative in 2009, and California, which launched its scheme in 2013 (Bigger 2016). Australia stands out as an example of a short-lived national cap-and-trade scheme. It initially began as a fixed carbon price in 2012 that was legislated to transform into an emissions trading scheme in 2015. The scheme was abolished in 2014 following a successful campaign against the carbon price by an incoming conservative government (Pearse 2017). Various other national schemes have been implemented, including in South Korea, New Zealand, Kazakhstan and a post-Brexit UK ETS, as well as city or region-level schemes such as in Tokyo and various Canadian provinces (Knox-Hayes 2016).

Carbon offsetting

Carbon offsetting schemes, sometimes called "baseline-and-credit", offer another market-based option for reducing emissions. Instead of governments creating permits equal to the overall cap on emissions, under carbon offsetting, emissions reduction projects – such as those promising to stop deforestation or to install renewable rather than fossil energy – are judged against a business-as-usual "baseline". If project emissions are below this baseline, they are awarded "credits" that can be sold to governments, companies or individuals to "offset" their emissions. The economic logic of carbon offsetting is that revenue from selling carbon credits incentivizes "additional" emissions reduction from projects compared to what would otherwise occur. These green projects may remove emissions, as in negative emissions technologies projects, or avoid emissions, as in energy efficiency projects. Offsetting projects need not be zero carbon – just lower carbon than they otherwise would be. In a geographical flattening, offset credits are presented as environmentally equivalent to the buyer reducing their own emissions.

Carbon offsetting occurs for both "compliance" and "voluntary" purposes. Compliance markets refer to the construction of carbon offsetting schemes to meet the compliance requirements of government-mandated climate policies – usually cap-and-trade schemes that allow the use of offset credits. Prior to the Paris Agreement, the largest compliance-based offsetting scheme was the CDM, which was created as a mechanism for wealthy countries with Kyoto Protocol commitments to source emissions reductions from developing countries. It grew rapidly after it linked with the EU ETS from 2008, which made CDM offsets, known as Certified Emission Reductions (CERs), substitutable with EU permits. By the end of 2012, there were about 7,000 registered CDM projects issued with over one billion carbon credits, each representing one tonne of avoided or removed carbon. The most common project type was renewable energy projects, while the most credits were issued to a small number of projects destroying potent industrial gases (UNEP DTU 2018). Demand for the CDM credits dissipated after the EU ETS gradually severed links with the Kyoto mechanisms from 2013 in the face of mounting controversies over their integrity and impact on carbon prices (Bryant 2016). However, other carbon markets continue to accept offsets for compliance purposes, including the Californian market and the Chinese market, which has a domestic system of China CERs closely modelled on the CDM (Xue 2022).

The voluntary carbon offsetting market is driven largely by corporate net zero and carbon neutrality pledges. It is much more fragmented than the compliance market, with many different platforms selling offsets that meet various climate, social and environmental standards, at different prices. The main offset registries are Climate Action Reserve, American Carbon Registry, Verified Carbon Standard and the Gold Standard. As net zero and carbon neutrality pledges have increased, so too has demand for voluntary carbon offsets. In 2021, 298 million voluntary credits were issued globally, up from 64 million in 2015. These credits were dominated by forestry and renewable energy projects located in the US, China and India (Berkeley Carbon Trading Project 2022). Buyers are dominated by energy companies; however, the Carbon Offsetting and Reduction Scheme for International Aviation scheme being developed by the aviation industry, after it successfully negotiated exemptions from Paris targets, represents a new source of demand.

The politics of precision in regulatory paradise

Across this variegated carbon market landscape, both emissions trading and carbon offsetting schemes have been troubled by over-allocation and over-crediting, leading to low and at times volatile prices. In 2021, the average carbon price in emissions trading schemes was €3.59, well below even conservative estimates of the social cost of carbon (OECD 2022b: 36). The EU ETS was plagued by over-allocation in the early years of its operation. Initially, permits were allocated to industry for free based on historical emissions, in a commonly used method known as "grandfathering", which delivered windfall profits to some of the biggest polluters in Europe. This, combined with the impact of the 2008 global financial crisis and widespread use of carbon offset credits, resulted in a chronic surplus of permits that saw prices crash from over €30 in 2008 to less than €10 and locking in single-digit prices for close to ten years (Bryant 2019: 104).

Carbon offset prices, both compliance and voluntary, were even lower. These vary according to project type and registry, but in 2019 offsets from renewable energy projects ranged from US$0.40–4.80 compared with US$1.90–10.70 for forestry offsets (Ecosystem Marketplace 2022). Over-crediting results from methodologies that enable carbon credits to be issued for "non-additional" emissions reductions that are the product of inflated baselines. This is an issue that has beset all carbon offsetting schemes that are predicated on avoiding future emissions. In the early period of the CDM, a disproportionate quantity of credits were issued to a tiny number of projects that destroyed HFC-23, a potent greenhouse gas produced as a by-product in the manufacturing of refrigerant gases. These projects were widely described as non-additional by experts and activists, who argued that the UNFCCC methodology perversely incentivized projects to increase production of refrigerant gases solely for the purposes of gaining CDM revenue from the destruction of HFC-23 (Bryant, Dhabi & Böhm 2015). Similarly, the large proportion of voluntary credits from renewable energy projects have been questioned on additionality grounds. Given new renewable energy is now cost competitive with fossil fuel-based power, further investment is unlikely to depend on climate finance from offsetting credits.

Carbon market reforms have sought to address these and other issues. This "politics of carbon market design" involves contestation between governments, industry and climate activists over the implementation of carbon markets (Bryant 2016). This contestation, Callon (2009) argues, occurs between the *in vitro* (theoretical) and *in vivo* (practical) experiments of carbon market making, or as precision markets encounter everyday politics. In the EU ETS, member states agreed to a series of carbon market reforms to address the glut of permits from 2010. Key reforms included greater use of auctioning rather than free allocation of permits, tighter emissions caps and limits on offsetting, and the implementation of a Market Stability Reserve in 2019 that automatically adds or withdraws permits from the market to avoid large surpluses and shortages building up. These reforms have been slow and uneven. Energy-intensive industries, such as steel and cement, have successfully lobbied to maintain free allocation on the basis that high carbon costs will force production to "leak" offshore. Nonetheless, combined with expectations of future climate policy, the reforms saw carbon prices reach highs of €100 in early 2023 (Hodgson & Sheppard 2023). Voluntary markets, too, have responded to criticisms with voluntary reform initiatives. Following a now well-trodden formula (see Chapter 3), Mark Carney established a Taskforce on Scaling Voluntary Carbon Markets as a private sector initiative to standardize offsetting methodologies.

Beyond reform, debates about the scope of emissions trading and carbon offsetting raise deeper questions about the equivalences, or "endless algebra" (Lohmann 2011), that enact carbon markets. The exact scope of equivalence is dynamic. Political pressure from both industry and movements has resulted in new equivalence methodologies being added and withdrawn. HFC-23 offsets were, for example, banned from the EU ETS from 2013. But all carbon markets depend on some degree of equivalence-making. MacKenzie (2009) describes the enormous work that goes into constructing the algebra of carbon markets as a process of "making things the same". This is the work of bureaucratic agencies that regulate carbon markets, auditors who measure and verify emissions and exchange platforms and banks who facilitate the trading of carbon-derived financial instruments.

Carbon markets operate through a series of abstractions that make greenhouse gases that are emitted or reduced by different companies in different sectors of the economy, in different places and at different points in time, "the same" – as tonnes of carbon dioxide-equivalent. Abstractions and equivalences are necessary for markets to function, to enable the "precise" trade-offs to find the optimal response to climate change. Indeed, from the perspective of conventional economics, the wider the scope of abstraction and equivalence (including by "linking" different schemes), the greater heterogeneity in abatement costs, leading to a more efficient outcome through trading (Cullenward & Victor 2021).

Political battles over the abstractions of carbon markets are not merely about getting the price right from the perspective of economic models. The abstractions of carbon markets format and redistribute carbon rents. The value of carbon permits and credits is always anchored in the burning of fossil fuels, without which there would be no demand for new carbon commodities (Andreucci et al. 2017; Felli 2014). The politics of carbon market design is therefore about the reach, force and priority afforded to the economic determinations of carbon markets in redistributing carbon rents between different actors in the market (Bryant 2016). More than this, the scale and scope of carbon pricing congeals expectations of the stringency and speed of future climate pathways, enabling financial actors to trade in speculative carbon-derived financial assets, such as carbon futures, swaps and options contracts (Bryant 2018; Christophers 2018b).

Carbon markets and their discontents

But are the abstractions of carbon markets really equivalent? Critics of carbon trading, especially of carbon offsetting, have argued that the approach facilitates a spatial displacement of action on climate change from north to south, resulting in "carbon colonialism" (Pearse & Böhm 2014). Indeed, offsets have been likened to modern-day versions of the "indulgences" sold by the medieval Catholic Church, where sinners could buy surplus good deeds from the clergy (Smith 2007). As a result, what is being sustained is not the climate, but consumption (Lovell, Bulkeley & Liverman 2009).

Forest-based offsets – such as REDD+, or Reducing Emissions from Deforestation and Forest Degradation in Developing Countries – have been particularly controversial, because their narrow focus on forests as carbon sinks has come into conflict with livelihoods of forest communities (Osborne 2015). Disney, for example, has financed a voluntary carbon offset project run by Conservation International in Alto Mayo, in the Peruvian Amazon, to offset its emissions from two of its Caribbean cruise ships, aptly named *Fantasy* and *Dream*. The project promises to reduce carbon emissions by partnering with a Peruvian government agency to stop land clearing by local farmers who had settled in the area. Many farmers signed up to the project, which encouraged them to shift to more sustainable coffee production. Yet, the project reportedly ignited land conflicts because it resourced the government to use carbon to assert territorial control over informally settled land (Mider & Quigley 2020). Even where offset methodologies are well-constructed, there are always uncertainties around permanence. For example, wildfires destroyed large tracts of forests in California and Oregon that were producing offsets purchased by BP and Microsoft (Choi-Schagrin 2021).

There are, however, examples of communities that have strategically used specific carbon offsetting projects as a tool for climate justice. First Nations- and Indigenous-led carbon offsetting projects seek to harness financial flows for different social, ecological and economic outcomes. In Australia, Indigenous carbon farming uses traditional cultural burning and other socio-ecological practices to reduce land-based emissions while supporting access to Indigenous land, or "Country", and formal employment for Traditional Owners (e.g. Aboriginal Carbon Foundation 2022). Similarly, academics at the University of California's Center for Climate Justice have been facilitating an Indigenous-led carbon burial project in Ecuador. The project mobilizes the University of California's endowment and net-zero commitments to support plans developed by the Indigenous peoples of Sarayaku for sustainable forest management that sequesters carbon, builds Indigenous knowledge and practice, and prohibits fossil fuel extraction in the eastern Amazon (UC Center for Climate Justice 2022). Both of these approaches resist the abstractions and equivalences of carbon offsetting through Indigenous community-determined methodologies and contracts. The case of the Yurok tribe in California, which has sold offsets in the state's cap-and-trade system and used the millions in revenue to reacquire territory under their sovereign control, illustrates the possibilities and tensions of this strategy on a broader scale (Manning & Reed 2019). While members of the Yurok celebrate that participating in California's cap-and-trade programmes has "revive[d] the economy in a way that align[s] with our cultural values" they also recognize that the gains are premised on a carbon market that ultimately allows "polluters to pollute" (Yurok elders in Kormann 2018).

Views about carbon markets ultimately hinge on competing visions of the climate transition as an incremental or transformative process. Economists are adamant that carbon pricing *works*. In a major econometric study of 142 countries, Best, Burke and Jotzo found that countries with carbon prices reduced fossil fuel combustion-based emissions by 2 per cent per year more than those without carbon prices. These reductions were described as "substantial" (Best, Burke & Jotzo 2020: 91). A review of similar studies by Green also found that carbon pricing schemes delivered emissions reductions of around 0–2 per cent per year. But Green (2021: 9, 14) described such impacts as "limited", producing incremental results rather than the 10 per cent reductions per year needed to reach the 1.5°C goal.

Contrasting views about the same evidence are grounded in different visions of climate transition. From the perspective of economists, incrementalism is a virtue, as carbon pricing is supposed to deliver least-cost climate action at the margin. Yet, from a perspective that views climate change as a structural problem, transformational change beyond carbon pricing is required. For example, there is agreement that many of the EU ETS emissions reductions came from "fuel switching" from coal to gas (Tvinnereim & Mehling 2018). Whether this is an efficient response or one that entrenches fossil fuels depends on your perspective about incrementalism or transformation. The risk of carbon markets, however, is that more transformational changes are traded for more incremental ones, driven by the "least-cost" logic of carbon trading that seeks to order the sequence of the transition according to the most profitable uses of carbon pollution (Bryant 2019).

INSURANCE

Insurance markets extend the calculative logic of precision markets from trading emissions reductions to pricing exposures to future climate risks. Insurance provides multiple functions for mediating finance and risk under climate change and disaster. Insurance works by collecting individual premiums from an uncorrelated population – that is, a population who face different distributions of risk of loss – and making payouts to cover the losses of a subset (hopefully) of that population following a trigger event. A policyholder purchases insurance from an insurance company, who then is reinsured through a reinsurer to try to spread risks. Because insurance and reinsurance are so tightly coupled, they are often referred to collectively as re/insurers.

Insurance collectivizes loss, spreading the negative financial impacts of a disastrous event across a population. For vulnerable people and places with limited ability to access quick cash reserves, insurance is also a method for rapidly releasing funds following a disaster. At the same time, because it estimates and prices risk through both the premiums paid for receiving insurance and geographical coverage, proponents of market-based forms of insurance argue that it incentivizes measures to mitigate risks or even encourage retreat. Insurance, in other words, is a "financial first responder" (Collier, Elliott & Lehonen 2021: 162) to the increasing severity and frequency of extreme events due to climate change, from the individual household to supranational regional scale.

But is climate change a financial problem, or opportunity, for insurance? As disasters such as tropical storms, floods and fires become both more frequent and intense, payouts increase proportionately. Global reinsurer Swiss Re reported that, in 2021, economic losses reached almost US$260 billion and insured losses US$112 billion, well above the ten-year average, and the fourth-highest annual cost since the 1970s (Swiss Re Institute 2021). Their analysis suggests that continued urbanization and wealth accumulation in vulnerable areas and climate change-induced extreme events are driving these losses. The increasing costs of responding to disasters looms for insurers, reinsurers and their broader financial entanglements. As a financial industry revolving around returns, solvency in this context requires re/insurers to increase premiums, create different kinds of financial products to address new scales and sites of risk, or withdraw coverage for particular kinds of events or locations. Indeed, the western US and Australia are facing the withdrawal of insurance for forest and bushfires.

Responding to climate risks, however, also offers opportunities for new insurance tools, programmes and collaborations and an expanded portfolio of potentially insurable populations and sets of catastrophic events. The industry sees unparalleled business opportunities in the climate crisis, not only through financial innovation and experimentation but as an innovator in producing new information about climate changes and as a leader in governing risk in the wake of governmental and intergovernmental failure. As discussed in the following two examples, Insurance-linked securities (ILS) such as catastrophe bonds and index insurance are demonstrative of insurance under climate change, showing the breadth of actors involved, the forms of prediction and precision on which it depends and the uneven and incomplete outcomes. Despite the calculative and scientific attributes of this position on precision, there are deep distributional and geographical implications.

Insurance-linked securities

ILS are an alternative asset class, most often comprising catastrophe bonds, or cat bonds. Insurance and reinsurance exposure to events such as earthquakes, flooding and wind impacts from tropical cyclones and storms, drought and fire have become targets for securitization. Catastrophe bonds are generally structured as three-year bonds by the issuing re/insurer, with investors receiving annual payments, and their principal only if no catastrophes have triggered a transfer of funds to the sponsor (Johnson 2013). Triggers can be either pre-specified physical measures of an event, as in parametric, or index, insurance, or based on losses or damage (common in residential insurance, but more complex in reinsurance and ILS markets). Following the creation of insurance-linked securitization after financial deregulation in the 1990s, this asset class has risen to prominence in the wake of the global financial crisis, as investors, particularly European and American institutional investors, are attracted by its "non-correlated" nature – a description that assumes climate disasters are disconnected from macroeconomic impacts and cycles. Despite claims of the potential to provide diversified and uncorrelated investments while covering multiple disasters globally, the vast majority of this market is concentrated in the US and more than half of current ILS capital securitizes residential insurance against Florida hurricanes (Taylor 2020).

The emergence of catastrophe bonds depends on making contingent futures fungible. Just as computational and technical innovation underpin financialization more broadly, the key enabling technology for ILS is catastrophe modelling. Insurance, in general, turns on probabilistic renderings of the future; probability "brings order to chaos" such that those known unknowns like extreme events and disasters "become, if not precisely predictable, at least patterned in ways that humans can understand and anticipate" (Elliott 2021: 5; see also Chapter 3). Despite depending on probability, re/insurance has long been unable to estimate or has underestimated, and therefore incorrectly priced, risks of losses from extreme events.

This problem is exacerbated by climate change. For insurers, catastrophe models address these problems by calculating and facilitating "actuarial" or "risk-reflective" pricing (rather than subsidized prices) and incorporating climate change forcing. Where probabilistic forms of insurance model risk by projecting forward from historical observations, the rarity of extreme events undermines any attempt to produce an accurate distribution of their occurrence or losses. Catastrophe modelling departs from actuarial, probabilistic models, instead using Monte Carlo simulations to produce "plausible, synthetic" historical disaster events and thereby transform a small data set into a large, albeit computer generated, one (Gray 2021). These forms of hazard modelling combine with estimates of damages to assets and indeed of the vulnerability of entire re/insurance portfolios to produce risk assessments and estimations. These more scientific forms of risk assessment have made catastrophe bonds and other market objects "exchangeable".

A preliminary assessment of the expanding re/insurance industry might find that it is particularly at risk amid the growing impacts of climate change and its wildly oscillating extreme events. More frequent and extreme disasters would warrant more unpredictable and larger claims, thereby undermining profitability for businesses and returns for investors. But this fundamentally misunderstands cycles of pricing and accumulation within the industry, which as geographer Leigh Johnson argues, are instead *secured* by catastrophe (Johnson 2015). Insurance is a highly cyclical industry, with prices for insurance and reinsurance low during periods without triggering events, and rents and returns ticking upwards after catastrophic losses. Overaccumulation can be resolved through geographical expansion, as in emerging forms of insurance explored below, new risks to be insured, or "the destruction of reinsurers' capital reserves through catastrophic losses" (Johnson 2015: 2508). Indeed, the 2004 and 2005 North Atlantic hurricane seasons, each the costliest on record when they occurred, were followed by the most profitable years for the insurance industry. Super-profits in the industry depend on oscillations between big insurance losses in one year and big returns the following.

The ultimate result of these catastrophic cycles, however, is splintered distributions of protection and, perversely, more vulnerability to disasters (Johnson 2014). If the profitability of re/insurance depends on exposure to disasters, this encourages more vulnerable built environments that command higher premiums and experience more "fixing" disasters. As with much of the financial industry, state and public funding play an active role in insurance, most obviously as a regulator, but also by providing economic subsidies and bailouts, or as an insurer of last resort (Collier, Elliott & Lehtonen 2021; Lucas & Booth 2020). In 2022 the Australian government funded an AU$10 billion reinsurance scheme intending to extend insurance coverage and reduce premiums against cyclones and flooding in northern Australia; but, as one industry insider describes, its projected reductions of 10 per cent in premiums are little against the 500 per cent increases over recent flood- and fire-hit years (Hannam 2022). The cost to consumers of insurance and reinsurance will only grow as climate extremes do.

The logic of precision in insurance markets cuts against the politics of residential property values. The cost of insurance in the US is determined by local regulators, who must manage complex and contradictory forces (Elliott 2021). On the one hand, their constituents do not want higher premiums for insurance for their property and they do not want their properties designated as at higher risk of loss because it would negatively affect their property values. These regulators, in turn, want to maintain high property values because it is the basis of their taxes, a particular problem in high-value coastal cities such as Miami, Florida. On the other hand, without risk-reflective pricing of premiums, the price signal of insurance cannot be incorporated into individual decisions about risk mitigation or indeed location – one of the key benefits of insurance according to market proponents. Subsidized premiums for insurance also facilitate ongoing development in vulnerable locations; indeed, commentators have described the expansionary motive of re/insurance as "underwriting to securitize" (Johnson 2014). As a result, expanded insurance and insurance-derived financial innovations narrow adaptation to climate risks to financial tools, and impede coordinated and pre-emptive discussions about retreat in the face of future climate risks.

Index insurance

The last decade of insurance experimentation has produced new forms of financialized protection in the Global South – principally through agricultural micro-insurance schemes and regional risk pools. Unlike residential insurance, which is based on experienced losses, index or parametric insurance for agricultural production is triggered by the occurrence of a predetermined physical observation. This technical development has facilitated the expansion of insurance to cover the agrarian livelihoods of the poor. In contrast to catastrophe bonds driven by financial institutions and re/insurers, the expansion of index insurance has been a project of humanitarian and development organizations expanding from the worlds of poverty finance (Bernards 2022). Proliferating particularly in sub-Saharan Africa, agricultural index insurance has primarily targeted individuals as a means to cultivate resilience in the face of weather risks and thereby govern climate change vulnerability and poverty. Thus, index insurance promises to cultivate "individual responsibility to secure assets and affairs from the whims of fate or change" (Johnson 2021: 250) with resulting economic and productivity dividends.

Despite the enthusiasm and experimentation with different forms, how-ever, index insurance has not delivered reduced risk and increased resilience. Often facilitated through behavioural economics-inspired experiments, through which potential consumers might play games of luck and chance as a method to learn the logics of insurance, these products seek to cultivate market subjects who securitize their own assets and futures. Critiques of these tools have identified that they undermine non-capitalist social relations of reciprocity and redistribution in agrarian livelihoods and increase inequality by providing material benefits to already wealthy rural producers (Müller, Johnson & Kreuer 2017). And yet both index insurance insiders and critics find that there are currently no commercially viable schemes. There is low demand for index insurance products from their supposed beneficiaries, des-pite ongoing experiments and subsidies to try to encourage uptake. Moreover, and reinforcing this low uptake, index insurance schemes have often failed to cover experienced losses, reflecting the complexity of parametric design, the poor design of the parameters of interest or a disconnect between the identified parameter and local experience. Like many other stylized financial innovations to address climate change, then, index insurance might better be conceived as an ideological commitment to the precision and efficiency of market mechanisms that deliver state (and development donor) subsidies. The result is a highly fragmented social safety net.

One of the outcomes of the failure of micro-scale forms of insurance has been an upwards rescaling into pooled insurance mechanisms, such as sov-ereign risk pools. Three major examples of these pooled insurance schemes include: The African Risk Capacity, Caribbean Catastrophe Risk Insurance Facility and the Pacific Catastrophe Risk Insurance Company (formerly the Pacific Catastrophe Risk Assessment and Financing Initiative, or PCRAFI) (Christophers, Bigger & Johnson 2020). While each of these models work somewhat differently, their overarching goals are the same – to collectivize insurance across a population of states that are differently exposed to cli-mate risks and thereby expand access to insurance and decrease the financial costs of disasters. For the relatively small states that usually incur losses that constitute a high proportion of their gross domestic product (GDP), pooled insurance is meant to provide quick financial resources following a disaster that spares their meagre cash reserves and avoids the vagaries of humani-tarian response. The regional nature of the facilities creates savings for states because risk is dispersed among a bigger population and the transaction costs of structuring the insurance product are reduced.

In several Pacific islands, for instance, there is high exposure to extreme events, particularly tropical cyclones, and there are high average annual losses from these disasters as a proportion of GDP. In its original design, the PCRAFI pooled risk for five Pacific islands countries and determined pre-specified parametric triggers for which payouts would be made. But there is a high degree of basis risk; that is, the difference between expected losses determined by the parametric model and those experienced during the event (Ramachandran & Masood 2019). In a high-profile outcome, the Solomon Islands withdrew from the scheme because two damaging disasters were not covered, one of which resulted in losses of almost 10 per cent of GDP (Westfall 2015). Across all the regional schemes, the payouts following disasters have not met the participants' expectations, reflecting trade-offs around regional cooperation, catastrophe modelling capacity and the costs of premiums.

In the wake of the multi-scalar failures of insurance to protect the vulnerable, a framework and set of claims around "loss and damage" has emerged. The idea of loss and damage crystalized in the Warsaw International Mechanism on Loss and Damage at the 2013 COP, due to lobbying from the Alliance of Small Island States over the two decades prior to centre the irreparable impacts of climate change for their members (Thomas, Serdeczny & Pringle 2020). Under this framework, loss and damage represents that "residual" beyond the limits of adaptation, including the excesses and fragmentation of insurance. Losses are considered permanent, whereas damages may be redressed. Rich countries have mostly rejected an engagement with the politics of loss and damage, due to any admission of culpability or liability for compensation and reparations. As a result, despite being a politically capacious demand from those feeling the brunt of climate change, loss and damage is often operationalized through the financial tools of risk transfer and risk retention, and particularly insurance as a quickly disbursing injection of cash following catastrophe. Developing and vulnerable countries, particularly Pacific island countries, went to COP27 in Sharm el-Sheikh (2022) ready and relentless about negotiating a financial mechanism for loss and damage. And while such a fund was established, it is meagrely capitalized, low on participation and as yet not operational.

Insurance is an inherently social and relational tool. The contemporary examples described here depend on social and scalar relations between individuals, states and markets. In its original design, the institution of insurance itself founded these social relations as mutualities and solidarities. Insurance, in theory, socializes risks by pooling them through a process of mutualization between the insured. But, rather than constituting mutualities through subsidies across social class, geographies and levels of risk on the understanding that risks are a collective social responsibility and coverage should be provided universally, the insurance of climate change and extreme events is renegotiating questions of inclusion and exclusion. There are glimmers of progressive redistributive potential – whether through the pooling of risk at regional levels to produce regional solidarities and reduce the costs of insurance and the burdens of disaster, in the welfarist tendencies of agricultural micro-insurance that secure subsidies for the poorest, or in the collective demands of compensation through loss and damage mechanisms. Ultimately, however, the re/insurance industry decides the distribution of costs and benefits and who bears the responsibility for managing risk, and the pool is increasingly narrowly defined and individualized for the benefit of cyclical accumulation.

CONCLUSION

Precision markets combine the scientific projections of climate modelling with mainstream economic methodologies in pursuit of least-cost and economically efficient decision-making pathways. These models – from Nordhaus's IAMs to the catastrophe modelling of ILS – performatively produce precision markets and marketized subjectivities in their own image, or at least they try to. Social costs of carbon methodologies aim to identify the right balance of greenhouse gas abatement activity to ensure cost-effective climate futures. More than producing a shadow price for carbon, carbon markets – as cap-and-trade or offset markets – price carbon directly, thereby allowing comparison of different climate action pathways through trading, allowing market exchange to discover the most efficient option for reducing emissions. Insurance against climate events also provides a price signal through its premiums for consumers to identify the most efficient risk mitigation measures. Computational and observational advances in precision modelling, including in catastrophe modelling and satellite measurements of agroecological conditions, have simultaneously provided opportunities for new financial tools.

Despite claims to precision, the assumptions of the economic and climatic models that underpin precision markets offer a window into the ideological commitments, contested goals and uneven outcomes of this position of climate finance on climate change, and the misfires and overflows of economic models. Examining assumptions about discount rates, for instance, demonstrates how IAMs value – or, indeed, do not – uncertain climate futures, making the outputs manipulable to suit predetermined climate policy goals. The promise of carbon markets to shift decision-making around climate action from the sphere of politics to market rationality is constantly undermined by political controversy around their perverse outcomes that demand regulatory redress. Climate disasters overflow from catastrophe models demanding a role for the state as climate insurer of last resort to make insurance payouts and fill gaps in the market. As described, these tools are currently producing splintered landscapes and policy worlds of least-cost carbon reduction, climate low-hanging fruit and ongoing insurance experimentation. But the fragments of political contestation on market terms are suggestive, whether through zero or negative discount rates that honour the future, the reparative reworking of Indigenous carbon farming, or socialities and communalities produced through lobbying on loss and damage. This chapter has oriented around the politics of precision in market design; the next considers an inherently imprecise position on climate finance: speculation.

CHAPTER 5

SPECULATIVE MARKETS

Over the last two decades, another phenomenon has competed with climate finance for the "cli-fi" abbreviation: climate fiction. Works of climate fiction are commonly explorations of the "near future" of climate change, set in post-apocalyptic landscapes in which social, economic and political systems have collapsed and are being reworked. The two cli-fis have occasionally converged. In Kim Stanley Robinson's *The Ministry for the Future* (2020) a new "carbon coin" currency is created linked to carbon removals. Margaret Atwood's *MaddAddam* trilogy, a dystopian series of books exploring a world transformed by pandemic and genetic engineering, is another prominent example of climate fiction. Atwood describes hers as *"speculative fiction"*: "things that really could happen but just hadn't completely happened when the authors wrote the books" (Atwood 2012: 6). Literary debates about genre categorization notwithstanding, Atwood's description captures the role of climate fiction in speculating about possible climate futures. This speculation is not limited to questions of technological development, but rather "human society and its possible future forms, which are either much better than what we have now or much worse" (Atwood 2012: 115).

The climate fiction of both Robinson and Atwood resonates with the approach taken to the other "cli-fi" in this book, where climate finance is understood as something that both reflects and shapes future climate pathways. This chapter focuses on forms of climate finance that, like climate fiction, take an explicitly speculative position on the future. As with precision markets, speculative markets seek to manage the future. But in contrast to the former, speculative markets do so in a way that is inherently *imprecise*. Actors in precision markets, such as climate economists modelling future climate costs, aim to discover the future using a set of axiomatic assumptions. Debate revolves around whose projected future most closely approximates the real one. Actors in speculative markets, such as the emerging class of green billionaires, are explicitly competing to generate climate futures in their own image. Rather than being discounted, the future gains more prominence as a site of speculative competition.

Speculation is a controversial topic in political economy and economic geography. Critics of finance often blame tendencies towards instability and crisis on the speculative nature of finance. Finance in this register represents "fictitious" value as opposed to the real value produced by industries that sit at the foundations of the economy, such as energy production. This line of critique owes a debt to the work of British economist John Maynard Keynes, who famously argued that financial actors were driven by "animal spirits—of a spontaneous urge to action" (2018: 141) to describe the mania and panics characterizing herd behaviour in financial markets. The Keynesian critique of finance as pure speculation shares elements with Marxist political economy approaches that categorize finance as unproductive of value and thus unearned income (Collins 2021), necessitating, as Keynes (2018: 334) quipped, the "euthanasia of the rentier, of the functionless investor".

An alternative view challenges the distinction between speculation and the "real" economy. This view argues that all economic activity is inherently speculative in the way it grapples with and feeds on future economic uncertainty. Rather than viewing speculative activity as a "fiction" that is disconnected from economic realities, speculation is understood as actively shaping economic pathways, for better or worse. Post-Keynesian economist Hyman Minksy – the figure behind the climate Minsky moment popularized by Mark Carney (see Chapter 3) – demonstrates both sides of the debate. Minsky is commonly viewed as a trenchant critic of speculation as leading to financial bubbles and bursts. Yet he also recognized that speculation is an inescapable element of capitalism that forces actors to take "*positions* in an uncertain world" (Minsky 1980: 515, emphasis added). A critical approach to speculation therefore recognizes "the constitutive, generative character of financial speculation" in shaping economic futures (Konings 2018b: 148). If climate change, as postcolonial theorist Chakrabarty (2009) argues, has upended our received notions of time, then speculation is one method through which the new temporalities of a climate-changing capitalism are being renegotiated. Central to this renegotiation is liquidity: the lifeblood of speculation, and the nexus on which the green dreams of climate speculators live and die (Konings & Adkins 2022).

There is an irony in Carney's climate Minsky moment. To recap, Mark Carney describes a climate Minsky moment as the point at which sudden climate change-induced devaluations of fossil fuel assets trigger systemic risks to global financial systems. These potentially "stranded" assets created by climate change and political responses to climate change – assets such as oil reserves and gas terminals – are those that were foundational to twentieth-century productive capitalism and at the heart of the undisputed "real", rather than speculative, economy. In response to the threats of a climate Minsky moment, a precision market approach seeks a gradual and incremental transition as investors incorporate transition risk. By contrast, a speculative market approach embraces the potential rapid and collective devaluation of these assets as an opportunity to take positions on climate futures that promise to create big winners and big losers by engineering – both technologically and financially – green "solutions".

In this chapter we explore three instances of speculative markets, starting with the green billionaires that have positioned themselves as purveyors of speculative and spectacular solutions to climate change. Second, we explore geoengineering and related technologies that are attempting to make the near futures of climate fiction a reality. Third, we explore the off-grid solar market, where speculation lies in the financial and network innovations to expand the reach of rather unspectacular renewable energy technologies. These examples are each different kinds of speculative markets, incorporating a range of technologies, financial strategies and classes of actors that indicate the breadth and variety of speculative positions on climate change. Our focus across each is the role played by financial ideas, instruments and institutions in mediating speculative positions on climate change. Paradoxically, the "disruptive" techno and financial fixes proposed by speculative markets often leave capitalism's existing power and socio-ecological relations largely intact: speculation is underwritten by states and tethered to ongoing resource extraction. Yet, they also illustrate how financing, via the liquidity it provides to speculative markets in the present, creates more and less desirable climate futures.

GREEN BILLIONAIRES

A class of green billionaires has emerged as the public face of speculative markets in climate finance. Green billionaires are ultra-high-wealth individuals with investments in clean-tech industries such as electric vehicles, batteries, renewable energy and green hydrogen. Beyond their specific investments, green billionaires have gained outsized influence in the political economy of climate change through their performance of speculative climate politics. Personifying the "solutions business", green billionaires offer techno-fixes for climate change powered by the entrepreneurial spirit of innovation.

One of the early green billionaires was founder of Virgin Group, Richard Branson. As a kind of prototype for the green billionaires that emerged in his wake, Branson adopted an "entrepreneurial performance" that was "heroic, splashy, highly public, mercurial, and (in significant ways) even macho fusions of adventure and business" (Prudham 2009: 1607). In the mid-2000s, Branson committed to reinvesting US$3 billion in profits from his airlines and trains business into the development of biofuels that could reduce greenhouse gas emissions and established a US$25 million prize competition for commercially viable carbon capture technologies (Klein 2014). In practice, Branson over-promised and under-delivered. He only invested a small fraction of the US$3 billion pledged for biofuels and the competition ultimately disappeared before a winner was announced. These speculative manoeuvres are less about technological, or even financial, success – let alone climate success – than they are about performing and building legitimacy for spectacular green capitalism.

The cultural niche previously occupied by Branson has been taken up by a new crop of green billionaires, led by Tesla CEO Elon Musk. In 2021, Musk headed Bloomberg's yearly list of the richest 15 green billionaires with a net worth estimated at US$288.3 billion (Pendleton 2021). Beyond Musk, the list was dominated by Chinese green billionaires, all of whom are investors in companies linked to either electric vehicles, batteries and/or solar panels or components. They were led by Zeng Yuqun who is the chairman of CATL, the largest supplier of electric vehicle batteries in the world. The wealth in speculative markets, as in the clean-tech sector, is highly volatile, rising and falling with sentiment in markets for climate technologies and wider financial and monetary conditions. The wealth of Bloomberg's top 15 green billionaires was estimated to be US$500 billion in 2021, but six months following the publication of the list they had collectively lost US$141 billion (Lee, Lee & Feng 2022). These losses were driven by Musk, who by January 2023 had lost more than half his net worth as Tesla's share price crashed and losses from his controversial takeover of Twitter were registered (Moloney & Hull 2023).

Beyond the Bloomberg list, there are a variety of other prominent billionaires, often working at the intersection of fintech and clean tech, who are intervening in speculative markets in climate finance. Microsoft founder Bill Gates established Breakthrough Energy Ventures at the Paris Climate Conference in 2015 to invest as venture capital in start-ups and other companies involved in technological innovation for climate change. Investors in the US$2 billion fund included Amazon's Jeff Bezos, Alibaba's Jack Ma and Richard Branson himself. Other green billionaires have taken a more activist route, such as Atlassian's Mike Cannon-Brookes. Cannon-Brookes is an Australian tech billionaire who in 2022 partnered with Canada's Brookfield Asset Management (of which Mark Carney is vice-chair) to take-over Australia's largest polluting company, AGL, in order to more rapidly phase out its coal-fired power generators and replace them with renewables. While the takeover bid was unsuccessful, Cannon-Brookes emphasized the political significance "on the national psyche" of his attempted investment, and subsequently engineered a partial takeover of the board on climate grounds (Hyland 2022). The move was not Cannon-Brookes's first financial speculative political intervention: during a significant energy crisis in 2017, he facilitated a bet between the South Australian state government and Elon Musk to deliver the then biggest battery storage system globally in 100 days, or it would be free.

Some green billionaires have followed a pipeline from extractive industries to climate tech. Another Australian billionaire, Andrew "Twiggy" Forrest, is chair of Fortescue Metals Group, one of the biggest iron ore miners in the world – the key input into highly polluting steelmaking. Forrest is renowned for his opposition to taxation in the mining industry and legal disputes over land with Indigenous Traditional Owners. But, in a 2021 public lecture titled "Confessions of a carbon emitter", Forrest outlined Fortescue's plans to dominate the global production of green hydrogen. This plan had been formulated during the Covid-19 lockdowns of 2020, when Forrest took his private jet on a scoping mission to almost 50 countries around the world. In outlining his vision, Forrest anticipated a battle with both legacy fossil capital – which he described as a "knife fight in a telephone box" – and with other green billionaires, including Elon Musk, who he bets will be thwarted by the ecological limits of battery production that only green hydrogen can overcome (Forrest 2021).

Contradictions of the green billionaire class

The rise of green billionaires is full of contradictions. Green billionaires present a narrative of entrepreneurial innovation solving climate change, acting in place of a state encumbered by bureaucracy and vested interests. However, green billionaires have attracted significant public finance and regulatory support from the state, such as loan guarantees, tax credits and research and development funding. Goldstein and Tyfield (2018: 84) describe this as "the venture capital state". Contradictions are also evident between the green billionaire image of "clean" innovation and wealth creation, moving beyond the dirty industries of the past, and the material basis of clean-tech industries. The batteries integral to electric vehicles and renewable energy storage depend on lithium extraction. But, in Chile for instance, lithium extracted through brine mining produces unsustainable impacts on water and ecosystems and violates Indigenous rights (Jerez, Garcés & Torres 2021). Chinese companies have established control over the minerals necessary for clean technologies, including lithium, cobalt, nickel and rare earth elements mined in Latin America and Africa (Riofrancos 2022), producing new geographies of "green extractivism".

For proponents of and practitioners in speculative markets, there are tensions over the relationship between technological and financial imperatives. Divisions have emerged between capital investments in the search for new technological miracles or the scaling up of existing ones. Bill Gates and his Breakthrough Energy Ventures falls into the former camp, stating "our investments don't just respond to today's circumstances – they also anticipate tomorrow's urgent needs" (Breakthrough Energy 2022). In his book, Gates outlines the speculative nature of his approach to technologies: "We can't be afraid to bet on some crazy ideas. It's the only way to guarantee at least a few breakthroughs" (2021: 84). Gates's approach to innovation has, however, been criticized by other entrepreneurs who, in response to China's competitive advantage in low-cost clean-tech production, have instead argued for a definition of "breakthrough" to include financial innovation that can make the deployment of existing technologies more profitable (Knuth 2018: 223).

More fundamentally, there are contradictions between the technological disruption and the socio-ecological continuity offered by green billionaires. Ultimately, the "planetary improvement" offered by clean-tech entrepreneurs is focused on "non-disruptive disruptions", or technologies as "solutions" that leave the causes of climate change untouched (Goldstein 2018). As Branson himself articulates, in his vision, the "'doom and gloom' scenario vanishes. We can carry on living our lives in a pretty normal way" (Branson 2011: 140). The status quo is just one miracle technology away. For Forrest, that technology is green hydrogen. As he concluded in his lecture: "There are two futures ahead of us. Fly less, drive less, live out in the open, or you're killing the planet. Or the alternative one that doesn't demand such austerity and sacrifice … I choose hydrogen. What will you choose?" (Forrest 2021).

Unwinding Musk's speculative climate future

Elon Musk, CEO of electric vehicle and renewable energy company Tesla, is emblematic of the latest wave of tech-turned-green billionaires. Musk's route to clean tech was fintech, as a founder of financial payments company PayPal, before becoming an early investor in Tesla. Musk's surge to become the world's richest person in 2021 came off the back of the astonishing growth in Tesla's share pricing during the Covid-19 pandemic, seeing a 1,400 per cent rise between March 2020 and November 2021. The astronomical increase in Tesla stocks reflected the speculative fervour surrounding the company and its CEO. Musk, the self-appointed "Techno-King" of Tesla, courts controversy through his inflammatory public comments and brash business and financial practices, all of which were evident in his 2022 takeover of Twitter.

The outsized influence of Tesla and Musk emerged, however, through the speculative position they took on the future of climate change. In an interview, Musk declared that "we will solve the climate issue. It is just a question of when. And that is like the fundamental goal of Tesla … to improve the quality of the *future*" (Döpfner 2022, emphasis added).

Tesla's share price performance is a classic case of financial speculation. Its November 2021 high elevated Tesla's market capitalization to over US$1 trillion – more than the next nine biggest car makers combined (McGee & Badkar 2021). According to standard financial benchmarks, Tesla's share price is massively over-valued relative to its earnings and its peers, measured in terms of cars sold and profits made. Yet, Tesla's share price is not driven by such "fundamentals", but by speculation on the place of Tesla, and electric vehicles, in the future of climate change. Tesla stock is popular with retail investors who are avid fans of the Musk personality cult (Hull 2020). Tesla does not pay dividends to the owners of its stock, who therefore take a purely speculative position on capital gains, rather than income generation. The liquidity and volatility of the stock has also been underpinned by extensive trading in options and other derivatives taking positions for and against Tesla, such that there is significant leverage attached to Tesla's share price movements (Wigglesworth 2021).

The speculative basis of Tesla's rise has been productive for the company, but also carries significant risk. The financial survival of the company has depended on leveraging its share price increases for liquidity at crucial moments. Tesla's constant struggles for liquidity began with its difficulty meeting production targets and turning a profit in its first decade. In response, Musk turned to financial innovation to raise cash needed for survival, using Tesla's stocks as collateral for margin loans, selling more stock, selling convertible bonds that can be repaid with stock and splitting stock so that it is more accessible to retail investors (Hull & Recht 2018). Each of these strategies is designed to leverage and inflate Tesla's share price. Still, Tesla's financial strategy faces risks if the strategy of continual share price inflation falters, as occurred across 2022 when tightening financial conditions, poor sales and increased competition from other electric vehicle companies combined to reduce Tesla's share price by more than two-thirds from its 2021 highs. These events threaten to unravel Musk and Tesla's nexus between speculation and liquidity because they can lead to creditor demands to pledge more stock to compensate for the devaluation of collateral (a financial process known as a "margin call"), which could trigger a downward spiral of illiquidity and insolvency (Moloney & Hull 2023).

However, assessments of the future prospects of the speculative markets of green billionaires cannot be limited to pure financial market mechanics. Both the development and survival of Tesla has been guaranteed by the state.

A US Department of Energy loan of US$465 in 2010 supported the development and manufacturing of the Tesla Model S, its first step towards a more mainstream product (Overly 2017). This public finance came in the wake of the global financial crisis when the auto industry was under severe stress and credit markets were tight. Tesla repaid the loan, which had a ten-year term, early, in 2013, using proceeds from stock offerings and convertible bonds. The early repayment of the loan, Tesla emphasized, was testament to its "scrappy and entrepreneurial" culture, unconstrained by "bureaucracy and a risk-averse profile that constrains break-through innovation" (O'Connell 2013). Tesla also secured a low-cost US$1.4 billion loan in 2019 from a consortium of Chinese state-owned banks to finance a new factory in Shanghai, which is central to the production and sale of its more mass-market Model 3 (Sun, Leng & Goh 2019). When Tesla did finally become profitable in 2020, regulatory credits were instrumental. Tesla gains significant revenue, beyond sales of its cars and battery systems, from selling tradeable regulatory credits to other car makers (an example of a precision market; see Chapter 4). Governments in Europe, California and elsewhere apply emissions standards to car makers across their entire fleets, and car makers can purchase compliance by buying credits from other car makers, such as Tesla. In 2020, when Tesla reported US$721 million in profit, this included US$1.58 billion from the sale of regulatory credits (Tesla Inc. 2021: 30, 41). Disruption, in Tesla's case, is a state-funded project.

Musk, Tesla and the green billionaire class's green vision is productive of a particular climate future that, paradoxically, largely maintains existing socio-ecological relations. As an electric vehicle company, Tesla offers a techno-fix to climate change that preserves private automobility as a pillar of contemporary capitalist life (Huber 2013). Musk's position on climate change avoids questions about how the necessity of zero-carbon transport presents opportunities to change, and even collectivize, mobility. These green contradictions are illuminated by Musk-as-speculative-performance. Musk openly acknowledges the environmental problems created by the minerals extraction on which Tesla batteries depend, but nonetheless encourages the expansion of nickel mining to reduce costs (Sun & Burton 2020). Controversially, in 2021 Tesla purchased US$1.5 billion of Bitcoin – the ultimate in speculative assets – as a way to "diversify and maximize returns" and as a prelude to accepting the cryptocurrency as payment (Tesla Inc. 2021: 23). The energy-intensive nature of Bitcoin mining, along with labour and product safety issues saw Tesla removed from a prominent ESG index. Musk's response that ESG is a "scam" (Norton 2022) is indicative of his divergent approach from the risk management climate future envisaged by ESG integration. Yet, while Musk's speculative markets valorize rather than manage risk, the end goals – a greener capitalism that is not fundamentally different to fossil-fuelled capitalism – ultimately converge. Similar debates are playing out over whether speculative climate engineering represents a break with or defence of the fossil economy, to which we now turn.

CLIMATE ENGINEERING

Climate engineering, or geoengineering, is the "intentional large-scale intervention in the Earth's climate system to counter climate change" (Union of Concerned Scientists 2017). The term commonly encompasses two broad technological practices: carbon removal, utilization and storage; and solar radiation management. These practices intervene very differently in the climate, but both imagine managing "an overshoot of temperature targets" (Buck 2019: 24). While sometimes presented as a technological fix for such overshoots, the imaginaries, accounting practices and financing of climate engineering are inherently political. Climate engineering is one of the clearest illustrations of the role of climate finance in shaping different climate pathways. Where the financing of carbon removal is tethered to ongoing fossil fuel use, these technologies can delay decarbonization. Alternatively, carbon removal can complement climate transitions where financing is targeted at cleaning up historical emissions, alongside rapid decarbonization. Whether private or public finance dominates, and how this financing is organized, shapes whether climate engineering technologies herald a privatization, or democratization, of governance over the climate.

The development of climate engineering is boosted by climate science research. Carbon dioxide removal includes "nature-based" terrestrial practices such as afforestation and soil carbon sequestration, and more capital-intensive practices such as direct air capture (DAC) with storage or utilization. The latter is gaining more interest due to the spatial limits of "nature-based solutions" for achieving large-scale removal. Direct air capture technologies suck carbon from the ambient air, which is then either stored underground or utilized, for example in enhanced oil recovery. The latest IPCC report concludes that the deployment of carbon dioxide removal is "necessary" to meet net-zero emissions and an "essential element" of limiting warming to 1.5–2°C (Intergovernmental Panel on Climate Change 2022b: 94).

Solar radiation management, or solar geoengineering, seeks to manage the climate effects of excess greenhouse gases in the atmosphere. This technology involves using different techniques to lessen and disperse the absorption of sunlight on Earth to lower temperatures. The most common proposed method is stratospheric aerosol injection of sulphur or other particles. Solar geoengineering has proven particularly controversial compared to carbon dioxide removal (Szerszynski *et al.* 2013; Yusoff 2013). The IPCC is more equivocal about the "uncertain side effects and thorny international equity and governance challenges" of solar geoengineering (Intergovernmental Panel on Climate Change 2022a: 26). Prominent climate and social scientists have forcefully taken up these concerns, describing solar geoengineering as a "risky and poorly understood set of technologies" and "politically [un] governable in the current context", and calling for an international non-use agreement on solar geoengineering (Biermann *et al.* 2021).

Climate engineering technologies are often criticized as tools of displacement and delay. Critics argue that both carbon removal and solar geoengineering offer a promissory "fix" for continued carbon emissions that risks keeping in place the structures of the fossil fuel economy as "an attempt to reconfigure the planet to avoid reworking the capitalist political economy" (Carton 2019: 674). Indeed, this is one of its appeals for prominent climate engineers. Physicist David Keith (2013: 143) – Harvard professor and climate tech entrepreneur of carbon dioxide removal and solar engineering – asks "must we fix capitalism in order to fix the climate?" His response: no, because climate engineering provides an alternative to the kinds of economic planning required to wean capitalism off its dependence on fossil fuels (Malm 2020).

Debates over climate engineering are, however, increasingly shifting from "for and against" arguments to discussion about the terms of their deployment. If limiting warming to 1.5–2°C is "virtually unattainable" without negative emissions technologies, the "how" will be crucial (Buck 2019: 7). Holly Jean Buck acknowledges concerns about the potential of climate engineering to delay climate transformations, but argues that this depends on the political-economic context in which the technology is deployed, rather than something that is inherent in the technology itself (Buck 2019). There are, Buck maintains, good reasons to "avoid the worst-case and go for the better-case ways of doing it"(2019: 26) Rather than counterposing climate engineering and systematic change, progressive visions of carbon removal and solar radiation management see structural reasons favouring better-case scenarios, because deploying these at scale is likely to require significant public oversight due to the need for public investment in renewable energy to power the technologies, democratic governance for global coordination, and local benefits to secure social legitimacy for development approval. Climate engineering might therefore be reimagined as a public service, organized through a public ownership model akin to the public utilities that manage urban sewerage systems (Buck 2021). Climate fiction writer Kim Stanley Robinson even describes publicly managed carbon removal as "Sewage Treatment for the Skies" (2020).

Financing direct air capture

The "how" of climate engineering is currently being shaped through the sources and terms of finance. As still speculative technologies, the coordinates of these competing possibilities are being worked out through intangible proposals and demonstration projects. Rather than big tech, the archetypical business of these speculative markets is the start-up: according to global professional services firm PwC, "climate tech" accounts for 14 cents in every dollar of venture capital financing (PwC 2021). However, while solar geoengineering remains a speculative proposition far from deployment at scale, DAC technologies are operational and are being scaled up. As we have outlined, the two technologies are distinct, and conclusions for DAC should not be conflated with solar geoengineering. Similarly, while there are some technological overlaps, DAC differs from carbon capture and storage approaches that capture carbon from emissions sources and which have struggled for commercial viability. In principle, DAC technologies can remove carbon that is already in the atmosphere from anywhere. In practice it is spatially bound by its significant renewable energy requirements and by the geography of geo-sequestration and utilization potentials (Buck 2021). These twin features, creating at once abundance and scarcity for the speculative futures of DAC, are reflected in the search to secure diversified revenue sources for carbon removal and sequestration.

Currently, there are three broad sources of revenue for DAC that project developers' leverage to attract equity investments and debt financing: government subsidies, demand for products made from carbon utilization and selling offset credits for carbon removal. First, government financing subsidizes research and development into DAC. In the US, the Bipartisan Infrastructure Law (2021) included US$3.5 billion in funding for DAC demonstration "hubs", and the Inflation Reduction Act (2022) increased tax credits available for DAC with storage to US$180 per tonne. Second, carbon utilization funds DAC through the demand for goods made using extracted carbon, such as aviation fuels, building products, plastics, chemicals and food and beverages. The largest area of carbon utilization is enhanced oil recovery, in which captured carbon is injected to extend the life of depleted oil wells – a practice that directly links DAC with the continuation of the fossil economy.

Third, revenues from selling carbon credits become possible as carbon offset methodologies have been extended to DAC. The purchase of carbon credits produced by DAC has a speculative quality. DAC carbon credits are a tiny proportion of the overall offsetting market owing to low volume and high price. Financial innovation has therefore focused on attracting buyers who are willing to pay a premium – around US$1,000 per tonne – to be able to publicize small-scale purchases of carbon removal-based credits. The Frontier fund established by online payments company Stripe, together with Alphabet, Meta, Shopify and McKinsey, is an example of financial innovation aimed at building carbon offsetting markets that can provide revenue for the scale-up of DAC. Stripe's Nan Ransohoff described Frontier as "a bit of a hybrid between philanthropy and an attempt to meet our own net-zero commitments" (Purdom & Zhou 2022). Frontier acts as both a purchaser and broker of DAC offsets, modelled on the advanced market commitments used in vaccine development and PPAs used for renewable energy.

Two prominent and advanced DAC start-ups – Carbon Engineering and Climeworks – illustrate how different forms of financing influence the place of DAC technology in climate futures. Founded by David Keith, introduced above for his vision of climate engineering as a means of avoiding structural change to fossil fuel use, Carbon Engineering is a DAC start-up based in Canada that is financially backed by Bill Gates. Carbon Engineering demonstrates how DAC can delay decarbonization. Carbon Engineering has run a pilot facility in Squamish, British Columbia since 2015 and is developing a plant in Texas that it claims will remove one million tonnes of carbon dioxide per year. In addition to securing finance from a range of venture capital, private equity and institutional sources, two prominent investors in Carbon Engineering are Chevron's Future Energy Fund and Occidental Petroleum's venture capital arm Oxy Low Carbon Ventures (Carbon Engineering 2019b). The interests of these fossil fuel companies is in carbon utilization through the production of synthetic fuels and in the injection of captured carbon for enhanced oil recovery (Carbon Engineering 2019a). CEO of Oxy, Vicki Hollub, described DAC with storage as a "waste of a valuable product. And it's something that we should not do on a large scale basis" (Rathi 2022). Carbon Engineering has also signed advanced contracts to supply both carbon credits and synthetic fuel to fossil fuel-dependent companies including aircraft manufacturer Airbus and oil company SK Innovation (Carbon Engineering 2022; Vahn & Lee 2022). Its CEO is explicit about the role of Carbon Engineering in managing the continued use of fossil fuels, saying "It's infeasible that we all stop using fossil fuels overnight" (Hook 2019).

Zürich-based Climeworks is, at the time of writing, the most advanced DAC start-up in terms of its development, and represents a somewhat different financing strategy to Carbon Engineering. In 2021, Climeworks opened its Orca DAC with storage plant in Iceland powered by geothermal energy, in partnership with the aptly named CarbFix, part of the publicly owned Reykjavík Energy Group, which oversees the storage. This is the first DAC with storage plant operating on a commercial basis that is financed by selling carbon removal credits to businesses. The plant is very small scale, with capacity to remove and store only 4,000 tonnes of carbon per year.

Future projects, including a new plant with 36,000 tonnes per year capacity under construction in Iceland, are notable for their use of highly publicized contracts for selling carbon credits. These deals have created a public spectacle around Climeworks, attracting significant media and celebrity attention, including from Leonardo DiCaprio's climate change documentary *Ice on Fire* and partially offsetting emissions from a tour of the band Coldplay. The offsets have also been used to leverage investment into Climeworks from various sources, including the Singapore government's sovereign wealth fund GIC, the world's largest reinsurer Swiss Re, asset manager Baillie Gifford and private equity firm Partners Group (Climeworks 2022b).

Climeworks sells future carbon credits for a premium rate of US$1,000 per tonne to both companies and individual consumers. The premium price paid for credits gives these contracts outsized financial weight for Climeworks compared to generic offset markets. Their approach to the creation of speculative markets in DAC technology is reflected in its position on climate futures, which focuses on removing "historic CO_2 emissions from the air" (Climeworks 2022a). Climeworks has deals to sell future carbon credits to various companies in the tech and finance sectors, including Microsoft, Boston Consulting Group, Swiss Re and more (Climeworks 2022c). The volume of these contracts is extremely small, mostly 1,000–2,000 tonnes, and their purchase is not driven by offsetting requirements. But it is exactly this exclusivity that comes with the scarcity of carbon removal that plays a performative role in the construction of a speculative market around carbon removals. This speculative dimension extends to Climeworks' carbon removal deals for individual consumption, including for instance: 300 tonnes of removal purchased by tech billionaire Chris Larson, "climate positivity" certificates sold directly from Climeworks' website on a subscription basis for as low as 1kg per month and carbon removal certificates issued to purchasers of high-end cosmetics products sold by La Prairie.

However, there are limits to the financing strategies being adopted by DAC start-ups for scaling up carbon removals, reflecting a "precarious economics of removal" (Carton *et al.* 2020: 10). Credits produced by DAC avoid problems associated with credits based on "avoided emissions" as in other forms of offsetting (see Chapter 4) because they remove actual, rather than counterfactual, carbon. Nonetheless, when used to offset real emissions they are at best carbon neutral, not carbon negative. Similarly, the potential market for carbon utilization products represents a small proportion of the total carbon removal challenge, at most less than 10 per cent of the "mitigation challenge", and is also not carbon negative (MacDowell *et al.* 2017).

The current financing strategy of the DAC industry does not appear to facilitate the scale of negative emissions needed to reach the industry's promises to address climate change. Buck (2019) describes this challenge as moving from the first stage of "niche, boutique, aesthetic, or symbolic" removals to the second stage of "climate significant" removals. While the first stage is currently financing the initial wave of DAC start-ups, the second stage is "a cleanup operation" (2019: 31–2), which may not produce commoditized products and services. To finance a public cleanup for the skies, a combination of public money from the state and state regulation to divert private money to climate repair is likely necessary. Beyond those private actors operating at the "frontier" of carbon removal as a speculative market, other private actors are unlikely to provide finance to draw down their historic emissions unless required to by state regulation. Further, there are good reasons for state money and state regulation to govern the socio-ecological risks of climate engineering. Carbon dioxide removal, and indeed solar geoengineering, are not one-off interventions, but rather ongoing processes requiring management over long time horizons that extend well beyond commercial forward contracts. The risks of failure, such as widespread carbon leakage, or an abrupt and uncoordinated halt to drawdown, would be catastrophic for the climate. Only the state can insure this level of climate risk.

OFF-GRID SOLAR

Beyond the expansion of innovative climate technologies such as DAC, speculative markets in climate finance are also oriented towards the geographical expansion of existing, even ordinary, climate technologies into new markets. In her anthropology of the making of the US electricity market, Özden-Schilling (2021) describes electricity as both ordinary and extraordinary. As with our other infrastructures or essential services, those of us in the "fully electrified world" take its seamless provision and ongoing accessibility as a given. This is not a universal experience; as the World Bank reports, some 10 per cent of the world's population do not have reliable access to electricity (as of 2020; this is of course much lower in some countries; World Bank et al. 2022). On the other hand, electricity is much more than mundane, both for the way it has thoroughly transformed social life and for its complex journey to market. Electricity is an unlikely commodity, difficult to store, transport or substitute; it was once considered a natural monopoly with its singular grid infrastructure. And yet, while requiring work, electricity is commoditized, marketized through competitive generation and supply markets and increasingly financialized through financial contracts and speculative virtual trading. Energy is productive of social forms and economic relations; the public-private, regulatory-financial dynamics that facilitate accumulation through electricity are spatially and temporally specific instantiations of "electricity capital" (Luke & Huber 2022).

The examples below explore the dynamic off-grid solar market in developing countries as one configuration of (renewable) electricity capital. Climate finance for off-grid solar takes a speculative position that seeks to leverage climate imperatives for expanding access to renewable energy technologies for rural and remote consumers in developing countries to expand market frontiers. In very different contexts than those described above, and with very different actors interpellated, the off-grid solar industry invites speculative investment, governance and action. Low electrification rates in some countries – particularly in sub-Saharan Africa where it is below 50 per cent – makes off-grid solar both an economic opportunity and humanitarian need while also reducing greenhouse gas emissions. Motivated to meet Sustainable Development Goal 7's commitment to universal access to electricity, off-grid solar PV systems work from the limits of grid-based, centralized electricity systems, especially for the world's poorest. Indeed, off-grid solar is often positioned as a pathway towards "electric modernity": "full electrification and modern energy services that can reliably drive upward social and economic mobility" (Cross & Neumark 2021: 919). Across the Global South, life unplugged is the contemporary condition of poverty and marginalization, but where the failures of both states and markets to provide grid-based energy is positioned as a "market opportunity" (Cross 2016). Indeed, the off-grid solar PV market, what energy financial analysts call "global energy access markets", is now one of the biggest solar markets globally, worth US$1.75 billion annually, with double digit growth year on year projected.

Financial and electrical engineering

A range of different physical and financial technologies are bundled under the umbrella of off-grid solar. At the smallest scale, these include single solar lanterns, which led the industry early in its evolution. Larger solar home systems have come to dominate sales, as integrated "plug-n-play" systems that include solar panels, batteries and several connection points (Munro, Jacome & Samarakoon 2022). These systems have become more complex over time, growing from lights and mobile phone charging connections to include more sophisticated and higher electricity-consuming devices such as televisions, fridges and fans. Solar microgrids are larger again, sometimes powering public services such as hospitals and schools or operating across villages with households and businesses connected to the systems as a kind of decentralized power plant. The financial terms of these physical systems are also diverse, most often including either "rent-to-own" or hire purchase payment systems. Accordingly, customers place an initial down payment and regular repayments over a set period of time, following which they would own the system. In the case of larger solar microgrids, customers pay for electricity consumed as measured through smart meters.

The industry sits at the productive intersection of fintech and clean tech. On the one hand, the mobile payment platforms and technologies driving "bottom billion banking" depend on electrification, and on the other hand, solar home systems and microgrids depend on mobile banking technologies and other smart infrastructures to monitor consumption and receive payments. These codependencies have expanded the webs of "lending, collecting, and monitoring" of customers and their consumption, producing precarious populations as "hidden reserves of creditworthiness" (Cross & Neumark 2021: 906).

The extraordinary growth of pay-as-you-go, or PAYG, systems is illustrative. These are predominantly rent-to-own systems that require a 10–20 per cent deposit, after which customers make regular payments through mobile banking. Crucially, the off-grid solar company can monitor these payments remotely and disconnect the system if payments lag. These systems have overwhelmingly driven recent growth in the industry, indeed obscuring decline across other parts of the sector. Their success stems in part from defraying the cost of integrated solar home systems for customers, but also the way that they draw on and produce new streams of data to create credit profiles of potential customers, enabling the predatory inclusion of low-income consumers. These systems have also become gateways to other consumer products, as well as financial products and services, such as insurance, that in turn produce new data streams (Baker 2022a).

Who are the investors taking positions on off-grid solar companies? Early experiments with off-grid solar technologies were first imagined by "graduate entrepreneurs" from engineering and business schools in the Global North. From the mid-2000s, these students combined their engineering skills with liberal economic development doctrines in search of less-polluting solutions to rural and remote electrification. For instance, founded by two Australian engineers, Barefoot Power created small solar lanterns in the hope of electrifying swathes of rural and poor Papua New Guinea; in 2007, some Stanford University students created d.light to sell solar lanterns in India and Tanzania (Munro, Jacome & Samarakoon 2022). While driven by humanitarian aims of tackling energy poverty and reducing pollution, these entrepreneurs also regurgitate assumptions about the limits of electricity as a public good and the failures of grid-based universal provision. As the World Bank describes, the advantages of off-grid electrification include that it "lightens" the load of financially precarious state-based utilities and "leverages" innovative financial investment all while being a more sustainable electricity alternative (Cogan *et al.* 2021: 2).

The financial model for off-grid solar has changed over the last two decades. In the market's initial stages, these graduate entrepreneurs were financially supported by impact investors, from individual investors to specialized funds with explicit social and environmental commitments (see Chapters 2 and 3). While securing initial financing was relatively easy, through angel investors, microfinance institutions and even prizes, securing markets for the off-grid solar product in rural and remote locations was less so (Munro, Jacome & Samarakoon 2022). As local staff were recruited, offices set up, technologies became more complex and the companies scaled up, investment became more traditional, including private equity and debt and venture capital (Baker 2022a). Off-grid solar mimics Silicon Valley-style faith in the power of angel investors and venture capitalists to spur innovation, particularly in clean tech. Indeed, many Bay Area investors sought out "emerging market" opportunities such as off-grid solar in the wake of failures of the global financial crisis of 2008 and Silicon Valley's own clean-tech failure. Since 2010 the off-grid solar industry has attracted more than US$2 billion in equity and debt financing; in 2021, pandemic notwithstanding, the industry attracted almost US$500 million in financing, more than two-thirds of this as debt commitments (GOGLA 2022). This market growth is banked by investors, facilitated by consumer credit and debt held by some of the most globally precarious customers.

Illiquid electricity

This story of growth and success – in ever-growing inflows of investment and ever-more complex debt arrangements and financial products – hides a more complex evolution and story. From around 2018 the industry has hit a series of speed bumps. Just as with the speculative positions of green billionaires or the products of climate engineering, very few off-grid solar companies are profitable. One of Africa's largest and most widely recognized off-grid solar companies, Mobisol, filed for preliminary insolvency in 2019. Having taken on up to US$100 million in debt and equity investment over the 2010s, by 2018 Mobisol was busy repossessing solar home systems on which East African customers had defaulted. Although armed with payment data and credit profiles at minute scales, with poor customers unable to pay, their "too good to be true" business model appeared exactly that (Cross & Neumark 2021). The peculiarities of financing off-grid solar are important to recognize here: the assets are not liquid, there are currency mismatches, there are long cash conversion cycles and the industry is consumer-finance heavy.

Ultimately, however, off-grid solar for poor customers is a "risky" investment because the customers cannot afford to pay the costs of the systems. The industry itself took off following the rapid fall in costs for the solar systems in the mid-2000s. Despite this, the costs of off-grid solar remain prohibitively expensive for consumers. In Uttar Pradesh, India, for instance, PAYG off-grid solar systems cost customers 100–200 rupees a month (US$1.50–$3.00), or "more than a half-day's wage for the poorest households" and are between two and four times more expensive than a grid connection (Balls & Fischer 2019: 470). In Kenya, PAYG expenditures are around US$6–15 a month, requiring increases in expenditure over other forms of energy (such as kerosene) and leading to reductions in other consumption expenditures (Zollmann *et al.* 2017). These precipitous costs for customers, and the work involved in securing payments to ensure liquidity, has undermined business models. In response, the big gamble of bottom of the pyramid off-grid solar has moved to surer bets, shifting from supplying "the poorest of the poor" (as described by an electronics engineer in Baker 2022a) to bigger systems and wealthier customers often in relatively well-connected urban areas. Some of these middle-class urban customers use off-grid solar to complement their unreliable grid-based electricity. Staying profitable and thus able to service investment obligations has required a substantial shift away from the humanitarian origins of the industry.

Off-grid solar shares with more spectacular forms of speculative climate finance a scepticism of "flabby states" (Mawdsley 2018) and their ability to deliver innovative social, economic and environmental outcomes fast. This has tended towards a kind of "cyber-libertarianism", zealously promoting the solutions of the "fintech-philanthropy-development complex" (Gabor & Brooks 2017). But the industry also shares with other speculative climate finance markets a reliance on public sector direct funding, subsidies and bailouts. The off-grid sector has always depended on direct grant funding and concessional lending. Multilateral and development finance institutions have also long played a prominent role in building the industry. The World Bank has acted as a key market-maker, hosting forums and expos, creating quality assurance systems and collating several state-of-the-market reports. The World Bank and other development institutions have also directly invested in the industry. With other stakeholders, the World Bank provided considerable concessional financing for "energy access companies" through the Energy Access Relief Fund in the wake of the Covid-19-induced economic shocks of 2020–21 (World Bank 2021). The economic impact of the pandemic further reduced customers' ability to meet their service payment obligations, causing "liquidity constraints" for off-grid companies; the World Bank projected that up to 85 per cent of them were not likely to withstand the crisis. The concessional facility addressed this squeeze, claiming the US$1m loans for off-grid solar companies would ensure the continued operation of the "vital" sector (SIMA 2022).

Predatory inclusion

Beyond its questionable financial success, the social and political effects of predatory forms of "digital-based" financial inclusion such as off-grid solar are profound. The remote lockout technology of PAYG systems has enabled the scale-up of financial investment, enticing investors with data streams and the disciplinary apparatus of the "lock". As the development research organization, CGAP, write, Harima in eastern Uganda experienced embarrassment and shame when her solar home system shut off after she failed to make a payment and all her neighbours could see her house in the dark. But without this action, how could her provider "be sure of recovering value on small-asset loans in remote areas, where repossessions are expensive, if they're even possible?" (Waldron & Swinderen 2018). Yet, there is no evidence that the locks increase payment rates and, as with repossession, they may be counterproductive. Locking solar home systems requires customers to spend on other kinds of energy, and where the systems are productive a shut off may limit income generation. Repossession of the solar devices is particularly illogical, costing both consumers, who lose their investment and are ashamed, and the companies who incur substantial costs to recover and store the system, which degrades over time. Unlike other assets, the solar home systems are not easily resold.

There is a mutual expansion of off-grid solar and financial technologies such as mobile banking and lending and indebtedness. The speculative nature of off-grid solar – working at an unproven frontier, on an experimental big bet – has required constant expansion to new customers to solve, or at least push into the future, its liquidity problem. The outcomes of the "adverse inclusion" of precarious populations is not electric modernity, but further exclusion and indebtedness. Fintech has been celebrated by the development industry for its transformative ability to reduce poverty through mobile banking and microcredit. M-Pesa in Kenya is exemplary: processing more than half of Kenyan GDP it is *claimed* to have lifted some 2 per cent of households out of poverty through its various loan infrastructures (Bateman, Duvendack & Loubere 2019). These analyses overlook their impact on indebtedness, for which M-Pesa and its off-grid affiliate M-Kopa have been labelled "merchants of debt" operating with a "battery of digital data and algorithms ... [and] a largely unregulated lending fronter ... at a premium so costly it would be illegal for a Kenyan bank" (Donovan & Park 2019). And who benefits from these fintech innovations with their high interest rate repayments and default? Their Silicon Valley investors.

Off-grid solar systems are socially transformative for households. They are safer, cleaner and more reliable, literally and figuratively illuminating for the lighting and the social connections through phones, radios and televisions. And yet the full realization of this promise remains constrained by their imbrication with forms of climate finance that take speculative positions investors have difficulty sustaining financially. Most companies are not returning profits, are no longer serving poor customers and are producing factories full of solar e-waste; some customers are not making their payments. Meanwhile, states and other sources of public finance continue to subsidize the ultimate investors in off-grid solar, while the systems themselves undermine efforts towards universal state provision, produce overlapping patchworks of service and escape regulatory oversight. Despite these adverse outcomes, the World Bank claims the industry is on the brink of success, just needing greater equity and debt investment (Cogan *et al.* 2021), another US$11 billion dollars to serve 132 million households by 2030. Rather than configured as failure, the industry identifies an opportunity to keep the speculative dreams alive, creating new sites for experimentation and innovation.

CONCLUSION

Elon Musk and his green billionaire class, climate geoengineering and off-grid solar infrastructure systems may seem unlikely case studies to collectively examine speculative climate finance. Musk and his ultra-high-worth colleagues and rivals harness their entrepreneurial spirit to seek "crazy", in Bill Gates's words, technological solutions at the scale of trillions; climate geoengineering is creating new, intertwined circuits of carbon and finance that work in and through an essential, and globally public, climate sewerage system; and off-grid solar targets the financial and electrical inclusion of the world's poorest through micro-technologies. The technologies, financial scales and consumers are worlds apart. And yet they each offer techno-financial fixes that promise a contradictory mix of currently unrealized climate futures that enable existing social and ecological relations to remain largely untouched. The futures envisaged by speculative markets are, however, anchored in the present through the constant search for liquidity. The cases all negotiate what Martijn Konings and Lisa Adkins call the "speculation-liquidity nexus" (Konings & Adkins 2022: 3): constantly seeking more finance and funding, evolving and expanding to new markets, sites and technologies in order to overcome the limited profitability of their products and services. This opens speculative markets to political contestation over how, and on what terms, liquidity is provided.

Each of the examples demonstrate how their speculative positions on climate finance fundamentally structure the climate futures they predict. It seems, at least in the immediate term, that battery technologies, DAC and off-grid solar systems in remote and rural areas will all play a part in climate transitions. All represent critically important climate technologies across different scenarios for reaching net-zero emissions. The exact nature of the climate solution on offer, and the winners and losers that follow, is being shaped by negotiations over whose visions of the future are embedded in the financing that provides the lifeblood of liquidity in speculative markets. Finance matters for questions of who gets access to climate technologies and who is excluded, whether climate technologies preserve or challenge dependence on fossil fuels and what governance and ownership arrangements apply. While on current trends the dominant future envisaged by speculative markets is a slightly greener although still wildly unequal and extractive capitalism, other political possibilities are also emerging. Rather than a simple rejection of different climate technologies, debates and struggles over speculative markets raise questions about the financial actors and institutions that could harness the generative potential of speculation for different ends.

Public financing of speculative markets provides a significant point of political leverage. Although each example has prominent actors representing techno-libertarian ideological scepticism of the state, they are fundamentally dependent on state subsidies and bailouts. In off-grid solar, financial innovation is a response to the absence of public provision of what are basic and essential technologies. The central role of concessional finance points to possibilities that international public climate finance could instead be used to reduce exploitative financial relationships and embed principles of universal service provision – an issue we return to in Chapter 7 on climate justice finance. There is a clear division between the use of DAC technologies for the drawdown of historical emissions or the maintenance of fossil fuels into the future. The bespoke nature of contracts for carbon removal has created scope for the embedding of socio-ecological safeguards and benefits (Purdom & Zhou 2022). But the limits of financing from offsetting and carbon utilization, and the need for scale in materially significant drawdown scenarios, is seeing a greater role for public financing that comes with governance requirements for community and labour representation (Office of Clean Energy Demonstrations 2022). The speculative visions of green billionaires are, however, largely antithetical to any kind of public oversight over the technologies being underwritten by state subsidies, loans and bailouts. This suggests the need for a shift to forms of public financing that challenge monopoly private control over important technologies such as batteries. The following chapter focuses squarely on the different roles of state actors and institutions in programming climate finance, examining the potential of the fiscal and monetary tools of big green states in configuring climate futures.

CHAPTER 6

BIG GREEN STATES

In many ways, the story of climate finance is that of financial restructuring in the wake of overlapping climate, environmental and economic crises. As the international climate finance regime was being established at the Copenhagen COP in 2009, the global economy was lurching from one crisis to another. Financial markets were still reeling from the effects of the 2008 crisis emerging from the US banking system, which was beginning to shift to a sovereign debt crisis in the eurozone that would strike with full force from 2010. Responses to these crises brought into sharp focus the role of state institutions in underwriting tightly interconnected systems of global finance. Decades of neoliberal reform had embedded rules ostensibly designed to enforce the trifecta of fiscal discipline: low spending, low taxation and low public debt. The 2008 global financial crisis revealed the extent to which constraints on state action in the neoliberal period had been selectively applied. The "rollback" of the state was visibly countered by the "rollout" of a potent set of new state powers (Peck & Tickell 2002). Confronted with prospects of a full-scale crisis, the fiscal and monetary arms of the US government, the Treasury and the Federal Reserve acted with enormous political discretion to bail out banks and put the global financial system on life support. However, the politics of fiscal austerity not only endured, but in many cases was redoubled as the effects of the crisis reverberated. In sharp contrast to the bailouts of Wall Street, an "extreme economy" of public austerity was entrenched across city, regional and national governments as banking crises were reformatted as public debt crises (Peck 2012).

The role of the state across each of the climate finance positions advanced in this book has been conditioned by the significant shifts in fiscal and monetary policy and politics seeded by this period of crisis. In a very direct way, the public spending and liquidity support provided by states in response to the global financial crisis – and rehearsed and refined in responses to the

Covid-19 pandemic and its economic impacts – had different levels of regard to climate change and prospects for a green recovery. There was significant variation in the level of "greenness" of stimulus delivered in response to each crisis across states. Less directly, but more importantly, contested state responses to crisis have set the political-economic parameters in which debates about climate finance are playing out. Political efforts to enforce budget and market discipline while implicitly and explicitly guaranteeing private finance are reflected in dominant climate finance positions that privilege private investment and relegate the state to "market correcting" or "de-risking" roles (Gabor 2021b; Mazzucato 2015). However, the scale and coordination of state firepower on display during the global financial crisis, and especially during Covid-19, inevitably raised questions about how the fiscal and monetary powers of states could be wielded in the fight against climate change. Both crises revealed the extent to which austerity was a political choice, and that other choices were politically possible.

This chapter examines the climate finance positions being developed by "big green states". Previous chapters have emphasized the crucial roles that states play in regulating and subsidizing celebrated private finance innovations in the climate policy sphere, despite purported independence from, even disdain for, state-centred actions. In this chapter we are explicitly concerned with how states, as public institutions, are using their own fiscal and monetary powers to actively shape future climate pathways. The big green state represents a pathway to decarbonisation that "puts the state firmly in the driving seat" (Gabor 2023: 24). We show that the big green state is a terrain of political contestation that is occurring across a wide spectrum of state action, from more incremental efforts to "green" fiscal and monetary policy, to programmes that take climate change as necessitating a more comprehensive role for the state in managing, even planning, investment. Climate finance is not only an inheritor of wider shifts in fiscal and monetary politics, but is a terrain through which those shifts are evolving, as competitive and democratic pressures are pushing states to take "big green" positions on climate futures.

The meaning of "big" in big green states is contested. Neoliberal states were never "small": state powers were not wound back but rather repurposed in the interests of private profits. "Freer markets", as Vogel (2018) explained, necessitated "more rules". Scaling up *public* finance to not only meet climate investment gaps, but actively shape *how* those gaps are filled, is nonetheless a crucial ingredient in many visions for big green states. As shown by responses to both the global financial crisis and Covid-19, state action through expansionary monetary and fiscal policy can dramatically shift the dial on what is financially possible. More than the scale of the state, however, contestation over "big" green states is about the creation of collective political spaces of democracy and accountability through which climate finance can be organized and extended in ways that reflect and advance distinctive "public" interests. One of the defining elements of neoliberal reform was to recast the state as just another market actor. In pursuit of "levelling the playing field" between public and private sectors, neoliberal reform served to hide and restrict the scope for democratic participation in the exercise of state finances (Spies-Butcher & Bryant 2023).

Climate politics is, however, putting the always "dynamic interface" between public and private finance further in flux (August *et al.* 2022: 527). Crises are always moments that reconfigure the role of the state in the economy, as states face acute tensions between reproducing capitalism (with its racialized, colonial, gendered and class oppressions) and securing democratic or political legitimacy (O'Connor 1998). These pressures are especially strong with the climate crisis. Pretences of "market neutrality" are difficult to maintain as activists and researchers highlight the role of fiscal and monetary policy in supporting fossil fuels. Similarly, commitments to "letting the market decide" appear increasingly at odds with the scale and scope of the climate transition challenge, which demand states either shape markets through, for example, green industrial policy, or consider non-market options such as public ownership.

We explore big green states as a position on climate finance through two broad sections that are organized according to the main ways that states alter the distribution of resources in an economy: monetary policy and fiscal policy. We ground our analysis in contestation over existing forms of climate finance statecraft to consider possibilities and limits for big green states in a capitalist economy, which sets the scene for our analysis of more radical, justice-aligned, even post-capitalist possibilities for climate finance, inside and outside the state, in Chapter 7. The first section on monetary policy introduces the role of central banks in contemporary capitalism before considering debates on the relationship between central banks and climate change and proposals to "green" central banks. These proposals all revolve around central banks differentiating between green and dirty assets in their monetary policy operations, to address current biases in favour of fossil fuels and shift the allocation of capital towards green investment. The second section on fiscal policy canvasses a greater range of state configurations that are being pushed to take a big green state position on climate change. We explore these configurations by looking at different policy instruments (fossil fuel subsidy reform and carbon taxation), institutions (state investment banks) and a comparison of fiscal support for renewable energy in the US and China.

GREEN MONETARY POLICY

Monetary policy is concerned with managing the supply of money and credit in an economy. The main tools of monetary policy are controlled by central banks. Central banks are public or quasi-public financial institutions that occupy a privileged position in national economies and global financial markets as issuers of currency and enactors of monetary policy. Central banks around the world have different mandates concerning inflation, unemployment, financial stability and other policy goals. They use a variety of tools of monetary policy to achieve these goals, including issuing currency, setting official interest rates, buying and selling financial assets and regulating the banking sector.

Central banks were, and are, central institutions in the development, evolution and reproduction of capitalism. More recently, central banks have assumed increasingly significant roles in the governance of neoliberalism, underpinning the liberalization of private finance. The quintessential features of neoliberal central banking are formal independence from government and an overarching focus on targeting low inflation over other goals, such as Keynesian-era goals of full employment (Best 2019; Krippner 2007). Following the global financial crisis, and then the Covid-19 pandemic, the role of central banks as crisis managers has come to the fore. With interest rates close to zero, limiting scope to use conventional crisis management techniques such as lowering interest rates, central banks turned to so-called "unconventional" monetary policy, such as quantitative easing (QE) and the creation of novel facilities to guarantee liquidity in financial markets (Langley 2015; Tooze 2018). Crises management techniques reflect the long-standing mission of central banks as "lenders of last resort". With the expansion of their role in backstopping systemically important securities markets, primarily US and other government bond markets, the purview of central banks has expanded to include being "market-makers" or "dealers" of last resort (Gabor & Ban 2016; Mehrling 2011). New techniques of central banking that emerged in 2008 and were consolidated during the pandemic reflect the increasing coupling of price stability and financial stability goals, the latter of which seeks to govern "systemic risk" (Musthaq 2021; Özgöde 2021).

The enrolment of monetary policy into debates about climate policy reflects the increasing significance of central banking in economic policy, both in the management of economic crisis and in debates about social and environmental issues. This has culminated in proposals for "green monetary policy". Monetary policy is a key pillar of climate finance from the position of big green states because it concerns the role of the state, via central banks, in managing the monetary systems of capitalist economies. Nonetheless, central banks are not representative of a monolithic state; they are a particular form of state power that is mobilized in a way that is deeply entangled with the private power of finance (Coombs & Thiemann 2022; Mann 2010). At present, central banks exercise power in the financial system by governing *through* financial markets. Rather than acting as outside regulators seeking to restrain finance, central banks rely on the market infrastructure of private finance – in particular, the growing "shadow" banking sector – to transmit monetary policy (Braun 2020; Braun & Gabor 2020).

Central banks and climate change

Proposals for green monetary policy are shaped and constrained by these developments in the political economy of central banking. Growing appreciation of the financial risks of climate change has led researchers, campaigners and some central bankers themselves to call for central banks to factor climate change into their monetary policy operations, as "climate governors of last resort" (Langley & Morris 2020). Disagreement from within and beyond central banks about whether to do so hinges on the relationship between their mandates and climate change. Monetary policy decisions such as whether to increase or decrease official interest rates have important implications for climate change, by affecting the cost of capital for green and fossil fuel investment alike. Do existing central bank mandates, which overwhelmingly target price and financial stability, warrant a focus on these climate change considerations in their monetary policy decisions? Or do central bank mandates need to be expanded to take on an explicit climate role? Currently, only a small minority of central bank mandates explicitly cover climate change. A study of 135 central bank mandates found only 12 per cent had sustainability elements, although 40 per cent made mention of broader government policy objectives, which can include climate policy (Dikau & Volz 2021).

The Bank of England recently changed its mandate to consider climate change. Typical of central banks around the world, the objectives of the Bank of England, according to the Bank of England Act 1998 section 11, are to "maintain price stability" and "subject to that, to support the economic policy of His Majesty's Government, including its objectives for growth and employment". Every year the Chancellor sends a "remit" letter on behalf of the Treasury specifying the exact price stability goal and the economic policies of the government that the Bank of England should factor into monetary policy. In 2021, in addition to the 2 per cent inflation target, the Chancellor added the "transition to a net zero economy" to the Bank of England's remit. However, the letter also affirmed the "primacy of price stability and the inflation target in the UK monetary policy framework", making clear that the two objectives are not on equal footing, and that the neoliberal focus on fighting inflation still reigned supreme (Sunak 2021:3, 5).

Not all central bankers have embraced calls to add climate change to their mandates. While supporting measures such as climate disclosure, former president of the German central bank, the Deutsche Bundesbank, Jens Weidmann, is resistant to the idea that existing central bank mandates extend to climate change. He expressed scepticism that central banks should stray too far from their inflation mandates, or abandon "market neutrality" principles by differentiating between green and dirty assets in their monetary operations. He argued: "It is not the task of the Eurosystem to penalise or promote certain industries. Our primary objective is to maintain price stability … Monetary policy has often been credited with extraordinary powers. That adulation has never really rung true. When it comes to saving the planet, central banks do not have a magic wand" (Weidmann 2020). US Federal Reserve Chair, Jerome Powell, echoed this sentiment. Powell has acknowledged the Fed has "narrow, but important" responsibilities supervising the financial risks of climate change, but argued that climate change is largely the responsibility of elected branches of government and fiscal policy. In short, Powell argues that the US Federal Reserve is "not, and will not be, a climate policymaker" (Smialek 2023).

However, the fact that powerful central bankers feel compelled to respond to climate questions is indicative of climate pressures on monetary policy. Some central banks are seeing climate change as relevant to their conventional mandates due to the implications of climate-related financial risks to price and financial stability. In 2017, over 100 national central banks and financial supervisors formed the Central Banks and Supervisors Network for Greening the Financial System. This is a voluntary network focused on sharing knowledge and practice around the management of climate risk as it relates to the operations of central banking and the regulation of financial systems.

Within green central banking, there is a divide between those institutions that take a more limited "risk exposure" approach and those that take a more expansive "systemic risk" approach (Dafermos 2022). The former is concerned with quantifying and managing climate-related financial risks to the financial system while leaving climate policy to executive government. The latter, acknowledging both the uncertainty and gravity of climate risk, envisions a role for central banks in actively reducing these risks by promoting low-carbon transitions. This systemic risk approach entails challenging the "myth" of market neutrality principles of central banks, by recognizing that its application has, in practice, underpinned the fossil fuel economy (van't Klooster & Fontan 2020).

The Bank for International Settlements – the international bank that is owned by, and coordinates between, the world's major central banks – has advanced a position that climate risks can and should be addressed within the financial stability mandates of central banks, and central banks should play an active role in coordinating the climate response. It published a report in 2020 warning that "climate change could lead to 'green swan' events and be the cause of the next systemic financial crisis" (Bolton *et al.* 2020: 1). A "green swan" is a climate inflection on the term "black swan" – unexpected and rare crises with wide-ranging impacts that can only be explained after the fact – which gained popularity in accounts of the global financial crisis. Accordingly, climate change is a potential green swan because high levels of uncertainty make risk management approaches based on extrapolating historical probabilities inappropriate. Further, these risks are both more complex and more severe than standard financial crises, due to the presence of "long" tail risks (see Chapter 4; Morris & Collins 2023). As a result, the report argues that central banks should not wait for governments to take action because this could lead to risks to financial and price stability that are at odds with their mandates. Waiting will force central banks to adopt an unwanted role of "climate rescuers of last resort"; unwanted because, although buying devalued assets may secure financial stability, it would not stabilize the climate. The approach advocated by the report is described as an "epistemological break" in central banking where monetary authorities, fiscal authorities and financial markets coordinate to meet their mandates in the face of climate risk.

Green central banking

Proposals for green central banking encompass a variety of tools of monetary policy, financial supervision and financial regulation to reduce the role of central banks in supporting fossil fuels and harness the power of central banks for climate ends. The most common climate initiative implemented by central banks has been extending prudential stress testing to climate risk (Morris & Collins 2023). A key tool of post-crisis financial governance, stress testing models the capacity of banks and the financial system as a whole to withstand shocks such as a sudden devaluation of asset values under different economic and financial scenarios as a measure of financial resilience in the face of different risks (Coombs 2020). Climate stress testing adds climate scenarios that involve different manifestations of physical and transition risk. It has been used or trialled by central banks including the European Central Bank (ECB), the Bank of England, the People's Bank of China and the US Federal Reserve. Such exercises have revealed limitations in the measurement and quantification of climate risks by the banking sector and potential for significant devaluations of banking assets. To date these stress tests have only been exploratory in nature and used to highlight the need for improved risk disclosure rather than regulatory measures by central banks and financial supervisors to reduce those risks. These limitations reflect broader criticisms levelled against stress testing as a relatively light-touch response that relies too heavily on markets to make self-adjustments in the face of new information, while excluding key parts of the financial system, including the shadow banking sector (Langley & Morris 2020).

Beyond scenario planning approaches such as stress testing, central banks are being pushed to adjust their own operations to support climate transitions. Scrutiny is being applied to the climate effects of three main tools: capital requirements, collateral frameworks and QE. Each tool plays a distinct role in the financial system, but proposals to "green" them share a similar logic. Green central banking proposals recognize that the existing application of these tools supports, however unintentionally, carbon-intensive assets by reducing financing costs for fossil fuel expansion and disadvantaging green investments. Hence, they propose differentiating between dirty and green assets, penalizing the former and/or privileging the latter, in order to shift the cost of capital in favour of climate-friendly investment. Although proposals to green capital requirements primarily target the traditional banking sector, the greening of collateral frameworks and QE is designed to filter throughout shadow banking systems and market-based forms of credit (such as corporate bonds) rather than conventional bank loans.

Capital requirements aim to reduce the systemic risks of leverage and liquidity by requiring financial institutions to maintain a certain ratio of liquid assets (i.e. assets easily tradeable for cash) relative to long-term illiquid assets. The risk weights of assets that determine capital requirements make some kinds of investments more favourable than others, because they require banks to hold greater or smaller levels of liquid assets. Applying a "dirty penalizing factor" to carbon-intensive assets, or alternatively a "green supporting factor" to green assets, would incentivize banks to shift their lending away from fossil fuels or towards green investments by increasingly or decreasing liquid capital requirements. While penalizing dirty assets promises to reduce the systemic risks of a climate Minsky moment, supporting green assets using lower capital requirements may work at cross purposes with financial regulation of conventional Minsky moments (see Chapter 3).

To date, there have been only very limited moves in this direction. The ECB has begun including climate risk in its bank supervision scores that impact capital requirements under Pillar II of the Basel II banking accord (Campiglio 2016; European Central Bank 2022b; see Chapter 3). The People's Bank of China has similarly added "green performance", such as levels of lending and green bond issuance, to its macroprudential assessment framework that governs capital requirements (Choi, Escalante & Larsen 2020: 10). Central banks in emerging economies, which usually have more traditional bank-based finance systems, have pursued policies akin to green capital requirements through tools that explicitly aim to direct the flow of credit towards green sectors. For example, the Bangladesh Bank mandates that 5 per cent of loans on the books of commercial banks are earmarked for green purposes (Bangladesh Bank 2020).

Collateral frameworks govern the type and quantity of assets that central banks require to be deposited with them from the banking sector in return for the liquidity they provide. Central banks have lists of what assets are eligible for collateral, and the "haircuts", or reductions, applied to their market value based on perceived risk. Assets that are eligible as central bank collateral, especially those with small haircuts applied, attract more favourable financing terms throughout the financial system. Proposals to green collateral frameworks argue that haircuts could be increased for dirty assets, or decreased for green assets, making the latter relatively more valuable as collateral than the former (Robins, Dikau & Volz 2021). A stronger approach would be a progressive removal of carbon-intensive assets from the list of eligible collateral (Dafermos *et al.* 2021).

There have been some moves in this direction. The People's Bank of China has focused on promoting the use of green assets as collateral. It expanded its list of eligible collateral for its lending facilities to include green credit and green bonds (Choi, Escalante & Larsen 2020: 10). The ECB, in contrast, announced it would limit the use of corporate bonds from carbon-intensive companies as collateral by banks from 2024. The announcement, however, showed the extent to which central banks remain tied to the principle of market neutrality. The ECB emphasized that the rule would not breach market neutrality because it would only set an overall limit on banks, without dictating eligible and ineligible assets on climate grounds. The ECB also announced that it would begin considering climate risk in haircut decisions and from 2026 require that all collateral comply with climate disclosure rules (European Central Bank 2022a).

QE refers to central bank purchases of financial assets, such as government bonds, corporate bonds and asset-based securities. QE is designed, especially in a low interest rate environment, as an alternative form of stimulatory monetary policy that puts downward pressure on interest rates and adds liquidity to key markets. But what are the climate implications of QE, particularly for programmes that involve corporate debt purchases, such as the ECB's? QE programmes, while being purportedly "market neutral", can reproduce the implicit carbon biases of the markets they are supporting, which do not always price carbon risk in a material way (Dafermos *et al.* 2020; see Chapter 3). Using a similar logic to collateral frameworks, "green QE" would shift corporate bond buying programmes to reduce purchases of high-carbon assets and increase purchases of green assets. This proposal could also have implications for turns to quantitative tightening, which would inform the order in which central bank's shrink their balance sheets by disproportionately selling, or choosing not to roll over, carbon-intensive assets.

Both the Bank of England and the ECB have begun to consider climate risk in the balance sheet operations that manage their QE programmes. This followed earlier moves by Sweden's Riksbank to negatively screen its corporate bond purchases according to sustainability norms. In response to its new net-zero remit, the Bank of England announced it would "tilt" its corporate bond purchases, aiming for a 25 per cent reduction in its total portfolio by 2025, and alignment with net zero by 2050, which would preclude further purchases of bonds from coal mining companies (Bank of England 2021). The ECB announced a similar "tilting" strategy, with an emphasis on reinvestment in bonds linked to companies with "better climate performance" when existing holdings are redeemed (European Central Bank 2022a). However, both central banks emphasized that climate goals are secondary to inflation considerations when making decisions on issues such as the total quantity of central bank asset purchases. Indeed, when the Bank of England began to unwind its corporate bond holdings in response to post-pandemic inflationary pressures, it ceased its "tilting" strategy and the carbon intensity of its balance sheet increased (Bank of England 2023). The ECB's tilting strategy was similarly short-lived as climate considerations were jettisoned in the turn to quantitative tightening (Dafermos *et al.* 2023).

The monetary politics of climate crisis

Experiments with green central banking demonstrate how understandings of climate change as a systemic risk create political imperatives to act. This impetus for action has driven moves to extend the power of modern central banks to govern climate change as a financial stability problem, with the aim of overseeing an orderly green transition. At present, green central banking is largely using the potential monetary powers of big green states to complement rather than challenge the nexus of climate capital and climate risk as positions of climate finance (Chapters 2 and 3). Because central banks want to govern *through* financial markets, green central banking shapes climate futures by encouraging financial markets to reprice assets in line with climate risk.

At the same time, using existing monetary tools for climate purposes, such as by treating green and dirty assets differently, represents a departure from the recent politics of central banking. The tools mobilized by central banks in response to recent crises represent an overarching concern with putting a floor under asset prices – often with a considerable degree of success, but at the expense of growing social, economic and spatial inequalities (August, Cohen & Rosenman 2022). Rather than reducing the prevalence of systemic risk, central banks have periodically bailed out financial institutions and asset classes deemed systemically important, or "too big to fail". As Konings (2018a: 119) argues, this strategy "involved lending not against good collateral but precisely against bad collateral". In the monetary politics of the climate crisis, central banks may be caught between using green central banking to manage or reduce the systematic financial risks of climate change, or bailing out institutions exposed to carbon-intensive assets in ways that threaten financial stability.

However, these are not the only possible climate finance positions of central banks. Central banks could adopt the position of big green monetary states by providing low-cost debt for private green investments that meet government policy goals or, more effectually, directly funding public green investment through the "monetary financing" of big green fiscal states. These actions would build on and expand central bank responses to the Covid-19 crisis, which saw the creation of various lending facilities and the monetization of public debt. The aim of these responses, however, was limited to stabilizing financial markets in turmoil, avoiding attempts to shape the nature of the recovery in a green direction (Gabor 2021a). Central banks could use these monetary powers to effectively create "climate money" to finance the transition in line with the climate policy goals of governments. Both the People's Bank of China and the Bank of Japan made small steps in this direction by establishing green credit facilities that finance green lending by banks at close to the official policy interest rate (Eames & Barmes 2022: 16).

Possibilities for more expansive use of monetary powers to finance climate remain constrained by the structure of central banking independence, which intentionally places monetary policy at arm's reach from democratic pressures that might push central banks in this direction (Mann 2010: 618). Paul Langley and John Morris (2020: 1477) therefore argue that a transformative climate monetary policy "will most likely necessitate the democratic transformation and fundamental repurposing of central banking itself". As we have argued in this book, finance is not only shaping the course of climate change; climate pressures are reshaping finance itself. Could climate change be the impetus for a democratization of central banking? Any such shift would likely emerge through pressures on central banks to coordinate climate responses with fiscal authorities, to which we now turn.

GREEN FISCAL POLICY

Fiscal policy influences the distribution of resources through the various powers of government to tax, borrow and spend. As with monetary policy, fiscal policy has both driven, and is being called on to address, climate change. Debates about the role of fiscal policy in climate change are unfolding in the context of the constraints on fiscal policy imposed by decades of neoliberalism. However, the scope of state responses to the global financial crisis and Covid-19 demonstrate that fiscal policy remains a contested and variegated sphere of state action. And, as across other axes of climate finance, climate change itself is driving transformations in fiscal policy. Climate change is providing the impetus for the phase-out of fossil fuel subsidies and carbon taxation as a strategy of green fiscal reform. States are also using various fiscal methods, from tax credits to state investment banks, to shape green investment patterns in industries such as renewable energy.

In this section we explore political-economic differences across strands of green fiscal policy that represent four existing state configurations that are being pushed to adopt the position of big green states: the market correcting state, the de-risking state, the green Keynesian state and state capitalism. The market correcting state is the fiscal expression of the logic underpinning precision markets (Chapter 4). Following orthodox, neoclassical economics, state fiscal action is justified in response to climate change only insofar as it corrects market failures by adjusting market prices. The de-risking state is the pillar of what Daniela Gabor (2021b) terms the "Wall Street Consensus", where the state uses its fiscal power to construct and underwrite new investable asset classes. The role of the state is therefore to take on risk on behalf of private investors to ensure that assets provide income streams and are protected from devaluation, such as in climate-resilient infrastructure (Chapter 2).

These market-based approaches are being challenged by imperatives to adopt big green state positions that build from elements of Keynesianism and state capitalism. The green Keynesian state uses the state's fiscal powers to play a more active role in steering markets. Influential twentieth-century economist John Maynard Keynes (2018: 336) called for a "somewhat comprehensive socialisation of investment" in which the state plays an enduring role in guiding investment without necessarily expanding public ownership. Heterodox economist Mariana Mazzucato's "entrepreneurial state" (Mazzucato 2015) articulates a modern and green version of this Keynesian state as an "investor of first resort" (Lederer 2019). The entrepreneurial state plays a more expansive role in shaping the direction of investment and technological innovation than both the market correcting state and the de-risking state by "not simply fixing market failures but by actively creating and shaping (new) markets, while regulating existing ones" (Mazzucato 2015: 6). Investment may be delivered through public-private partnerships, but rather than the state de-risking private sector investment plans, the private sector is mobilized in service of state-defined "missions" such as climate change.

State capitalism represents another configuration of state fiscal power, defined broadly as "configurations of capitalism where the state plays a particularly strong role as promoter, supervisor and owner of capital" (Alami & Dixon 2023: 76). Accordingly, states seek to exert greater control over markets through institutions such as planning authorities, sovereign wealth funds, national development banks and state-owned enterprises. The expansion of "state-controlled capital", state-capital "hybrids" and other "muscular" forms of statism, has been termed the "new" state capitalism (Alami & Dixon 2023: 75). The impulses towards the expansion of state capitalism are varied, and its climate potential is contested, as models developed to support fossil fuels, such as national oil and gas production, are extended to climate infrastructure.

Green fiscal reform and carbon taxation

The fiscal powers of states have been a key driver of climate change. The International Energy Agency and OECD estimated that governments of 51 major global economies provided fossil fuel subsidies worth US$697 billion in 2021 (OECD 2022e). These subsidies include fiscal support such as tax concessions or direct government payments to producers and consumers, which function to lower the price of coal, oil and gas relative to alternatives. State-owned enterprises in the fossil fuel industry have made outsized contributions to climate change: 41 per cent of carbon dioxide and methane emissions from fossil fuel and cement producers released globally between 1854 and 2010 can be traced to state-owned "carbon majors" (Heede 2013). In 2009, G20 governments committed to "phase out inefficient fossil fuel subsidies", a commitment that was reiterated in the 2021 Glasgow Climate Pact that emerged from COP26. However, OECD and International Energy Agency data show that subsidies for fossil fuels in major economies, although fluctuating with movements in the oil price, largely remain in place (OECD 2022e).

Carbon taxes complement and take further the market correcting logic of fossil fuel subsidy reform, by not only removing government "distortion" in favour of fossil fuels, but also making fossil fuels more expensive relative to alternatives. Carbon taxes place a government levy on emissions, or carbon-intensive output or consumption. By 2022, 37 carbon tax schemes had been implemented at national and subnational levels globally (World Bank 2022: 15).

According to the logic of orthodox economics (detailed in Chapter 4), carbon taxes should be set to equal the unpaid costs – or "externalities" – of climate change. In practice, political pressures have resulted in wildly different carbon tax levels and levels of sectoral coverage: in 2022 they ranged from less than US$10 per tonne in Poland, Argentina, Columbia, Mexico, Ukraine, Japan, South Africa and Singapore, to more than US$100 per tonne in Uruguay, Switzerland, Sweden and Liechtenstein (World Bank 2022: 19). Varying levels of sectoral coverage often reflect lobbying from industry arguing that carbon taxes will place them at a disadvantage compared to international competitors, creating the risk of "carbon leakage" where carbon-intensive production migrates to carbon-tax-free jurisdictions. This often leads to exceptions for industries deemed to be "trade exposed". An alternative fiscal approach, which has been implemented in the EU, is to impose "border adjustment taxes" on imports of carbon-intensive goods from countries with less stringent climate policies.

Carbon taxes also have a fiscal logic as a form of government revenue that can be used to redistribute resources. In 2022, carbon taxes around the world raised US$28 billion (World Bank 2022: 27). This so-called "double dividend" of carbon taxes may be used as another source of consolidated government revenue, earmarked for climate and environmental programmes or used to reduce other taxes, such as on labour or capital. Canada and Switzerland distribute a "carbon dividend" payment direct to citizens funded by their carbon taxes in an effort to increase public support for the policy (Mildenberger et al. 2022). There is, however, an inherent trade-off in the revenue-raising logic of carbon taxes from a climate perspective. A carbon tax cannot be both a strong disincentive to continue burning fossil fuels and a potent revenue source for too long: the better it is at one thing the worse it is at the other.

Despite offering a seemingly simple, even "elegant" solution to climate change, the politics of carbon taxation are fierce (Cullenward & Victor 2021). Carbon taxes have been criticized for shifting the cost of climate change on to ordinary households through increased power bills and other essential areas of spending. Indeed, the economic theory behind carbon taxes expects costs to be passed on to end consumers to send economy-wide signals for decarbonization. In practice, whether carbon taxes are regressive – meaning that poorer households pay a higher share of their income richer households – is a question of policy design. In the short-lived Australian carbon tax, in place from 2012 to 2014, carbon revenues were directed to compensate low and middle-income earners. However, these policy design features were not enough to overcome an effective political campaign to "axe the tax" (Pearse 2017). The political limits of carbon taxation are one reason behind state efforts to use their fiscal power in a more active way to shape climate outcomes, including via state investment banks.

Green state investment banks

National state investment banks (also referred to as development banks or policy banks), are potentially key institutions of big green fiscal states. State investment banks are state-owned institutions that lend or invest public money in line with public mandates. They can be already established state investment banks that move towards a green mandate or newly established dedicated green investment banks (Geddes, Schmidt & Steffen 2018). Green investment banks can expand the fiscal space available to states to publicly finance green investments. Because they provide public finance in the form of state-backed credit or by taking an equity stake, they can build public green wealth, while avoiding some of the fiscal constraints that are applied to government spending, borrowing and taxing. However, green state investment banks are currently caught between competing models of (big) green fiscal states.

Green state investment banks in advanced capitalist countries are currently dominated by a de-risking logic that reflects the "gap talk" approach to climate finance. These institutions are tasked with filling market gaps by mobilizing and leveraging private capital (OECD 2017a: 2). The key de-risking metrics of green investment banks are the leverage ratio of public to private investment and the rate of return delivered to the state compared with commercial benchmarks. Australia's Clean Energy Finance Corporation (CEFC) and the UK's Green Investment Bank, both created in 2012, were established with an explicit de-risking purpose. For example, the CEFC's objective is to "catalyse and leverage an increased flow of funds" for clean energy via "targeted commercial investments, to counter market failures and financing impediments and to generate positive public policy outcomes" (Clean Energy Finance Corporation 2021: 2). These objectives combine the possibility of both commercial and broader public policy goals. The CEFC's positive returns for the budget have been used in Australia to defend it against the same political attacks that led to the abolition of the carbon tax. However, it also makes it a potentially attractive candidate for privatization. Indeed, the UK's Green Investment Bank was sold to the Macquarie Group in 2017 and renamed the Green Investment Group.

From a green Keynesian perspective, state investment banks can provide "patient capital" that takes on risks to create social value. As public institutions, state investment banks can be designed to follow long-term public missions (Mazzucato 2015). Rather than simply filling gaps in private capital markets, Mazzucato and Penna (2016) outline an expansive set of roles that state investment banks can play in meeting public missions, including: countercyclical lending, long-term project finance, socializing benefits, and coordinating with other public institutions. They argue that

121

the mission-oriented structures of Germany's KfW, and Brazil's National Bank for Economic and Social Development go some way to achieving these goals. Both were established in the years immediately following the Second World War to support the state development goals of post-war reconstruction and agricultural industrialization, respectively. While these institutions also adopt de-risking approaches, their climate mandates have seen them coordinate investment in the renewable energy transition in their national economies. For example, KfW's sustainability mission specifies that a minimum of 35 per cent of new investment should be climate and environment related and excludes coal investment (KfW 2022).

The China Development Bank is exemplary of the "state-constituted market" nature of Chinese state capitalism (Weber & Qi 2022). The China Development Bank is one of three policy banks in China, which sit alongside the four big state-owned commercial banks. Founded in 1994 with national and regional development objectives, the China Development Bank is a major source of infrastructure lending both in China and internationally (Williams, Robinson & Bouzarovski 2020). It is an active state participant in markets, "creating, empowering, and most importantly, composing a competitive market where the main players – regulators, buyers, sellers – are state actors" (Chen 2020: 457). Since the late 2000s, the China Development Bank has adopted a green growth strategy (while continuing to finance fossil fuels) that in coordination with other state authorities has successfully established China as the leading manufacturer and installer of renewable energy technologies. We turn to public financing of renewable energy, contrasting the approach of China with the US, in more detail now.

Public finance for solar power in China and the US

The solar power sectors in the US and China illustrate and reflect different movements towards big green fiscal states. The US, with Germany and Japan, was an early leader in the production of solar technologies. Over the course of the 2010s, China emerged as the dominant global producer of solar technologies, controlling at least 80 per cent of every major part of the supply chain for manufacturing solar panels (International Energy Agency 2022: 7). The US and China have adopted different models of fiscal support for solar, with the former relying on tax credits and loan guarantees for innovation and the latter relying on loans from state investment banks to support mass production as a state strategic priority.

Tax credits have been the primary fiscal support provided by the US government to renewable energy and other climate technologies. Tax credits use the fiscal powers of the state in a way that avoids direct forms of expenditure.

They have their genesis in, and continue to be used by, wealthy individuals and households (Tapp 2019). Crucially, tax credits are effectively sellable, which allows renewable energy businesses that are yet to make a profit, and therefore have no tax liability, to sell them to "tax equity" investors, such as banks and corporations that purchase the credits as tax shelters. Developers sell, or "monetize", the tax credits to these investors at a discount in return for upfront capital, in a process that has led wind and solar farms to be pejoratively described as "tax farms". Reliance on tax credits means that a portion of the fiscal subsidy is diverted away from investment in renewable energy and creates a bias in favour of large-scale privately owned projects designed as special purpose vehicles over smaller-scale community or publicly owned renewables (Knuth 2021).

When the global financial crisis hit, the Obama administration responded with a package of green stimulus within the wider American Recovery and Reinvestment Act of 2009. The green stimulus component of this $780 billion bill included $90 billion for clean energy primarily through a combination of loan guarantees and tax credits (Mulvaney 2019: 22, 51–2). The stimulus package extended a pre-existing Department of Energy loan guarantee programme for fossil and nuclear energy to renewable energy. The programme is not a state bank, as it is administered by a government department and is focused on loan guarantees, but it nonetheless has bank-like characteristics. The programme embeds principles of the de-risking state. It was designed to underwrite the risks of financing gaps that occur in the "valley of death" stage of innovation.

The same Department of Energy loan programme was behind loans to Tesla (Chapter 5). It is best known, however, for the controversy surrounding the $535 million in loan guarantees provided to solar manufacturing business Solyndra in 2010. Solyndra's strategy was to manufacture thin film solar modules as an alternative to polysilicon-based modules. But they ultimately went bankrupt in 2011 as Chinese-produced polysilicon modules came to dominate the global market (Caprotti 2017). The Solyndra episode was weaponized by Republican politicians and conservative media as evidence that the government should not be in the game of "picking winners". While a US Government Accountability Office found problems in the administration of the Solyndra loan, the programme on a whole delivered an overall return to the state and supported other successful solar businesses (Mulvaney 2019: 53, 62). Nonetheless, the case shows how the de-risking state socializes risks and privatizes profits, because the Solyndra loans were structured so that private creditors were to be paid before the government (Mulvaney 2019: 206).

Chinese fiscal support for renewable energy reflects the Chinese state-constituted market model of state capitalism that combines state planning and liberalized markets through a "dual-track" price system (Weber 2021). In this dual-track system, the Chinese state distinguishes between sectors that are, and are not, what it deems to be "systemically significant" (Weber & Qi 2022: 5). Although the non-systematically significant sectors have been progressively liberalized, the state has maintained control over systemically significant sectors, including renewable energy, through policies such as price controls and state ownership.

The rapid expansion of the Chinese solar industry has been coordinated through national planning authorities and policies that have directed state finance to publicly and privately owned renewable energy manufacturers and developers. In contrast to US bets on innovation by new technology start-ups, the overarching strategy of China's solar policy is to gain global market dominance through the mass production of existing solar technologies. The Chinese government established the renewable energy industry as a systemically important strategic industry in various policy documents (Allen *et al.* 2021; Chen & Lees 2016; Huang *et al.* 2016). For example, the 2005 Renewable Energy Law gave renewable energy "national priority status", requiring national grid operators to connect new renewable energy installations to the grid and state-owned utilities to purchase electricity from renewable sources. Periodic five-year plans set targets for solar PV cell production, followed by solar supply chain targets and then utility-scale installation targets. These targets empowered the National Development and Reform Commission to play a steering role in the renewable energy sector, controlling prices and overseeing investment direction.

Through the China Development Bank and other sources of public finance, fiscal policy has been mobilized to support solar at different stages of development. Initially, support was aimed at solar manufacturers that were primarily producing for export markets in Europe and the US, which have implemented their own installation subsidies. The China Development Bank established various large-scale lending programmes to key solar manufacturers, worth over US$5 billion each (Sanderson & Forsythe 2013: 151). These loans were bolstered by tax rebates from provincial governments for establishing solar manufacturing locally. Following the global financial crisis, fiscal support for the Chinese solar industry shifted towards support for domestic installation. The financial crisis reduced demand for exports, which, combined with increasing scales of production in China, created a global glut of solar technology. The impact of the global glut was a "solar trade war", where the EU and the US commenced anti-dumping actions by using fiscal powers to impose tariffs on imports of Chinese solar technologies (Caprotti 2015). The Chinese government responded with public finance to support domestic installation to substitute for the loss of global demand through programmes such as Golden Sun and Solar Roofs, which supported large-scale and rooftop installation with feed-in tariffs (Huang *et al.* 2016; Zhang, Andrews-Speed & Ji 2014).

The Chinese state capitalist model of fiscal support has successfully driven down the global costs of solar and established China as the leading producer, and installer, of renewable energy, at levels far exceeding other economies. In 2022, US$546 billion was invested in the energy transition (predominately across renewable energy and electrified transport), representing half the world's total, and well above the US$141 billion invested in the US (BNEF 2023). China's nationally coordinated renewable energy strategy, has, nonetheless been criticized for at times "erratic" implementation locally and regionally, due to abrupt policy changes and the failure of some renewable energy companies (Zhang, Andrews-Speed & Ji 2014). A deeper problem is that state coordination of renewables investment has not translated to the general decarbonization strategy. The China Development Bank, along with other state-owned banks, were major financers of new coal-fired power plants within China and internationally, at the same time as they were providing finance to renewables (Hervé-Mignucci & Wang 2015; Hervé-Mignucci et al. 2015). Campaigners and researchers have also raised concerns about environmental pollution, worker and community health and safety hazards and forced labour of Uyghurs across the polysilicon supply chain (Mulvaney 2019: 26–33; Murphy & Elima 2021).

Competition with China provided a major impetus for the US to turn towards "green industrial policy" in its post-Covid-19 climate bill (Allan, Lewis & Oatley 2021). The Inflation Reduction Act had its genesis in the Biden administration's post-pandemic 'Build Back Better' plans, which were ultimately thwarted by fiscally conservative Democratic Senators in the context of a spike in inflation. The eventually successful, but smaller, Inflation Reduction Act was heavily focused on climate change, although contained elements of support for fossil fuels too. The bill relied on the two central de-risking tools – tax credits and loan guarantees – but these were designed with far greater conditions to "steer", in a partially green Keynesian manner, public and private investment towards creating domestic supply chains in clean energy.

Motivated by twin goals of countering China's dominance in the clean energy market and securing public support for spending on the climate transition, the bill demonstrated possibilities for doing green industrial policy through and beyond the tools of the de-risking state. The bill significantly increased the Department of Energy's existing loan programmes while creating new programmes targeted at retrofitting existing energy infrastructure. At the core of the bill were tax credits to subsidize the manufacturing and take-up of solar PV, wind turbines, batteries and electric vehicles. Various conditions were placed on access to these credits, such as domestic mining, processing and manufacturing, local production in disadvantaged and historically fossil fuel-dependent communities and minimum labour standards around wages and training. Some of the tax credits were also made "direct pay", bypassing the need for tax equity investment, and potentially opening up their use to public and community models of ownership. However, ongoing reliance on tax credits nonetheless remains biased towards private models of renewable energy development, from household solar PV to the utility-scale, in contrast to the emphasis on reducing inequality and expanding public ownership in proposals for a GND, which we turn to in the next chapter (Bigger *et al.* 2022; Jenkins *et al.* 2022).

CONCLUSION

The green monetary and fiscal policies of "big" green states explored in this chapter do not necessarily imply "small" markets. In current examples, such as central banks greening their QE programmes or state investment banks making green investments, states continue to govern through markets while exerting varying degrees of "public" control over the climate futures being produced. The positioning of big green states in the world of climate finance is being negotiated out of existing state configurations, which remain heavily influenced by market correcting and de-risking ideas alongside Keynesian and state capitalist impulses. However, states have fiscal and monetary capacities that well exceed these roles, and the climate finance positions of big green states – as custodians of *public* climate finance – need not be limited by existing models of statecraft.

The "publicness" of big green states as a position on climate finance is, or at least could be, distinct from the other positions on climate finance discussed so far in this book. First, it embraces the distinctiveness of state finance in capitalist economies, due to the privileged monetary powers of central banks and the unique fiscal capacities of treasuries to finance climate expenditure on more favourable terms than the private sector. Public climate finance has the capacity to exercise state power over the role of markets in the climate transition, while also extending non-market forms of climate finance. For the most part, climate finance influenced by big green state thinking has sought to embed and transmit public climate goals in and through markets. Policies such as the Inflation Reduction Act in the US have mostly sought to incentivise public climate goals with carrots that reward private capital with access to public finance for meeting social and environmental criteria (Gabor 2023: 18). States have been more hesitant to implement sticks that restrain and direct private fossil and climate finance and build separate circuits of public climate finance, through, for example, using central banks to penalize dirty investment, removing public subsidies for fossil fuel investment, or creating fully public green investment banks. These state powers are also unevenly held across the global political economy, with developing and emerging economies having significantly less fiscal and monetary space, which intersects with the historical inequalities of climate change. Whereas this chapter has primarily focused on public climate finance within national borders, in the next chapter we discuss international public climate finance initiatives that aim to address international climate inequalities.

Second, the "public" position of big green states overtly politicizes public climate finance. Public money is subject to democratic politics and other forms of public accountability in a way that private money is not. A key project of neoliberalism was to conceal the role of public money in subsidizing private capital (Spies-Butcher & Bryant 2023). The de-risking state can be understood in these terms. Underwriting the risks of public-private partnerships is treated as a contingent liability not public expenditure in public budgets, despite significant public finance commitments (Gabor 2021b: 439). Other state models, such as green Keynesianism or (green) state capitalism, are more explicit about the state goals that are embedded in public climate finance, as with ambitions to develop national industries such as renewable energy. The extent to which these goals are shaped by democratic input differs across policy domains and geographies. There is scope for big green states to create more political space for participatory and collective decision-making over the design and allocation of climate finance than is currently the case. In the next and final chapter we consider more radical positions on climate finance that centre claims for justice.

CHAPTER 7

CLIMATE JUSTICE FINANCE

Climate justice is a capacious demand, movement and framework. This is borne out of the foundational inequalities at the heart of climate change, that those countries and communities least responsible for the climate crisis through historical and contemporary greenhouse gas emissions are feeling the brunt of its impacts while being the least able to cope. In the 1990s and 2000s a predominantly philosophical inquiry into the moral and ethical implications of climate inequalities emerged, which attempted to incorporate theories of justice into global climate policy (Schlosberg & Collins 2014). Beyond this more academic area of research, social movements, environmentalists and developing country coalitions have mobilized around climate justice to highlight the way climate change exacerbates existing and creates new inequalities – both through climate impacts themselves, as well as the distributional and procedural implications of responses to climate change. In feminist geographer Farhana Sultana's (2022: 118) evocative phrasing, climate justice wants to expose "the fault lines of suffering across sites and scales", and asks us to respond in ways that redress this uneven burden.

Recognition of and responses to climate injustice have been incorporated into the international climate regime, including through the principle of "common but differentiated responsibility". Within the UNFCCC, its Kyoto Protocol and subsequent agreements, developed and developing countries have been assigned different responsibilities for reducing emissions, mobilizing climate finance and transferring technology in recognition of variegated needs and capabilities. Developing countries and social movements lobbied for these international governing institutions to recognize per capita and accumulated historical emissions and uneven abilities to cope with vulnerabilities and risks. These procedures and demands reflect a commitment to the "polluter pays" principle and the distributive justice dimensions of climate change. More modestly, the UNFCCC has embedded procedural and recognition justice through the "one member, one vote" mechanisms of the

UN system and has recognized the differential capabilities for participation of some nation states and non-nation-state actors.

The ambition to account for distributive injustice in international climate frameworks has undoubtedly fallen short. In part, this is because the clear lines between developed and developing country responsibilities and impacts have eroded over time, with rapidly growing emissions in some parts of the developing country bloc, especially in Asia, the impacts of climate change multiplying around the world and inequalities within countries, rather than between countries, increasing. These changes undermine the bifurcated division between developed and developing country obligations within the international climate regime. More importantly, however, developed countries have abrogated their commitments and weakened their responsibilities throughout the tenure of the UNFCCC and its agreements. At different times led by different obstructionist states, developed countries have exchanged the ethic of differentiated responsibilities for a strategy of "shifted responsibilities" (Okereke 2015), failed to meet their emissions reductions commitments through accounting tricks and not mobilized pledged climate finance. The justice elements inherent to the UNFCCC are beginning to unravel.

Climate justice movements have mobilized alongside the international regime – including through side events, conventions, principles and declarations that mimic those of the UNFCCC – and in response to its failures. These diverse climate justice movements have evolved from environmental justice movements that have highlighted environmental racism and the uneven burdens of toxicity and anti-globalization social movements. More recently, climate justice campaigns have multiplied and been emboldened, from anti-pipeline activism, broad-based youth climate strikes, to Extinction Rebellion civil disobedience. Despite differences in aims across the movements, climate justice has coalesced into a set of demands about: abandoning fossil fuels and market-based mechanisms as climate solutions, payments of climate finance according to historical responsibility and sovereignty over land, food, and Indigenous knowledges and practices (Schlosberg & Collins 2014). At their core, rather than seeing climate change as a technical or governance problem requiring a fix, climate justice movements see climate change as another symptom of capitalism and imperialism, and its production of uneven power relations across race, class, gender and other axes of marginalization.

Across these different domains, claims for climate justice mobilize redistributional, procedural, recognition and capabilities elements of justice (Schlosberg 2012). This broad framework has successfully identified the collection of countries, fossil fuel majors or class of consumers responsible for causing climate change. On the other side of the ledger, however, identifying the "victims", the "most vulnerable", is more complex, and attempting to redress these inequalities through legal climate justice frameworks risks veering into inherently limited liberal ideas of justice (Thomas & Rhiney 2022). In contrast to this liberal justice is transformative climate justice, which focuses on the political-economic structures and systems producing and reproducing injustice, including capitalism, colonialism, racism and patriarchy.

This chapter investigates the potential for climate justice finance positions on climate change, and movements that are working towards this goal. Climate justice finance places climate change in the context of historically produced and ongoing structural violence, while working towards climate futures with equality, liberation and democracy. We start by exploring the justice-based origins of bilateral and multilateral international climate finance institutions and their chequered record on climate justice. These flows of international public climate finance often dominate popular understandings of climate finance. We then move through proposals for climate debt relief, climate reparations, the GND and degrowth, to understand how justice claims on climate finance might, in political economists Raj Patel and Jason Moore's language, remake capitalism's ecology through monetary and nonmonetary redistributions and reparations (Patel & Moore 2017). These climate justice claims and models do not often, or explicitly, position themselves as forms of climate finance. Indeed, claims for climate debt reform and reparations seek to fundamentally restructure existing relations and institutions of finance. Models for a GND or degrowth similarly imagine a greater disciplining of private finance and the financial system and increased role for democratic states and communities in climate finance. Nonetheless, examining climate justice *finance* demonstrates how its forms take financial positions on climate change, contest climate finance and open real possibilities for our climate futures.

INTERNATIONAL PUBLIC CLIMATE FINANCE

In popular analysis, climate finance tends to stand for international transfers of money from rich countries to vulnerable countries through the UNFCCC mechanisms (see Chapter 1). The first climate finance mechanisms were introduced at the Rio Earth Summit in 1992 along with the UNFCCC itself. Since this time, climate funds and related institutional forms, if not flows, have proliferated. Within the UNFCCC, climate funds include the GCF, the GEF, the Adaptation Fund and many others beyond. One of our arguments in this book is that the singular focus on finance associated with formal political treaties obscures the variety, reach and futures embedded in existing climate finance institutions, flows and configurations. Nonetheless, this form of climate finance remains politically and publicly imperative in international struggles over climate inequalities and injustices.

We call this form of climate finance "international public climate finance". This name recognizes the international nature of these flows, while positioning them as public finance, as a collective political demand and as the terrain on which substantial state and extra-state politicking takes place. While not often described in these terms, this climate finance is distinctly public because it is based on collective and democratic claims about what is owed to developing and vulnerable countries from developed ones. In short, international public climate finance is embedded in claims about *climate justice* (Gifford & Knudson 2020). This is one of the reasons the question of who owes what and how we know is so intensely contested in debates over accounting for climate finance. But the public nature of this finance is at risk, undermined by a complex and burdensome bureaucracy that prioritizes donor rather than recipient interests. At the same time, being subject to domestic and international politics, international public climate finance is mediated by powerful interests, which are not always democratic or progressive. The increasing prevalence of non-concessional loans and other forms of state-led de-risking evidence erosion in the "publicness" at the centre of international public climate finance.

As a mechanism for reckoning with the inherent inequalities of climate change, the politics of accounting for international public climate finance are hard-fought. And yet they focus more on questions of how much international public climate finance is mobilized than they do on how the money itself is spent and what its impacts are. As we discussed in the introduction to this book, through the UNFCCC, developed countries committed to mobilizing US\$100 billion per year by 2020 and each year after to finance mitigation and adaptation activities in developing countries; this pledge is a pillar of recognition of the differentiated responsibilities for climate change and abilities to respond to its encompassing impacts. This commitment was not met, with international public climate finance reaching around US\$80 billion by 2019. In response, a delivery plan was developed that maps a pathway to the US\$100 billion target, suggesting that the target will be reached imminently. Meanwhile, developing countries have upped their demands for international public climate finance. As the UNFCCC Standing Committee on Finance finds, up to US\$6 trillion may be needed to pay for only half of the actions in official climate plans by 2030 (Gabbatiss 2022).

Counting international public climate finance

Despite figures about international public climate finance circulating widely, how precisely these are measured and what counts remains contested. There are three main forms of international public climate finance: bilateral, multilateral and multilateral development bank. The OECD collates countries' reported climate finance; in 2020, it reported that US$46 billion in bilateral finance was committed that was significantly or principally related to climate change, compared to US$7.2 billion that was committed through multilateral funds and development banks (OECD 2022c). Bilateral flows, the simplest and biggest form of international public climate finance, flow from one country to another, often through bilateral development assistance institutions or regional or national funds. The nearly £6 billion UK International Climate Finance Initiative or the Indonesian Climate Change Trust Fund, which receives support from both bilateral and multilateral sources, are illustrative examples. The multilateral climate funds, including the GEF, GCF, the Climate Investment Funds (World Bank) and others, take international public climate finance from contributing countries and their bilateral institutions and programme projects in recipient countries or regions. These funds are rapidly growing, institutionally and financially. The multilateral development banks play a key role as intermediaries and programmers; they are, along with the UN agencies, implementing entities or administrators for the vast proportion of the multilateral funds, while also investing their own resources as climate finance.

There are two broad instruments that comprise international public climate finance: grant-based instruments and debt instruments advanced on either a concessional or non-concessional basis. The OECD data shows that there are many more grant-based projects than loan-based projects, but that they are much smaller in financial terms than that financed through loans (OECD 2022d). As a result, only 28 per cent of climate-related official development assistance is in grants, and 64 per cent in debt instruments, with most of the remainder in hybrid debt/equity instruments. Although the amount of international public climate finance as grants has remained fairly consistent over the last decade, that provided as loans and other non-grant instruments has dramatically increased, particularly on the back of increases in non-concessional loans. The international development NGO, Oxfam, claims in its "Climate Finance Shadow Report" that the true figures for international public climate finance are perhaps only a third – around US$20 billion rather than US$60 billion in 2020 – of that estimated by the OECD once the "grant equivalent" value of loans (that is, without non-concessional repayments and interest) and other inaccuracies are accounted for (Carty, Kowalzig & Zagema 2020).

The growth of loans, including non-concessional loans, in climate finance has been challenged on climate justice grounds. Many countries report their non-concessional loans as international public climate finance, including some of the biggest reported contributors: Japan, Germany and France. Developing country governments and climate justice advocates have argued that these loans are increasing debt burdens among the most vulnerable countries rather than facilitating responses to climate change (Thomas & Theokritoff 2021). These country-scale dynamics are mirrored at a micro scale. International public climate finance has recently started investing in microfinance programmes as a tool for adaptation, touted to increase financial inclusion and household resilience amid climate shocks and stresses (see also Chapter 5). However, rather than cultivating adaptive capacity across scales, microfinance programmes are increasing debt within vulnerable rural households and undermining adaptation (Guermond *et al.* 2022).

There are also debates about how international public climate finance might be tracked: there are multiple different methodologies, countries interpret reporting requirements differently and these change over time (Weikmans & Roberts 2019). The lack of consistency and transparency hinders meaningful tracking and comparison. For instance, one of the main tools (reported above) is the OECD Rio Markers. The OECD tracks official development assistance through its Development Assistance Committee. Through this, bilateral contributors can mark their contributions as having principal or significant mitigation and/or adaptation objectives. But this method relies on developed countries self-reporting their contributions, and in doing so they significantly over-estimate their contributions to addressing climate change: of the 5,000 adaptation projects report to the OECD in 2012, only about a quarter of the US$10 billion pledged was found to genuinely contribute to adaptation (Weikmans *et al.* 2017). Moreover, these are only measures of pledges rather than disbursements, and there is no assessment of whether these climate funds are "new and additional" to official development assistance.

The Green Climate Fund

Contests over what counts as international public climate finance, how to measure it and in which mechanisms all come to a head in the GCF, the biggest contemporary multilateral climate fund. The number and form of climate funds has proliferated over the last three decades, but since its creation the GCF has become the principal intermediary for international public climate finance. The GCF was established as a financial mechanism of the UNFCCC to serve the US$100 billion pledge of the Paris Agreement, although it remains legally independent. It is principally capitalized through public contributions, predominantly from developed country governments pursuant to their commitments under the UNFCCC. Nonetheless, and like the Wall Street Consensus of multilateral development banks and associated institutions, the GCF is increasingly seeking to leverage private sources of co-financing in support of its mitigation and adaptation projects.

The GCF was originally celebrated by developing countries and activists as representing a more transparent, more democratic form of international public climate finance. Developing countries and civil society organizations were dissatisfied with the other financial mechanisms and the overwhelming control given to donors rather than recipients, emphasis on private and market-based responses and burdensome administrative processes. There was optimism that the GCF would facilitate a more "nationally owned" and therefore equitable approach to climate finance. The GCF was hailed as a "paradigm shift" away from the World Bank, the GEF and associated mechanisms, and towards "a people's alternative" that centres local engagement and priorities (Bruun 2017). However, these hopes have been dashed: the World Bank became trustee of the fund, only half of project funds have been allocated for particularly vulnerable countries and commitments to fund adaptation equally to mitigation have not yet been met.

One of the innovations in the GCF to improve country and local ownership was to allow national actors, rather than only multilateral development banks and UN agencies, to act as accredited agencies that directly receive funding to pursue nationally aligned projects. This is known as direct access. As yet, only 6 per cent of countries have used nationally accredited entities to receive GCF funding and around only 20 per cent of eligible countries had accredited entities (Garschagen & Doshi 2022). Moreover, the vast majority of projects implemented through nationally accredited entities have been only micro or small projects (US$0–10 million or US$10–50 million respectively) compared to the large projects (US$250+ million) implemented by international entities. National accreditation was also intended to address the complex bureaucracies of the funds that limit access for the most vulnerable. Yet, as the Taskforce on Climate Finance reporting to COP26 in Glasgow in 2021 described, accessing climate finance through organizations such as the GCF continues to be "often slow, complex, resource intensive, uncertain, and highly projectized, presenting significant barriers to access and constraints on delivery" (UK Government & Steering Committee Members 2021: 3). Burdensome schemes of access, administration and reporting for recipients primarily satisfy the domestic political interests of bilateral donors. The capacity for democratic deliberation over how international public climate finance is used remains unrealized, with questions of "how much?" dominating questions of "how good?" A view on the quality of investments, rather than just on tracking financing needs and flows shows the GCF as an operation of developed country power that is overly expensive, bureaucratic and overlooking its most vulnerable people and countries.

Democratizing public international climate finance

International public climate finance is essential political and economic terrain because it is constituted by flows over which policymakers and publics might "exert direct control" (Amerasinghe *et al.* 2017). Indeed, national and localized climate funds have been formulated as more transparent and democratic forms of international public climate finance. National development banks can access international public climate finance through the GCF and its national accreditation schemes, but many continue to report difficulties in accreditation and minimal concessional finance. National climate funds are also emerging in some developing countries to integrate and coordinate multiple funding sources in support of national priorities in a more programmatic rather than piecemeal, project-based fashion. These climate funds have received funding from bilateral sources and from institutions such as the GCF, and some from fiscal revenue streams. National climate funds have the potential to achieve identified adaptation and mitigation goals at scale, support public goods; coordinate otherwise piecemeal investments and thereby realize the public mandate of this finance. However, they are ultimately the outcome of political priorities negotiated across scales.

Alongside nationalization, localization is often presented as a means of progressively transforming international public climate finance. Accordingly, this finance should be invested in projects and policies that are locally led, thereby reaching the communities most vulnerable to climate impacts. For instance, the Least Developed Country Group of the UNFCCC calls for 70 per cent of international public climate finance to reach the local level to ensure transformative and localized adaptation (Soanes *et al.* 2021). The GCF is not currently configured to facilitate this: there is no mechanism for local actors to access funding and no framework for recognizing or identifying local actors and their potential. Moreover, while there is a focus on transparency and accountability for the GCF as a whole, this is largely centred on reporting to donor countries rather than on the outcomes of these investments for locally led adaptation. One example of a locally led and implemented climate fund is the "People's Survival Fund" of the Philippines, which exists to provide domestic and international public climate finance to frontline communities (see Bhandary 2022). Still, accessing this fund itself requires substantial submissions from local governments, suggesting political will but less institutional power to deliver on the community-based promise of this fund.

Across local, national and international scales, the outcomes of international public climate finance are in flux. These are flows of finance over which states and publics might have considerable control. They are also flows of climate finance predicated on global claims for climate justice. They come with the potential for, but no guarantees of, more democratic, progressive climate futures. The current failures and injustices of the international public financial regime have led climate movements, and some developing country governments, to call for more radical forms of climate justice finance that challenge historical climate debts and call for climate reparations.

CLIMATE DEBT AND REPARATIONS

For many developing countries and climate justice activists and advocates, climate change is a debt relation. The idea of climate debt references the inherent inequalities in the benefits of fossil fuel production and consumption and the resulting climate change effects. These are the base injustices introduced earlier in the chapter: that developed countries have gotten rich on greedy exploitation of fossil fuels, while developing countries have contributed little to the cause of climate change and are least able to cope with its effects. Moreover, responding to climate change has monetary costs – from reducing emissions while continuing economic development and poverty reduction measures, rebuilding after catastrophic events or investing in proactive adaptation measures. As such, the Global North has accrued a "climate debt" to the Global South.

Claims for recognition and repayments of climate debts emerge out of longer activism around the "ecological debt" accrued over centuries of colonial extraction and dispossession. In the lead up the Copenhagen COP to the UNFCCC in 2009, Bolivian representatives applied the logic of ecological debt to climate change, arguing that developed countries "have used up two thirds of the atmospheric space, depriving us of the necessary space for our development and provoking a climate crisis of huge proportions. [...] We are not assigning guilt, merely responsibility. As they say in the US, if you break it, you buy it" (Climate Justice Now in Pickering & Barry 2012: 673). Infamously, representatives from the US rejected "guilt or culpability or reparations" under the guise that much of these emissions occurred before full understanding of their effects on climate (Pickering & Barry 2012). The People's Agreement of Cochabamba – a declaration that emerged out of a social movement and civil society climate conference held in Bolivia in 2010 – was premised on the repayment of climate debts owed by the Global North to the Global South. It included provisions to differentiate emissions debt according to shares of atmospheric space and adaptation debts to pay the victims of climate change.

Calculating climate debts

Climate, or carbon, debts are "financially complex, but morally simple" (Ross 2013: 33): they reference a basic inequality, while raising calculative questions and political possibilities. In his expansive history, David Graeber described debts as "the obligation to pay a certain sum of money" (2011: 18), implying a precise quantification of what is owed, and the clear identification of creditor and debtor. How might this climate debt be calculated, and those owing and those owed assigned? Under the current UNFCCC process, the principle of common but differentiated responsibilities is translated into mitigation commitments according to current territorial emissions. But for measuring the impacts of and responsibilities for climate change, annual emissions are far less important than the accumulation of them in the atmosphere. From which date would you begin to measure a country's emissions? What is a "fair share" of emissions for each country and what is the total carbon budget to be distributed? And should producers or consumers be accountable for associated emissions?

These appear to be technical emissions accounting questions, but they are also deeply political ones, implicating the assignment of creditors and debtors and the scale of their liability for debts. For instance, climate scientist Damon Matthews (2016) calculates carbon and climate debts based on territorial emissions from 1960 and 1990, separating out those countries whose per capita emissions exceed the global average (debtors) and those who fall below this average (creditors). Identified debtors include the US, Russia, Brazil, Canada and Germany, and major creditors include India, China, Bangladesh, Pakistan and Nigeria. In contrast, Jason Hickel (2020b) argues that 1850 is the appropriate date to start assigning accumulated emissions, and that, where possible, consumption emissions should be used to account for the outsourcing of emissions-producing activities to developing countries through intensified globalization. Moreover, countries should be assigned to debtor or creditor status based on their exceedance of a per capita safe emissions budget – a measure of responsibility for climate breakdown. This method shows the increased climate debt of rich countries; the calculations indicate that the G8 countries are collectively responsible for 85 per cent of climate breakdown. Accordingly, emissions debts produce a kind of calculable moral claim that can be linked to demands on financial resources.

The impacts of climate change also create real financial debts for countries and households. The V20 – Vulnerable 20 Group of Ministers of Finance of the Climate Vulnerable Forum – calculates that between 2000 and 2019 their (at the time) 55 member countries lost a fifth of their GDP directly from climate change (V20 2022). Debt skyrockets in vulnerable countries and for vulnerable people in response to climate disasters, as governments and households take on debt to pay for needed physical and social repair. The World Bank estimates that public debt grows by 2.3–3.6 percentage points for the three years after disasters, while real GDP collapses by 1.3 percentage points in the year of a disaster, worsening debt to GDP ratios – a common measure of sovereign debt distress (Fan *et al.* 2022). The costs of debt are also higher for more vulnerable countries: the V20 group pays, on average, a 1.174 percentage point higher cost of debt than less vulnerable countries (Kling *et al.* 2018). The financial impacts of overlapping and multiple crises – Covid-19 pandemic, food and fuel price hikes, monetary tightening by central banks and debts driven by climate disasters – has produced a landscape of debt distress among low-income and even middle-income countries, reducing their ability to invest in adaptation and other necessary social services and infrastructures.

Repaying climate debts

Calculations of climate debts facilitate political claims based on a moral common sense that what is owed must be paid (Graeber 2011). If northern countries and international financial institutions, including the IMF and World Bank, continue to insist on the proper repayment of sovereign debts (and at other scales and in different institutions, personal and household debt) – despite their extraordinary terms and public illegitimacy – to uphold a kind of moral good standing and the promises of the original loan, then should these same actors not make good on their debts? These political claims are made possible by engaging in the financial logics of debt, in the words of anti-debt organizers, as "a new strategy for collective economic power ... made possible in the age of finance and its inverse, debt" (Appel, Whitley & Kline 2019: 36). But how might climate debts be repaid? Concerns from both creditors (including private creditors, multilateral institutions, the World Bank and bilateral partners) and debtors about the abundance of debt distress and its connection to climate change has raised the potential for sovereign debt restructuring or cancellation as a means of investing in climate resilience. This restructuring and cancellation could take a variety of forms.

Debt-for-climate swaps propose to address unsustainable sovereign debt while reducing climate risks by restructuring existing debt obligations and their terms in exchange for spending on climate mitigation or adaptation. Debt-for-nature swaps first emerged as a tool of conservation policy in the 1980s. Using debt swaps linked to the secondary debt market, NGOs and other actors bought discounted debt, swapped it for local currencies and used these to fund conservation projects. More recently, huge environmental NGOs have negotiated debt-for-nature swaps attached to climate change.

In the Seychelles, Belize and Barbados, the conservation NGO the Nature Conservancy claims to have leveraged $500 million of debt into $230 million investment in conservation and climate adaptation (White 2022). The V20 and others have proposed coordinated and structured climate debt swaps that offer debt restructuring across creditor classes.

The Pacific region is facing a growing sovereign debt crisis that is eroding the fiscal space needed to address climate disasters. According to the Pacific Island Forum Secretariat, Pacific countries "are easily trapped in the 'borrowing-rebuilding-further borrowing' cycle" (Deputy Secretary General of PIFS in Ligaiula 2022) with growing debts and constraints on capacities to invest in durable, proactive adaptation and resilience measures. As a result, several organizations have advocated for bilateral/direct or third-party debt swaps in the Pacific that funnel funds from partially cancelled or restructured publicly held debt into a climate finance fund: the Pacific Resilience Facility (PIFS 2021). The Pacific Resilience Facility is designed as a Pacific-"owned, led and designed" facility, not dependent on the specifications of donors or multilateral partners, with the goal of facilitating sustained resilience-building activities for the most vulnerable without contributing to existing sovereign debt burdens. The goal is that climate debt swaps may facilitate longer-term investments and budget support.

The actual debt relief offered in these instances, however, is limited. These swaps generally lower interest rates or offer a longer loan tenor but have minimal impact on overall debt burdens and currency risks. The Seychelles case exemplifies this (Silver & Campbell 2018): through its debt swap for marine conservation and climate adaptation, the government bought back about US$21.6 million of its debt for US$20.2 million, with the money for repurchase coming from a US$5 million philanthropic grant and a US$15.2 million loan from the Nature Conservancy. In return, the Seychelles committed to repaying the US$15.2 million loan and putting US$6.4 million into a conservation and adaptation fund; the biggest component of the deal was therefore a debt-for-debt swap, and the country's total debt burden was not significantly reduced. The deal also took four years to negotiate, demonstrating the high transaction costs of setting up such swaps and monitoring their climate and environmental outcomes. Several proposals argue for climate conditionalities to be embedded in climate swaps to verify outcomes are real, additional and aligned with the Paris Agreement. These conditionalities are not only reminiscent of but are modelled on the kinds of conditionalities imposed through the Structural Adjustment Programs of the IMF in response to debt relief in the 1970 and 1980s (Volz et al. 2020). The Structural Adjustment Programs induced structural economic changes, including mass privatization and reductions in social spending, with devastating impacts.

Most importantly, however, these limited visions for debt restructuring and climate swaps fail to invert prevailing debtor and creditor relations – to recognize the climate debts owed from the Global North to the Global South. Indeed, discussions of climate debt swaps and sovereign debt distress rarely consider "the other debt crisis": the debt the Global North owes for "plunder, extraction and climate pollution" (Táíwò & Bigger 2021: 5). These historical and ongoing transfers from the Global South to the Global North are integral to the strictly financial debt crisis currently unfolding. Climate change, therefore, provides renewed impetus for debt cancellation, such as that which occurred through the Highly Indebted Poor Countries Initiative. Coordinated by international financial institutions since the late 1990s, the initiative has offered full debt relief for eligible countries. Climate debt justice through comprehensive debt forgiveness begins a programme of climate reparations.

Climate reparations

The devastating flooding in Pakistan in mid-2022 forcefully laid out the case for climate reparations and ignited a public debate about climate debtors and creditors. Sustained monsoonal rains throughout July and August flooded more than a third of the country, displaced more than 9 million people and killed more than 1,600, destroyed over 2 million homes, 30,000km of roads and other infrastructure and 4 million hectares of crops, causing estimated damage of between US$30–35 billion (Ellis-Petersen & Baloch 2022). While flood levels receded, humanitarian and health crises proliferated. Meanwhile, like many other climate-vulnerable countries, growing debt servicing commitments throughout the pandemic and interests rate spikes constrained the fiscal capacities of the state to respond. Pakistan's Climate Change Minister, meanwhile, argued that the country is owed climate reparations for the costs of losses and damages caused not by their own meagre contributions to greenhouse gas concentrations. These reparations "must – finally – address the root causes": a "legacy of a colonialism ... [and its] justification to exploit, plunder and create the climate catastrophe we see" (Qureshi 2022).

Debt cancellation and debt justice are first steps towards substantive climate reparations for climate debts. Existing financial institutions will need to be restructured and new financial institutions will need to be created. Climate justice activists have proposed reallocating special drawing rights – the international reserve assets of the IMF – away from wealthy countries most responsible for climate change and towards poorer countries as an initial funding source for climate reparations (Franczak & Táíwò 2022). Keston Perry (2020) suggests that new institutions might include a global climate stabilization fund to address the combined impacts of colonialism, climate change and financial distress, collecting dues from new taxation regimes in response to tax havens and un/under-taxed natural resource extraction, or a resilience funding programme for loss and damage. These new institutions could pay for unconditional adaptation, resilience and emergency responses while contributing to compensation for climate debts and both the shorter- and long-term work towards climate reparations.

Although climate reparations does require redistribution, it is not only a monetary payment for past wrongs. Instead, climate reparations is, as philosopher Olúfẹ́mi O. Táíwò writes, a "forward looking target" that is part of a "larger and broader worldmaking project … [to build] the just world to come" (2022: 70, 74). Táíwò's is not a concrete or comprehensive plan, as worldmaking projects require organization and mobilization of supporters to implement reparations within their particular political, cultural and geographical circumstances to have democratic legitimacy. The challenge is to connect tactics representing collective actions for now with longer-term targets of where we might hope to get. One example in this vein is to pair conventional climate justice finance claims for sustained, unconstrained, predictable and larger flows of international public climate finance with unconditional cash transfers for individuals, households and communities (Táíwò & Bigger 2021). Finance provided as unconditional cash transfers is not conventionally understood as climate finance, but can become such when provided through a climate justice logic that reverses the usual direction of conditionality in recognition of historical climate debts at multiple scales. Some of these ideas have also been taken up by advocates for a GND and degrowth, to which we now turn.

GREEN NEW DEAL AND DEGROWTH

A Green New Deal

GND is an umbrella term for large-scale programmes of state-led investment in climate and other infrastructure that seek to simultaneously counter climate change and inequality. Proposals for GNDs come in different shapes and sizes, but all combine climate goals with broader social, economic and environment justice goals (Ajl 2021; Pettifor 2019). The rationale for the GND is that the crisis of climate change is inextricably linked with social and economic crises such as wage stagnation and job insecurity, poverty, inequality, gender and racial discrimination, the ongoing colonization of Indigenous peoples and the erosion of democracy (Fraser 2021: 96). Addressing these social and economic crises through climate policy is, according to GND proponents, necessary not only to deliver on normative commitments to climate justice, but also to win public support for climate transitions (Aronoff *et al.* 2019).

At minimum, GNDs prioritize state-led climate investment programmes that rapidly scale up green jobs with good pay and secure conditions, rejecting "jobs versus environment" framings of climate politics, through policies such as a job guarantee for displaced fossil fuel workers (Sturman & Heenan 2021). These investments are directed towards building and retrofitting climate-friendly infrastructure in sectors such as energy, transport and housing, but also social and ecological infrastructure through investment in care work and environmental repair, which are reframed as low-carbon industries that enhance health and wellbeing (Battistoni 2022). A distinguishing feature of the GND is scale: "size matters" because "the problems the Green New Deal addresses, in short, are problems where *bigger is better*" (Hockett 2020: 2, emphasis added). GNDs tend to envisage transformation across the economy as a whole – mostly national economies, but also globally – requiring planning for both a significant mobilization of resources and coordination across different spheres of investment. The state is viewed as the key, or only, institution capable of mobilizing and coordinating resources and investment on the scale demanded by a GND.

The historical antecedent of the GND is the New Deal enacted by President Franklin Delano Roosevelt in the US in the 1930s and 1940s. The New Deal was instituted in response to the Great Depression and then the Second World War. Under the New Deal, the federal government embarked on a social and economic agenda of public investment in infrastructure (including energy, transport and housing), welfare programmes, regulation to protect labour and constrain finance, and industrial production for the war effort. Although it transformed the institutions of American society, the New Deal largely preserved its gendered and racialized hierarchies. Reflecting on these issues, proponents of a radical GND in the US, Kate Aronoff, Alyssa Battistoni, Daniel Aldana Cohen and Thea Riofrancos (2019: 5), argue "the point isn't to repeat the past, but to remember what concerted public action can do".

GNDs are more than large-scale climate planning; they have an ambition to reshape the socio-ecological relations of the economy in a more just direction. The meaning of, priority given to and pathway for achieving justice through GNDs is, however, contested: the GND is amenable to different political orientations (Sturman & Heenan 2021: 151). The European Green Deal, approved by the European Commission in 2020, is an example of a policy framework that adopts a more market-oriented approach that is geared towards mobilizing private investment for "green growth". Our focus is on "radical" GNDs that embed the principles of distributive, restorative and procedural justice. Radical GNDs tend to emphasize the power of organized labour and the interests of workers in the climate transition. In doing so, they promise to de-commodify the provision of infrastructure and services, reducing the market dependence of people in their everyday life and in climate policy. In contrast to private forms of climate finance that seek the most profitable climate actions, radical GNDs assert democratic control over climate plans across workplaces and policymaking processes.

The GND has a longer history, first gaining prominence as a response to the global financial crisis (Luke 2009). But it was the resolution introduced by Alexandria Ocasio-Cortez (AOC) and Edward Markey to the US Congress in 2019 that elevated the GND into public consciousness and animated progressive debate over its radical potential. The resolution itself was non-binding and did not pass Congress but sets out a framework for the GND. The resolution links the climate crisis with "several related crises" and notes that climate change is exacerbating "systemic injustices" in a way that disproportionately affects "frontline and vulnerable communities". It proposes a "10 year national mobilisation" with the goals of decarbonizing the economy through a "fair and just transition" while creating millions of good jobs, investing in infrastructure, securing rights to a healthy environment, and "promot[ing] justice and equity by stopping current, preventing future, and repairing historic oppression of ... frontline and vulnerable communities" (Ocasio-Cortez 2019).

Paying for the Green New Deal

Debates over financing GND proposals are struggles over how climate finance should be configured to reflect climate justice goals. Reflecting the emphasis on public climate finance in the GND, and the desire to restrain private climate finance, these debates are primarily framed in terms of *funding*, or "paying for", the GND within the US federal government's budget. Soon after the resolution was released, a conservative think tank estimated that the AOC/Markey GND would cost an astronomical US$51–93 trillion over ten years. This number was widely derided as a political attack, not least because the resolution lacked the policy detail necessary to undertake costings. The Bernie Sanders presidential primary GND, which largely translated the AOC/Markey resolution principles into policy, while more directly targeting fossil fuel producers for penalties and restrictions, claimed to be fully costed at US$16.3 trillion over 15 years. It was to be financed through a combination of cuts to spending on fossil fuel subsidies and the military and increased revenue from higher taxes on wealthy individuals and corporations, the creation of new taxpaying jobs and lower unemployment and new revenue from government-owned renewable energy providers (Galvin & Healy 2020: 4).

Progressive economists, including those who subscribe to modern monetary theory (MMT), argued that given the unlimited capacity of the US government to issue US dollars, there was no technical financing constraint. The real constraint was a resource one, which would determine whether GND plans would outpace the capacity of the economy to deliver, creating inflationary dynamics. Such constraints, argued MMT economists, were manageable through targeted anti-inflationary measures such as taxation and price controls (Nersisyan & Wray 2021). AOC advisor Robert Hockett (2020: xviii) outlined an approach to financing the GND that centred the challenge of "marshalling and channelling" resources in the economy, rather than balancing the budget. This was, in essence, a coordination challenge that only the public sector – across federal, state and local governments – could achieve. Rather than seeking to "level the playing field" between public and private sectors, Hockett's position on financing the GND embraces the "comparative advantages" of the state through, for example, a national investment council to oversee the financial architecture of the GND (2020: 31, 37). Hockett's (2020: 26) proposal for a "people's Fed" in which the US Federal Reserve would transform to provide reserve accounts direct to citizens, allowing the central bank to do "QE for the people" in service of the goals of the GND, demonstrates how the GND can change finance itself (see Chapter 6).

Public ownership as climate finance

The GND envisages a significant shift towards public ownership across the economy. The AOC/Markey resolution did not preclude private sector involvement but called for a GND that "ensures that the public receives appropriate ownership stakes and returns on investment" (Ocasio-Cortez 2019). In principle, public ownership has the potential to replace metrics such as profit and shareholder value with democratically determined goals. In practice, most state-owned enterprises, including in the energy sector, have become increasingly corporatized, meaning the democratization of public ownership is a prerequisite for the democratization of climate finance. Banking and energy are two sectors of the economy that are targeted by GND advocates for (re)nationalization or (re)municipalization. Public ownership, in this line of thinking, can become a powerful source of climate finance to drive GND plans.

Systems of public banks are envisaged as means to direct low-cost credit in ways that are coordinated with GND plans. Local or state/regional government ownership could ensure that finance is responsive and accountable to local and regional communities through democratic governance structures that represent their constituencies. The Bank of North Dakota is often given as an example of a public bank that could be multiplied or expanded as part of a system of public banking within a GND. The bank is the only substantial state-level public bank in the US, and was originally established in the early twentieth century to support economic democracy and public ownership in the agricultural industry. Public banking scholar and advocate Thomas Marois (2021: 168–72) argues that the Bank of North Dakota has developed a successful strategy of "definancialization", working in tandem with the state government, focused on spatially fixing the provision and benefits of finance in local communities.

The case for public ownership of power utilities is to accelerate the transition from fossil fuels to renewables beyond that which is being delivered by the private sector. In addition, public ownership is a favoured means to secure a just transition for both displaced fossil fuel workers and renewable energy workers, the latter of which have faced insecure and temporary contracts in the private sector (Pearse & Bryant 2022). Rather than being simply granted by the state, socialist geographer Matthew Huber (2022: 235–7) argues that such goals need to be won politically by workers, building on the existing strengths of unions in power utilities. The Tennessee Valley Authority, the largest electric utility publicly owned by the US government, has been put forward by GND activists as an existing institution that could be become a renewable energy-focused public option across the US. The Tennessee Valley Authority was established during the New Deal as part of a programme of "electricity for all". Mobilizing the Tennessee Valley Authority for the GND would leverage the political potential inherent in its publicly owned structure via changes to its governance, to create a "green" Tennessee Valley Authority (Bruenig 2019).

Beyond an American GND

The US origins of dominant strands of GND thinking have been criticized for being insufficiently internationalist or global. Rural sociologist Max Ajl (2021: 12) argues that "existing GND proposals are broadly Eurocentric and rest on continued global inequality" and as a consequence are not sufficiently ambitious or just for people in countries in the Global South. Global perspectives on the GND have pointed out the need to contend with issues such as the prominent place of informal labour and agricultural livelihoods in the Global South (Chen & Li 2021). Ajl (2021: 166) proposes an alternative "People's Green New Deal", led by social movements in the Global South, which seeks to challenge extractive South-North production networks underpinning green transitions.

Indigenous scholars and activists have raised similar concerns about the implications of GND proposals for Indigenous rights (Indigenous

Environmental Network 2019). The Red Nation, an Indigenous-led activist coalition cofounded by Nick Estes, a citizen of the Lower Brule Sioux Tribe, proposed the "Red Deal" as a framework that is not counter to but goes beyond the GND, with a focus on "Indigenous treaty rights, land restoration, sovereignty, self-determination, decolonization, and liberation" (The Red Nation 2021: 18). The "Red" in the Red Deal signifies both this focus on Indigenous rights and its eco-socialist political orientation. The Red Deal framework envisages a programme of divestment and reinvestment: divestment from fossil fuels as well as the carceral-colonial institutions of the military, police and prisons and reinvestment in what is called the "caretaking economy", modelled on the caretaking labour of Indigenous societies. This language is more than metaphorical. It expresses a demand that climate finance, delivered as climate reparations for Indigenous people, should do more than fund expansive GND-like programmes; financial resources must also be delinked from climate colonization, actively undoing harms while creating a funding source at the same time.

Degrowth

"Degrowth" perspectives fold concerns about possibilities that a GND will increase environmental pressures in the Global South and on Indigenous land into a more general critique of growth. This critique targets even progressive and transformative agendas that do not challenge growth, because they are understood to be premised on unsustainable resource use (Schmelzer, Vetter & Vansintjan 2022: 3). However, the bigger target of degrowth, to which we now turn, is the "green growth" ideology that sits behind many of the configurations of climate finance that we have canvassed in this book.

The tools of green finance promise to reconcile continued economic growth with sustainability goals. However, degrowth researchers argue that green growth is an impossibility because economic growth is both socially and ecologically damaging and ultimately self-destructive (Dale, Mathai & de Oliveira 2016). Degrowth points to the need to dismantle the structures, ideas and practices that orient capitalist economies towards growth and replace them with a degrowth economy with smaller throughput of energy and resource use alongside "global ecological justice" (Schmelzer, Vetter & Vansintjan 2022: 3).

The aim of degrowth is not necessarily to reduce the flows of national income that are measured in GDP, and therefore engineer an economic recession. Instead, degrowth aims to reduce that material throughput of energy and resources in an economy, so that economies operate within ecological limits. This overall goal is combined with a global justice perspective that would see wealthy countries contract their resource use faster and to a greater extent than poor countries. Still, degrowth economists recognize that degrowth would inevitably result in lower GDP, as economic growth is closely coupled with material throughput, including, in practice, carbon emissions (Hickel & Kallis 2019).

Degrowth represents, on one level, a challenge to the very topic of this book. Degrowth seeks to reduce the role of finance, as a mode of economic calculation, in favour of measures of material resource use. As degrowth scholars Schmelzer, Vetter & Vansintjan (2022: 32) explain:

> In essence, the degrowth vision is about pushing back against the dominant economic logic and economic calculation – namely, the question of whether everything pays off financially – as the dominant basis for decision-making in society. The aim is thus to repoliticize and democratize social institutions as well as power and property relationships, in order to abandon the social dominance and logic of "the economy".

Profit-based modes of calculation are, of course, capitalist modes of calculation. In practice, degrowth thinking cannot avoid questions of finance, and has instead looked to create alternative modes of calculation that are compatible with a degrowth economy.

Degrowth finance

Policies and practices of degrowth finance generally reflect one of two strategies: structural reforms to existing institutions of finance or building new small-scale alternative economy experiments. Examples of the former have significant overlaps with many GND proposals, such as public and community ownership of essential services, including energy and banking; universal basic income and universal basic services; a shift in labour from extractive to caring and creative industries, with a shorter working week, heavy regulation and taxation of fossil fuels and reparations for climate debt (Kallis 2018; Schmelzer, Vetter & Vansintjan 2022).

There are, however, subtle differences between degrowth and GND policies that reflect substantive political disagreements. Take the example of housing. A GND for housing would transform the financial relations of housing through an expansion of public housing and housing cooperative models on an energy-efficient and needs-basis (Cohen 2022). While degrowth housing policy echoes elements of the GND for housing, such as rights to housing and ecological redesign of housing stock, principles such as "voluntary simplicity" and deurbanization reflect a more voluntarist and decentralized politics (Nelson & Schneider 2018). Degrowth thus tends to favour more localized, distributed and "diverse" (Gibson-Graham 2008) forms of production, exchange and consumption than the GND.

Chief among the financial transformations envisaged by degrowth advocates is a change in monetary relations. The creation of money by private banks in the form of credit is understood to be a central driver of climate-damaging growth. Accordingly, indebtedness drives growth on two levels. First, the need to make interest repayments forces businesses to expand in order to make profits so they can repay their debts. Second, on an economy-wide level, growth is necessary to keep debt levels – usually measured as a ratio of debt to GDP – sustainable. The role of public- and community-owned banks in degrowth is, most importantly, to disentangle money creation from debt expansion through, for example, regulations requiring 100 per cent reserves or prohibiting the charging of real interest rates (Liegey & Nelson 2020: 148).

Rather than transforming existing banking structures, another approach is to build alternative forms of exchange that can shift units of measure towards the principles of degrowth. These usually take the form of local or complementary currency systems, such as timebanks or local exchange trading systems that attempt to facilitate exchange between members of a self-organized community by accounting for practices defined by that community as contributing to wellbeing and sustainability (Liegey & Nelson 2020: 149–50). However, they face criticism that they cannot "turn around the ocean liner" that is economic growth by winding down fossil fuels without a regulatory force such as the state (Hornborg 2017). Blockchain technology is sometimes put forward as a solution to the problem of scaling up degrowth practices. Blockchains are distributed ledgers that can securely record transactions or other data. The degrowth promise of blockchain is the potential to facilitate non-profit-based units of account, and therefore non-growth-based forms of value creation (Howson 2021). However, blockchain technologies for decentralized finance sit uneasily with degrowth principles, due to the energy use involved in maintaining and validating blockchain ledgers, and connections with speculative cryptocurrency bubbles.

Green New Deal or degrowth?

In recent years, cases for climate-driven transformation of the economy have tended to coalesce around either the GND or degrowth. As we have already touched on, there are substantive differences between the two camps. Whereas the emphasis of the GND is on bigger-scale interventions, degrowth focuses on reducing the scale of impact: "bigger is better" versus "less is more" (Hickel 2020a; Hockett 2020). Nonetheless, there are examples of rapprochement between both schools, such as degrowthers advocating for a "Green New Deal Without Growth", and GNDers calling for one "last stimulus" before the economy can "jump off the growth treadmill" (Aronoff *et al.* 2019: 30; Mastini, Kallis & Hickel 2021).

Degrowth provides a set of ecological principles for climate finance to follow, while the GND provides a political platform for challenging the financial institutions driving and blocking action on climate change. Although neither the GND nor degrowth are being adopted wholesale, their influence can be located in the shifted and broadened debates about the possibilities across different climate finance positions. This can be seen from the role of the GND in germinating and legitimizing the turn to green industrial policy, or references to degrowth in the IPCC's most recent influential discussions of climate scenarios and financial instruments (Intergovernmental Panel on Climate Change 2022a). The GND and degrowth, and their intersections, are playing key roles in the politics of climate finance, creating political possibilities for climate justice finance.

CONCLUSION

In this chapter we have explored a range of justice-based positions on climate finance. International public climate finance, although premised on justice-based claims, has so far failed to deliver on them. Beyond the ensuing debates about *climate finance justice* (Gifford & Knudson 2020), we have focused on "climate justice finance", which shapes climate futures both by financing climate justice and seeking to embed climate justice principles within finance itself. Claims for the repayment of climate debt, and climate reparations, seek to build new financing mechanisms for climate justice outside of existing forms of international public climate finance, while challenging the north-south financial relations of credit and debt that generate climate inequalities. The GND and degrowth both represent critiques of the injustices of dominant forms of "green finance" and offer alternative programmes for embedding climate justice within and through state and community finance to address the social and ecological challenges of climate change.

Rather than uncritically promoting climate justice represented in abstract proposals or small-scale experiments, our goal here is to examine climate justice finance in its complexities, contestations and potentials. Just as in the positions outlined previously in the book, we extend a political economy and economic geography lens to examine how climate justice is a contested sphere of climate finance that, like the other positions, is shaping contingent climate futures. Indeed, each of the climate justice visions outlined have more or less just outcomes, socially and for the climate. The politics of international public climate finance has largely been waged over how much finance there is and how to count it, rather than on how to finance climate transitions and transformations for the most vulnerable. While debates about climate debt have moved from an intellectual exercise to real negotiations over debt restructuring and cancellation, the spectrum of actual debt relief offered is narrow, and *climate* debts have largely not yet entered discussions. And although GNDs, degrowth and climate reparations draw out plans for democratization and equality, they must progress from programmatic demands to transformative movements. Realizing climate justice finance, then, will ultimately depend on building the political power of these movements, not simply the financial positions on climate change being advanced.

CHAPTER 8

CONCLUSION: TAKING A POSITION ON CLIMATE FINANCE

THE LONG AND SHORT OF CLIMATE FINANCE

In this book we have traversed the dizzying array of ideas, instruments and institutions that make up the world of climate finance. Our contention is that as finance is increasingly *positioned as* the solution to climate change, different *positions of* climate finance are an increasingly powerful indicator and mediator of possible climate futures. In the terminology of financial markets, traders "open" and "close" their market positions. Traders can either go "long", or "short" depending on whether they stand to profit if the market goes up, or down, respectively. To borrow this terminology, the six climate finance positions we have outlined in this book each take long and short positions on how the relationship between capitalist economies and climate change might evolve. In so doing, the ideas, actors and institutions that are positioning climate finance in particular ways are opening up some possible climate futures while foreclosing others.

To begin, we examined the climate finance positions of "climate capital" and "climate risk". These positions are two sides of the same climate capitalist coin. Climate capital is a position that goes long on climate as an asset class, while going short on climate investments that do not promise profits. As a result, climate capital opens up climate futures that allow some wealthy actors to seize on the financial opportunities of the climate crisis. This can mobilize capital for much-needed climate investment, whether as equity, such as via sustainable investment funds, or debt, such as via green bonds. However, as the cases of the financing of resilient infrastructure and renewable energy assets showed, climate capital can close off the wider possible social and environmental benefits of the climate transition, especially if they are less profitable or deemed too great an investment risk.

Climate risk takes a long position on managing the risks of climate change to finance and a short position on the risks posed by finance to the climate.

Climate risk initiatives such as climate disclosure and ESG integration seek to open up future climate pathways that are orderly, smooth and, above all, market-controlled. At the same time, framing investments in fossil fuels as climate risks has given climate activists, such as the divestment movement, a new set of "risky" tactics to drive climate action. Still, climate change is much more than a financial risk; this positioning can close down avenues to address climate impacts that are financially immaterial to investors.

"Precision markets" and "speculative markets", in contrast, represent opposing positions on the knowability and controllability of climate futures. Precision markets go long on pricing climate efficiency, while going short on climate uncertainties. For example, social cost of carbon estimates, carbon trading and climate insurance markets all envisage a predictable climate future that can be incentivized with the right calculative tools. These tools make the costs and benefits of climate change more visible, opening up climate pathways that are ordered by economic logics of optimality and efficiency. However, the precision impulse – to get the price right so as to achieve just the right balance of emissions reductions and climate damage – closes down precautionary climate futures that prioritize a safe climate in the face of incalculable and seismic potential change.

Speculative markets are long on technological solutions, but short on transformative change. The protagonists – from green billionaires to start-ups and social entrepreneurs – are producing climate futures through their high stakes techno-financial bets. Critical climate technologies, such as batteries, carbon removal, and off-grid solar, are currently being developed and propagated through speculative markets. Yet, the radically open climate futures implied by the wide variety of speculative market positions are simultaneously closed off because it serves to reproduce existing patterns of extraction, exploitation and exclusion in the image of speculators. In contradiction with their ideological underpinnings, speculative markets are usually produced with substantial state support.

"Big green states" and "climate justice finance" are positions that represent a spectrum of explicitly political forms of climate finance. "Big green states" hold a long position on the capacity of the state to provide public climate finance as big green carrots, but are currently short on the wielding of big green sticks against private fossil and climate finance. Nonetheless, states have the potential to open up big green climate futures that mobilize the financial firepower of fiscal and monetary policy in service of public climate goals. Those goals could work to close off some of the more privatized climate futures built on financial structures such as public-private partnerships. To date, however, big green states have largely only gone as far as greening existing forms of statecraft, such as central banks, state investment banks and taxation systems. As such, big green states remain caught between state imperatives to save capitalism from climate change as climate manager of last resort and the potential to democratize public climate finance, and the climate futures it is creating.

Finally, climate justice finance is long on the strength of normative claims of justice, but remains short on political power. International climate funds, calls for the repayment of climate debt and climate reparations, and campaigns for a GND or degrowth, each have their genesis in a recognition of the inherent inequalities and injustices of climate change. Climate justice finance, then, seeks to open up climate futures to the demands of developing country governments and environmental, labour, feminist, anti-racist and Indigenous movements, within the structures of international public climate finance. Such demands are often at odds with – and if enacted would close down – market-based climate futures that rely on, for example, carbon offsetting. However, reflecting the power imbalances of climate finance, currently these demands are either subsumed into market paradigms or remain unmet.

THE STATE OF CLIMATE FINANCE

Initiatives and experiments in climate finance are notoriously fickle. The coalitions, funds and policies that make up climate finance come and go. In this book we have mapped the variegated landscape of existing climate finance in terms of the *positions* they take on climate futures. This acts as a guide for examining still emerging climate finance experiments. Each position, from climate capital to climate justice finance, represents a configuration of ideas, instruments and institutions that orients climate finance, and therefore climate futures, in a certain direction. In practice, climate finance initiatives tend to blend and bind elements across several of the climate finance positions we have outlined. Climate futures are being shaped through these combinations.

Across each of our six climate finance positions – and those that exist at their interstices – the landscape of climate finance is dominated by efforts to green the existing capitalist economy. As a result, climate finance remains structured by ideas, instruments and actors emanating from the centres of global finance in the Global North. This is obvious in the positions of climate capital, climate risk, precision markets and speculative markets. But even big green states and climate justice finance positions remain constrained by the green capitalist imaginary. The balance of our analysis of climate finance in this book, therefore, is reflective of the balance of political-economic forces in the world of climate finance. And yet, the boundaries between climate finance positions are malleable and evolving; contestation and contingency indicates a different set of possibilities.

As this book goes to press, the Glasgow Financial Alliance for Net Zero (GFANZ) and the Just Energy Transition Partnerships (JETPs) it has closely supported are some of the most recent high-profile international climate finance initiatives. They may become pillars of the international climate finance regime, or make way for the next round of experimentation. Either way, GFANZ and the JETPs encapsulate the state, contradictions and geography of climate finance as revealed by our six positions. GFANZ is an alliance of the largest financial institutions in the world that was formed at the COP26 climate conference, held in Glasgow in 2021. There, negotiations on the US$100 billion per year goal of North-South international public climate finance continued to stagnate. Developing countries demanded the doubling of this target while a post-Covid sovereign debt crisis began to brew in many of their economies. And yet, the US$100 billion target for 2020 has still not been met, and recent estimates indicate that finance needs for adaptation in developing countries alone will perhaps reach ten times existing flows (UNEP 2022).

At the same time, Mark Carney, Larry Fink and their peers such as Bloomberg CEO Michael Bloomberg and CEO of Citigroup Jane Fraser were extolling their $130 trillion-plus GFANZ launched earlier that year. GFANZ is structured as an umbrella alliance of a range of sector-specific alliances, such as the Net Zero Asset Manager Alliance. Members of GFANZ are taking what is an increasingly hegemonic position on climate finance. The Alliance is made up of over 500 financial companies including institutional investors, asset managers, banks, insurers and other financial services providers. The $130 trillion-plus figure refers to the total assets under management by these companies; this represents about 40 per cent of global financial assets, though there is significant double counting because one member may manage another member's assets. As members of the GFANZ, companies commit to aligning their portfolios and operations in line with net zero by 2050 goals.

GFANZ represents the shifting centre of gravity of climate finance. It adopts language that spans each of our six positions on climate change. Its framework for net-zero talks about "mobilizing capital", "risk mitigation", "pricing the externalities of carbon emissions", "climate solution technologies", "engagement with government" and "smooth and just transition" (GFANZ 2022a). But its main commitment is to facilitating an "orderly" transition to net zero, indicative of its overarching orientation towards the greening of capitalism. From the framework developed in this book, GFANZ can be understood as a process of subsuming climate change within existing structures of global financial markets. Where climate finance emerged, at least in principle, from a commitment to the justice and equity principles of the international climate accord, the social relations and geographies of power have shifted to the financial centres of global capitalism. Governments are increasingly directing international public finance through initiatives such as GFANZ, despite their limited connections with institutions in developing and emerging economies.

The hegemonic position on climate finance represented by GFANZ is demonstrated in another key COP26 announcement: JETPs. JETPs are a financial mechanism established by the International Partners Group (IPG) of wealthy country donors, which includes the US, the UK, France and Germany. GFANZ will play a key role in financing the JETPs. They are intended to fund transitions in some of the world's most fossil fuel dependent economies, including South Africa, India, Indonesia, Senegal and Vietnam. South Africa was the first to launch its JETP Investment Plan at COP26, followed by Indonesia and Vietnam in late 2022. As the name indicates, JETPs are a response to demands for justice in climate transitions from developing countries. JETPs meet these demands with a mix of both public and private finance, reflecting the extent to which the justice-based origins of climate finance have been incorporated into existing power inequalities of global finance.

The JETPs are predicated on a co-financing arrangement in which public finance leverages an equivalent amount of private finance. The public finance component is overwhelming being delivered as commercial loans rather than as concessional loans or grants. In South Africa's JETP, only 4 per cent of total public finance was delivered in grant form, with the remainder being delivered in different kinds of loans (Archer 2022). GFANZ supports this "capital mobilization" for the Indonesian and Vietnamese JETPs. Through a working group of its members including Bank of America, Citi, Deutsche Bank, HSBC, Macquarie, MUFG and Standard Chartered, GFANZ committed to mobilize at least $10 billion in co-financing for Indonesia's JETP deal, matching the public finance commitment. The role of GFANZ in the Indonesian JETP is to identify barriers and necessary reforms to "crowd in" private finance, under the proviso that governments commit to policy reform, provide catalytic public finance and come up with investable projects (GFANZ 2022b).

The formation of GFANZ and the JETPs have been heavily contested from different political positions, and are indicative of the extent to which climate politics is now being fought over financial terrain. Climate activists have used the formation of GFANZ as a basis to place political pressure on its members to divest from fossil fuels and implement more stringent climate goals. On the eve of COP26, a coalition of international environmental and climate NGOs, including Greenpeace, Environmental Defense, 350.org, Bank on the Future and the Sunrise Project, ran full page advertisements in newspapers drawing attention to the ongoing fossil fuel financing by GFANZ members and demanding that "greenwashing must end" (Bank on the Future

157

and the Sunrise Project 2021). The NGO Reclaim Finance released a series of research reports describing GFANZ members as "climate arsonists" for their role in financing fossil fuels despite net-zero pledges (Harvey 2023).

Civil society groups have similarly levelled criticisms against the GFANZ backed JETPs. They have criticized the partnerships for their reliance on loan over grant-based public finance, which established debtor relations inverse to historical climate debts. The President of South Africa, Cyril Ramaphosa, who signed up for a JETP, echoed this criticism of the reliance on loans and argued South Africa required US$83 billion over five years – far more than the US$8.5 billion in public climate finance secured by the JETP (AFP 2022). Civil society groups argue that the reliance on private co-financing results in overly secretive contractual arrangements that exclude civil society deliberation over the plans and precludes the wider benefits of just transitions for community development (Wemanya *et al.* 2022).

Pressure on GFANZ has also come from conservative political forces. The Republican campaign against sustainable finance in the US asserted that membership of GFANZ, with its affiliation with the UN's Race to Zero campaign, and associated net zero and 1.5°C goals, risked falling afoul of antitrust laws that prevent businesses from colluding with each other. Financial institutions including JPMorgan, Morgan Stanley and Bank of America all threatened to leave GFANZ for this reason. Race to Zero responded by updating its criteria to reduce any sense of compulsion for members' pathways to net zero, removing, for example, mentions of "no new coal". Nonetheless, GFANZ ultimately dropped the requirement for its members to join Race to Zero. Political controversy around GFANZ has led to some high-profile defections from the alliance, including asset manager Vanguard, pension funds Cbus and Bundespensionskasse, and insurers Munich Re and Zurich Insurance Group. The tensions facing GFANZ point to the limits of coordinating collective action on climate change through the dominant actors and institutions of finance capital.

THE POLITICS OF CLIMATE FINANCE

Taking a financial position on climate change is inherently political. The example of the GFANZ and JETPs demonstrates that climate finance is, in turn, becoming a key site of contestation for climate politics for actors from the political left and right. No longer limited to the negotiating rooms of international climate conferences, the politics of climate finance are being fought in green standards, shareholder meetings, climate economics models and technology labs. These contests, in one way or another, always relate to the role of the state in underpinning climate finance in its various positions: from the de-risking state of climate capital, the risk manager state of climate risk, the regulatory state of precision markets, the subsidy state of speculative markets, and the more overt forms of public climate finance provided in the positions of big green states and climate justice finance.

The politics of climate finance is also increasingly contested by organizations and activists in the climate movement. These movements have long demanded increases in public climate finance over private climate finance as the best way to address historical climate injustices through unconditional transfers of resources from Global North to South. In this book we have also documented new financial tactics and strategies for climate movements to advance their political positions. On the one hand, this might involve using the language and tools of mainstream climate finance to influence the "greening" of finance. On the other hand, the imperatives of climate change are a basis to challenge and build different kinds of climate finance specifically, and financial systems generally, that transform the relationship between capitalism and climate change.

Our own position emerging from the analysis in this book is that climate finance must be reconfigured towards a greater role for public climate finance that combines the fiscal powers of big green states and the democratic and internationalist potential of climate justice finance in order to meet climate and socio-ecological goals. This would entail a rebalancing of the current private sector dominated positions on climate finance, and a reorientation of states away from their current focus on least-cost and de-risking logics towards a willingness to direct private capital and expand public wealth for climate ends. It would also require a reworking of state institutions, such as central banks or state-owned enterprises, to enable democratic engagement and public deliberation, especially from workers and affected and marginalized communities. Perhaps most importantly, this position expands the social, temporal and spatial horizons of climate finance to recognize historical and geographical responsibilities and obligations. This means paying climate debts as reparations incurred through the intersections of rapacious, extractive colonialisms, racial-capitalist formations and the uneven impacts of the resulting climate change.

Meeting this internationalist, reparative, publicly funded and democratically enacted position on climate finance will be worked out on and from the existing terrain of climate finance. Each of the identified positions on climate finance contain possibilities, tensions and contradictions, which require analytical and political engagement. Indeed, there are now a wide variety of tactics being pursued by different actors to both achieve goals within green financial reform agendas and use climate as a basis for financial system change. Unions and environment movements are campaigning for the asset classes of climate capital, from green bonds to renewable energy, to be negotiated with labour rights clauses and environmental protections. Divestment activists have mobilized climate risk, a seemingly apolitical and technical framing of climate change, to shift investment. Even the carbon offsetting schemes of precision markets, the traditional villain of climate justice, are being used by Indigenous communities to advance claims on land and receive reparative financial flows. And critical conversations about the need to finance, and thus govern, speculative technological solutions such carbon dioxide removal as a public utility are beginning to emerge.

Climate finance is a fast-moving and multi-faceted arena. The proliferation of new instruments, institutions, frameworks and deals can be mystifying in their technical detail. Against reified framings of climate finance as an autonomous driver of climate action, our message has been that different forms of climate finance are products of real contestation over climate change. The state of climate finance is a stark indicator of the balance of power in climate politics. Climate change, of course, is much more than a financial issue. But the coalescing of climate politics around financial questions reflects the centrality of finance in mediating political-economic responses to climate change in the contemporary capitalist economy. The upshot of our analysis is that there exist a range of positions of climate finance that imply very different responses to climate change. The politics of taking a financial position on climate change cannot remain obscure as climate finance plays an ever-widening role in configuring our collective climate futures.

REFERENCES

Aboriginal Carbon Foundation 2022. *Aboriginal Carbon Foundation: Community Prosperity, Carbon Farming*. Aboriginal Carbon Foundation. https://www.abcfoundation.org.au/

Adkins, L., M. Cooper & M. Konings 2020. *The Asset Economy*. Cambridge: Polity.

AFP 2022. "S. Africa to press rich nations for more money at COP27". France 24, 4 November. https://www.france24.com/en/live-news/20221104-s-africa-to-press-rich-nations-for-more-money-at-cop27

Ajadi, T. *et al.* 2020. *Global Trends in Renewable Energy Investment 2020*. Frankfurt School-UNEP Collaborating Centre for Climate & Sustainable Energy Finance and Bloomberg New Energy Finance.

Ajl, M. 2021. *A People's Green New Deal*. London: Pluto.

Alami, I., J. Copley & A. Moraitis 2023. "The 'wicked trinity' of late capitalism: governing in an era of stagnation, surplus humanity, and environmental breakdown". *Geoforum*, 103691.

Alami, I. & A. Dixon 2023. "Uneven and combined state capitalism". *Environment and Planning A: Economy and Space* 55(1): 72–99.

Allan, B., J. Lewis & T. Oatley 2021. "Green industrial policy and the global transformation of climate politics". *Global Environmental Politics* 21(4): 1–19.

Allen, M. *et al.* 2021. "State-permeated capitalism and the solar PV industry in China and India". *New Political Economy* 26(4): 527–39.

Ameli, N. *et al.* 2020. "Climate finance and disclosure for institutional investors: why transparency is not enough". *Climatic Change* 160(4): 565–89.

Amerasinghe, N. *et al.* 2017. *Future of the Funds: Exploring the Architecture of Multilateral Climate Finance*. World Resources Institute. https://www.wri.org/research/future-funds-exploring-architecture-multilateral-climate-finance

Anderson, B. 2010. "Preemption, precaution, preparedness: anticipatory action and future geographies". *Progress in Human Geography* 34(6): 777–98.

Andreucci, D. *et al.* 2017. "'Value grabbing': a political ecology of rent". *Capitalism Nature Socialism* 28(3): 28–47.

Ansar, A., B. Caldecott & J. Tilbury 2013. "Stranded assets and the fossil fuel divestment campaign: What does divestment mean for the valuation of fossil fuel assets?" Smith School of Enterprise and the Environment.

Appel, H., S. Whitley & C. Kline 2019. *The Power of Debt: Identity and Collective Action in the Age of Finance.* Luskin Institute on Inequality and Democracy.

Archer, S. 2022. *12-Month Update on Progress in Advancing the Just Energy Transition Partnership (JETP).* UN Climate Change Conference (COP26) at the SEC Glasgow 2021. 10 November. https://ukcop26.org/12-month-update-on-progress-in-advancing-the-just-energy-transition-partnership-jetp/

Aronoff, K. *et al.* 2019. *A Planet to Win: Why We Need a Green New Deal.* London: Verso.

Atwood, M. 2012. *In Other Worlds: SF and the Human Imagination.* New York: Anchor.

August, M. *et al.* 2022. "Reimagining geographies of public finance". *Progress in Human Geography* 46(2): 527–48.

August, M., D. Cohen & E. Rosenman 2022. "Walls of capital: quantitative easing, spatial inequality, and the winners and losers of Canada's pandemic-era housing market". *Cambridge Journal of Regions, Economy and Society*, 16(1): 225–38.

Backus, M., C. Conlon & M. Sinkinson 2021. "Common ownership in America: 1980–2017". *American Economic Journal: Microeconomics* 13(3): 273–308.

Baker, L. 2022a. "New frontiers of electricity capital: energy access in sub-Saharan Africa". *New Political Economy* 28(2): 1–17.

Baker, L. 2022b. "Procurement, finance and the energy transition: between global processes and territorial realities". *Environment and Planning E: Nature and Space* 5(4): 1738–64.

Balls, J. & H. Fischer 2019. "Electricity-centered clientelism and the contradictions of private solar microgrids in India". *Annals of the American Association of Geographers* 109(2): 465–75.

Banga, J. 2019. "The green bond market: a potential source of climate finance for developing countries". *Journal of Sustainable Finance & Investment* 9(1): 17–32.

Bangladesh Bank 2020. *Sustainable Finance Policy for Banks and Financial Institutions.* https://www.bb.org.bd/mediaroom/circulars/gbcrd/dec312020sfd05.pdf

Bank of England 2021. *Greening our Corporate Bond Purchase Scheme (CBPS).* 5 November. https://www.bankofengland.co.uk/markets/greening-the-corporate-bond-purchase-scheme

Bank of England 2023. *The Bank of England's Climate-Related Financial Disclosure 2023.* 6 July. https://www.bankofengland.co.uk/climate-change/the-bank-of-englands-climate-related-financial-disclosure-2023

Bank on the Future and the Sunrise Project 2021. *A Letter to Mark Carney: We are Running Out of Time.* Stand.Earth. November. https://stand.earth/resources/a-letter-to-mark-carney-we-are-running-out-of-time/

Bateman, M., M. Duvendack & N. Loubere 2019. "Is fin-tech the new panacea for poverty alleviation and local development? Contesting Suri and Jack's M-Pesa findings published in *Science*". *Review of African Political Economy* 46(161): 480–95.

Battistoni, A. 2022. "A green new deal for care: revaluing the work of social and ecological reproduction". In C. Calhoun & B. Fong (eds), *The New Green Deal and the Future of Work*, 103–41. New York: Columbia University Press.

Baysa, N. *et al.* 2021. *Global Landscape of Climate Finance 2021*. Climate Policy Initiative.

Behrsin, I., S. Knuth & A. Levenda 2022. "Thirty states of renewability: controversial energies and the politics of incumbent industry". *Environment and Planning E: Nature and Space* 5(2): 762–86.

Berg, F., J. Kölbel & R. Rigobon 2020. "Aggregate confusion: the divergence of ESG ratings". SSRN Scholarly Paper ID 3438533. Social Science Research Network.

Berkeley Carbon Trading Project 2022. *Voluntary Registry Offsets Database*. https://gspp.berkeley.edu/faculty-and-impact/centers/cepp/projects/berkeley-carbon-trading-project/offsets-database

Bernards, N. 2022. *A Critical History of Poverty Finance: Colonial Roots and Neoliberal Futures*. London: Pluto Press.

Best, J. 2019. "The inflation game: targets, practices and the social production of monetary credibility", *New Political Economy*, 24(5): 623–640, DOI: 10.1080/13563467.2018.1484714

Best, R., P. Burke & F. Jotzo 2020. "Carbon pricing efficacy: cross-country evidence". *Environmental and Resource Economics* 77(1): 69–94.

Bhandary, R. 2022. "National climate funds: a new dataset on national financing vehicles for climate change". *Climate Policy* 22(3): 401–10.

Biermann F. *et al.* 2021. *Open Letter: We Call for an International Non-Use Agreement on Solar Geoengineering*. Solar Geoengineering Non-Use Agreement. https://www.solargeoeng.org/non-use-agreement/open-letter/

Bigger, P. 2016. "Regulating fairness in the design of California's cap-and-trade market". In S. Paladino & S. Fiske (eds), *The Carbon Fix: Forest Carbon, Social Justice, and Environmental Governance*, 143–58. Abingdon: Routledge.

Bigger, P. 2017. "Measurement and the circulation of green bonds". *Journal of Environmental Investing* 8(1): 273–87.

Bigger, P. 2018. "Hybridity, possibility: degrees of marketization in tradeable permit systems". Environment and Planning A, 50(3): 512–530.

Bigger, P. *et al.* 2022. *Inflation Reduction Act: The Good, The Bad, The Ugly*. Climate and Community Project.

Bigger, P. & N. Millington 2020. "Getting soaked? Climate crisis, adaptation finance, and racialized austerity". *Environment and Planning E: Nature and Space* 3(3): 601–23.

Bigger, P. & S. Webber 2021. "Green structural adjustment in the World Bank's resilient city". *Annals of the American Association of Geographers* 111(1): 36–51.

Birch, K. & F. Muniesa 2020. "Introduction: assetization and technoscientific capitalism". In K. Birch & F. Muniesa (eds), *Assetization: Turning Things into Assets in Technoscientific Capitalism*, 1–41. Cambridge, MA: MIT Press.

Birch, K. & C. Ward 2022. "Assetization and the 'new asset geographies'". *Dialogues in Human Geography*, 20438206221130810.

BlackRock 2020. *Global Renewable Power Insight 2020. Winds of Change: How to Invest in Renewables Today.*

BlackRock's Big Problem 2021. *BlackRock Can Become a Visionary Climate Leader*. BlackRock's Big Problem. https://blackrocksbigproblem.com/the-solutions/

Block, F. 2019. "Problems with the concept of capitalism in the social sciences". *Environment and Planning A: Economy and Space* 51(5): 1166–77.

Blok, A. 2011. "Clash of the eco-sciences: carbon marketization, environmental NGOs and performativity as politics". *Economy and Society* 40(3): 451–76.

BNEF 2023. *Energy Transition Investment Trends 2023.* Bloomberg New Energy Finance.

BofA Global Research 2020. *Emission Impossible? Global Climate Change Primer.* BofA Securities. https://www.bofaml.com/content/dam/boamlimages/documents/articles/ID20_0540/Climate_Change.pdf

Bolton, P. *et al.* 2020. *The Green Swan: Central Banking and Financial Stability in the Age of Climate Change.* Bank for International Settlements.

Boyd, E., M. Boykoff & P. Newell 2011. "The 'new' carbon economy: what's new?" *Antipode* 43(3): 601–11.

Boykoff, M. *et al.* 2009. "Theorizing the carbon economy: Introduction to the special issue". *Environment and Planning A* 41: 2299–304.

Branson, R. 2011. *Screw It, Let's Do It: Lessons In Life* (special edition). Virgin Digital.

Braun, B. 2020. "Central banking and the infrastructural power of finance: the case of ECB support for repo and securitization markets". *Socio-Economic Review* 18(2): 395–418.

Braun, B. 2021. "Asset manager capitalism as a corporate governance regime". In J. Hacker *et al.* (eds), *American Political Economy: Politics, Markets, and Power.* Cambridge: Cambridge University Press.

Braun, B. & D. Gabor 2020. "Central banking, shadow banking, and infrastructural power". In P. Mader, D. Mertens & N. van der Zwan (eds), *The Routledge International Handbook of Financialization.* Abingdon: Routledge.

Breakthrough Energy 2022. *Investing in Innovation.* https://www.breakthroughenergy.org/investing-in-innovation/investing-in-innovation

Bridge, G. *et al.* 2020. "Pluralizing and problematizing carbon finance". *Progress in Human Geography* 44(4): 724–42.

Bruenig, M. 2019. *Fighting Climate Change with a Green Tennessee Valley Authority.* People's Policy Project. https://www.peoplespolicyproject.org/project/fighting-climate-change-with-a-green-tva/

Bruun, J. 2017. Governing Climate Finance: Paradigms, Participation and Power in the Green Climate Fund. PhD thesis, University of Manchester. https://www.research.manchester.ac.uk/portal/files/184631124/FULL_TEXT.PDF

Bryant, G. 2016. "The politics of carbon market design: rethinking the techno-politics and post-politics of climate change". *Antipode* 48(4): 877–98.

Bryant, G. 2018. "Nature as accumulation strategy? Finance, nature, and value in carbon markets". *Annals of the American Association of Geographers* 108(3): 605–19.

Bryant, G. 2019. *Carbon Markets in a Climate-Changing Capitalism.* Cambridge: Cambridge University Press.

Bryant, G., S. Dabhi & S. Böhm 2015. "'Fixing' the climate crisis: capital, states and carbon offsetting in India". *Environment and Planning A* 47(10): 2047–63.

Buck, H. 2019. *After Geoengineering: Climate Tragedy, Repair, and Restoration.* London: Verso.

Buck, H. 2021. *Ending Fossil Fuels: Why Net Zero is Not Enough*. London: Verso.

Bulkeley, H. & P. Newell 2015. *Governing Climate Change*. Second edition. Abingdon: Routledge.

Buller, A. 2020. *"Doing Well by Doing Good"? Examining the rise of Environmental, Social, Governance (ESG) Investing*. Common Wealth.

Buller, A. 2022. *The Value of a Whale: On the Illusions of Green Capitalism*. Manchester: Manchester University Press.

Bullock, S., M. Childs & T. Picken 2009. *A Dangerous Distraction: Why Offsetting is Failing the Climate and People: The Evidence*. Friends of the Earth England, Wales and Northern Ireland. http://www.foe.co.uk/resource/briefing_notes/dangerous_distraction.pdf

Bumpus, A. & D. Liverman 2008. "Accumulation by decarbonization and the governance of carbon offsets". *Economic Geography* 84: 127–55.

Cahill, D. & M. Konings 2017. *Neoliberalism*. Oxford: Wiley-Blackwell.

Caliskan, K. & M. Callon 2009. "Economization, part 1: shifting attention from the economy towards processes of economization". *Economy and Society* 38(3): 369–98.

Callon, M. 1998. "The embeddedness of economic markets in economics". In M. Callon (ed.), *The Laws of Markets*. Oxford: Blackwell.

Callon, M. 2009. "Civilizing markets: Carbon trading between in vitro and in vivo experiments", *Accounting, Organizations and Society*, 34 (3–4): 535–48.

Callon, M. 2010. "Performativity, misfires and politics". *Journal of Cultural Economy* 3(2): 163–9.

Campiglio, E. 2016. "Beyond carbon pricing: The role of banking and monetary policy in financing the transition to a low-carbon economy", *Ecological Economics*, 121: 220–30.

Caprotti, F. 2015. "Golden sun, green economy: market security and the US/EU–China 'solar trade war'". *Asian Geographer* 32(2): 99–115.

Caprotti, F. 2017. "Protecting innovative niches in the green economy: investigating the rise and fall of Solyndra, 2005–2011". *GeoJournal* 82(5): 937–55.

Carbon Engineering 2019a. "Investment from Oxy Low Carbon Ventures and Chevron Technology Ventures". Carbon Engineering, 9 January. https://carbonengineering.com/news-updates/investment-announcement/

Carbon Engineering 2019b. "Carbon Engineering concludes USD$68 million investment round". Carbon Engineering, 21 March. https://carbonengineering.com/news-updates/68-million-investment/

Carbon Engineering 2022. "1PointFive announces agreement with Airbus for the purchase of 400,000 tonnes of carbon removal credits". Carbon Engineering, 17 March. https://carbonengineering.com/news-updates/1pointfive-airbus/

Carbon Tracker 2011. *Unburnable Carbon: Are the World's Financial Markets Carrying a Carbon Bubble?* https://carbontracker.org/reports/carbon-bubble/

Carney, M. 2015. "Breaking the tragedy of the horizon: climate change and financial stability". Speech at Lloyd's of London, London, 29 September. https://www.bis.org/review/r151009a.pdf

Carney, M. 2019. "Remarks given during the UN Secretary General's Climate Action Summit". Climate Action Summit, UN General Assembly, New York, 23 September. https://www.bankofengland.co.uk/-/media/boe/files/speech/2019/remarks-given-during-the-un-secretary-generals-climate-actions-summit-2019-mark-carney.pdf

Carton, W. 2019. "'Fixing' climate change by mortgaging the future: negative emissions, spatiotemporal fixes, and the political economy of delay". *Antipode* 51(3): 750–69. https://doi.org/10.1111/anti.12532

Carton, W. *et al.* 2020. "Negative emissions and the long history of carbon removal". *WIREs Climate Change* 11(6): e671.

Carty, T., J. Kowalzig & B. Zagema 2020. *Climate Finance Shadow Report.* Oxfam. https://www.oxfam.org.uk/media/press-releases/poorer-nations-expected-to-face-up-to-55-billion-shortfall-in-climate-finance/

Castree, N. & B. Christophers 2015. "Banking spatially on the future: capital switching, infrastructure, and the ecological fix". *Annals of the Association of American Geographers* 105(2): 378–86.

CDP 2020. *The Time to Green Finance: CDP Financial Services Disclosure Report 2020.*

CDP 2021. "What CDP does". https://www.cdp.net/en/info/about-us/what-we-do

Chakrabarty, D. 2009. "The climate of history: four theses". *Critical Inquiry* 35(2): 197–222.

Chen, G. & C. Lees 2016. "Growing China's renewables sector: a developmental state approach". *New Political Economy* 21(6): 574–86.

Chen, M. 2020. "State actors, market games: credit guarantees and the funding of China Development Bank". *New Political Economy* 25(3): 453–68.

Chen, Y. & A. Li 2021. "Global green new deal: a global south perspective". *Economic and Labour Relations Review* 32(2): 170–89.

Chenet, H., J. Ryan-Collins & F. van Lerven 2021. "Finance, climate-change and radical uncertainty: towards a precautionary approach to financial policy". *Ecological Economics* 183: 106957.

Choi, J., D. Escalante & M. Larsen 2020. *Green Banking in China: Emerging Trends.* Climate Policy Institute.

Choi-Schagrin, W. 2021. "Wildfires are ravaging forests set aside to soak up greenhouse gases". *New York Times,* 23 August. https://www.nytimes.com/2021/08/23/us/wildfires-carbon-offsets.html

Christophers, B. 2017. "Climate change and financial instability: risk disclosure and the problematics of neoliberal governance". *Annals of the American Association of Geographers* 107(5): 1108–27.

Christophers, B. 2018a. "Risk capital: urban political ecology and entanglements of financial and environmental risk in Washington, DC". *Environment and Planning E: Nature and Space* 1(1–2): 144–64.

Christophers, B. 2018b. "Risking value theory in the political economy of finance and nature". *Progress in Human Geography* 42(3): 330–49.

Christophers, B. 2019. "Environmental beta or how institutional investors think about climate change and fossil fuel risk". *Annals of the American Association of Geographers* 109(3): 754–74.

Christophers, B. 2021a. "Fossilised capital: price and profit in the energy transition". *New Political Economy* 27(4): 1–14.

Christophers, B. 2021b. "The end of carbon capitalism (as we knew it)". *Critical Historical Studies* 8(2): 239–69.

Christophers, B. 2022. "Taking renewables to market: prospects for the after-subsidy energy transition". *Antipode* 54(5): 1519–44.

Christophers, B. 2023. Our Lives in Their Portfolios: Why Asset Managers Own the World. London: Verso

Christophers, B., P. Bigger & L. Johnson 2020. "Stretching scales? Risk and sociality in climate finance". *Environment and Planning A: Economy and Space* 52(1): 88–110.

Clean Energy Finance Corporation 2021. *CEFC Investment Policies*. Australian Government. https://www.cefc.com.au/media/1sbjb5qb/cefc-investment-policies-april-2021.pdf

Climate Bonds Initiative 2022. *Market Data*. Climate Bonds Initiative. https://www.climatebonds.net/market/data

Climate Jobs NY 2021. *Statement on New York's Historic Renewable Energy Job Standards*, 6 April. https://www.climatejobsny.org/news/2021/4/6/cjnys-statement-on-new-yorks-historic-renewable-energy-job-standards

Climate Policy Initiative 2022. *Global Landscape of Climate Finance: A Decade of Data 2011–2020*. Climate Policy Initiative. https://www.climatepolicyinitiative.org/wp-content/uploads/2022/10/Global-Landscape-of-Climate-Finance-A-Decade-of-Data.pdf

Climeworks 2022a. "Permanent CO_2 storage solutions". https://climeworks.com/co2-storage-solutions

Climeworks 2022b. "Climeworks raises CHF 600 million (US \$650 million) in equity". 5 April. https://climeworks.com/news/equity-fundraising

Climeworks 2022c. "Latest news about Climeworks and Direct Air Capture". 18 July. https://climeworks.com/news-and-press

Coase, R. 1960. "The problem of social cost". *Journal of Law and Economics* 3: 1–44.

Cogan, D. *et al.* 2021. "Funding the sun: new paradigms for financing off-grid solar companies". SSRN Electronic Journal.

Cohen, D. 2022. "A green new deal for housing". In Calhoun & Fong (eds), *The Green New Deal and the Future of Work*, 235–54. New York: Columbia University Press.

Cohen, D. & E. Rosenman 2020. "From the school yard to the conservation area: impact investment across the nature/social divide". *Antipode* 52(5): 1259–85.

Cohen, R. 2020. *Impact: Reshaping Capitalism to Drive Real Change*. New York: Random House.

Collier, S., R. Elliott & T.-K. Lehtonen 2021. "Climate change and insurance". *Economy and Society* 50(2): 158–72.

Collins, J. 2021. *Rent*. Cambridge: Polity.

Colven, E. & D. Tri Irawaty 2019. "Critical spatial practice and urban poor politics: (re)imagining housing in a flood-prone Jakarta". *Society + Space*. https://www.societyandspace.org/articles/critical-spatial-practice-and-urban-poor-politics-re-imagining-housing-in-a-flood-prone-jakarta

Coombs, N. 2020. "What do stress tests test? Experimentation, demonstration, and the sociotechnical performance of regulatory science". British Journal of Sociology 71(3): 520–36.

Coombs, N. & M. Thiemann 2022. "Recentering central banks: theorizing state–economy boundaries as central bank effects". Economy and Society 51(4): 1–24.

Corbet, J. 2020. "Climate protesters call out 'hot air' of financial giant during BlackRock annual meeting". Common Dreams, 21 May. https://www.commondreams.org/news/2020/05/21/climate-protesters-call-out-hot-air-financial-giant-during-blackrock-annual-meeting

Corporate Leaders Group on Climate Change 2009. The Copenhagen Communiqué on Climate Change. https://www.corporateleadersgroup.com/reports-evidence-and-insights/publications/publications-pdfs/the-copenhagen-communique.pdf

Cousins, J. & D. Hill 2021. "Green infrastructure, stormwater, and the financialization of municipal environmental governance". Journal of Environmental Policy & Planning 23(5): 581–98.

Cross, J. 2016. "Off the grid: infrastructure and energy beyond the mains". Infrastructures and Social Complexity: A Companion, 198–210.

Cross, J. & T. Neumark 2021. "Solar power and its discontents: critiquing off-grid infrastructures of inclusion in East Africa". Development and Change 52(4): 902–26.

Cullenward, D. & D. Victor 2021. Making Climate Policy Work. Cambridge: Polity.

Curran, G. 2020. "Divestment, energy incumbency and the global political economy of energy transition: the case of Adani's Carmichael mine in Australia". Climate Policy 20(8): 949–62.

Dafermos, Y. 2022. "Climate change, central banking and financial supervision: beyond the risk exposure approach". In S. Kappes, L.-P. Rochon & G. Vallet (eds), The Future of Central Banking, 175–9. Cheltenham: Elgar.

Dafermos, Y., D. Gabor & J. Michell 2021. "The Wall Street Consensus in pandemic times: what does it mean for climate-aligned development?" Canadian Journal of Development Studies / Revue Canadienne d'études Du Développement 42(1–2): 1–14.

Dafermos, Y. et al. 2020. Decarbonising is Easy: Beyond Market Neutrality in the ECB's Corporate QE. New Economics Foundation.

Dafermos, Y. et al. 2021. Greening the Eurosystem Collateral Framework: How to Decarbonise the ECB's Monetary Policy. New Economics Foundation.

Dafermos, Y. et al. 2023. "Broken promises: The ECB's widening Paris gap", SOAS University of London, University of Greenwich, University of the West of England, and Greenpeace, https://www.greenpeace.de/publikationen/EZB_Report%20_Broken_promises.pdf

Dale, G. 2018. "The Nobel Prize in climate chaos: Romer, Nordhaus and the IPCC". The Ecologist, 12 October. https://theecologist.org/2018/oct/12/nobel-prize-climate-chaos-romer-nordhaus-and-ipcc

Dale, G., M. Mathai & J. de Oliveira (eds) 2016. Green Growth: Ideology, Political Economy and the Alternatives. London: Zed.

de Coninck, H. *et al.* 2018. "Strengthening and implementing the global response". In *Global Warming of 1.5°C. An IPCC Special Report on the impacts of global warming of 1.5°C above pre-industrial levels and related global greenhouse gas emission pathways, in the context of strengthening the global response to the threat of climate change, sustainable development, and efforts to eradicate poverty.* Intergovernmental Panel on Climate Change. https://www.ipcc.ch/site/assets/uploads/sites/2/2019/02/SR15_Chapter4_Low_Res.pdf

Dempsey, J. & D. Suarez 2016. "Arrested development? The promises and paradoxes of 'selling nature to save it'". *Annals of the American Association of Geographers* 106(3): 653–71.

Derickson, K. 2018. "Urban Geography III: Anthropocene urbanism". *Progress in Human Geography* 42(3): 425–35.

DeSantis, R. 2022. *Governor Ron DeSantis Eliminates ESG Considerations from State Pension Investments.* https://www.flgov.com/2022/08/23/governor-ron-desantis-eliminates-esg-considerations-from-state-pension-investments/

Dessai, S. *et al.* 2009. "Climate prediction: a limit to adaptation". In W. Adger, I. Lorenzoni & K. O'Brien (eds), *Adapting to Climate Change: Thresholds, Values, Governance.* Cambridge: Cambridge University Press.

Dikau, S. & U. Volz 2021. "Central bank mandates, sustainability objectives and the promotion of green finance". *Ecological Economics* 184: 107022.

Donovan, K. & E. Park 2019. "Perpetual debt in the Silicon Savannah". *Boston Review*, 20 September. https://www.bostonreview.net/articles/kevin-p-donovan-emma-park-tk/

Döpfner, M. 2022. "Elon Musk discusses the war in Ukraine and the importance of nuclear power – and why Benjamin Franklin would be 'the most fun at dinner'". *Business Insider*, 27 March. https://www.businessinsider.com/elon-musk-interview-axel-springer-tesla-war-in-ukraine-2022-3

Eames, N. & D. Barmes 2022. The Green Central Banking Scorecard 2022 Edition. *Positive Money.* https://positivemoney.org/publications/green-central-banking-scorecard-2022

Ecosystem Marketplace 2022. *Credit Prices and Volumes (2019), By Project Type.* EM Data Intelligence & Analytics Dashboard – Public Version 1.0. https://data.ecosystemmarketplace.com/

Edgecliffe-Johnson, A. & B. Nauman 2019. "Fossil fuel divestment has 'zero' climate impact, says Bill Gates". *Financial Times*, 17 September.

Ehlers, T., F. Packer & K. de Greiff 2021. "The pricing of carbon risk in syndicated loans: which risks are priced and why?" *Journal of Banking & Finance*: 106180.

Elliott, R. 2021. *Underwater: Loss, Flood Insurance, and the Moral Economy of Climate Change in the United States.* New York: Columbia University Press.

Ellis-Petersen, H. & S. Baloch 2022. "Pakistani PM says he should not have to beg for help after catastrophic floods". *The Guardian*, 6 October.

Environmental Protection Authority 2022. *EPA External Review Draft of Report on the Social Cost of Greenhouse Gases: Estimates Incorporating Recent Scientific Advance.* https://www.epa.gov/system/files/documents/2022-11/epa_scghg_report_draft_0.pdf

Ervine, K. 2018. *Carbon*. Cambridge: Polity.

European Central Bank 2022a. "ECB takes further steps to incorporate climate change into its monetary policy operations". 4 July. https://www.ecb.europa.eu/press/pr/date/2022/html/ecb.pr220704~4f48a72462.en.html

European Central Bank 2022b. "ECB sets deadlines for banks to deal with climate risks". 2 November. https://www.bankingsupervision.europa.eu/press/pr/date/2022/html/ssm.pr221102~2f7070c567.en.html

European Commission 2021. *Corporate Sustainability Reporting Directive Proposal*. 21 April. https://ec.europa.eu/commission/presscorner/detail/en/QANDA_21_1806

Fan, R. *et al.* 2022. "On calamities, debt, and growth in developing countries". World Bank blogs, 7 June. https://blogs.worldbank.org/developmenttalk/calamities-debt-and-growth-developing-countries

Fancy, T. 2021. "Financial world greenwashing the public with deadly distraction in sustainable investing practices". *USA Today*. 16 March. https://www.usatoday.com/story/opinion/2021/03/16/wall-street-esg-sustainable-investing-greenwashing-column/6948923002/

Felli, R. 2014. "On climate rent". *Historical Materialism* 22(3–4): 251–80.

Fiedler, T. *et al.* 2021. "Business risk and the emergence of climate analytics". *Nature Climate Change* 11(2): 87–94.

Financial Stability Board 2011. *Thematic Review on Risk Disclosure Practices: Peer Review Report*. https://www.fsb.org/wp-content/uploads/r_110318.pdf

Fink, L. 2020. "A fundamental reshaping of finance" [Annual Letter to CEOs]. January. https://www.blackrock.com/americas-offshore/en/larry-fink-ceo-letter

Fletcher, L. & J. Oliver 2022. "Green investing: the risk of a new mis-selling scandal". *Financial Times*, 20 February.

Forrest, A. 2021. *Oil vs Water: Confessions of a Carbon Emitter* [Sound]. ABC Radio National; Australian Broadcasting Corporation. 22 January. https://www.abc.net.au/radionational/programs/boyerlectures/oil-vs-water-confessions-of-a-carbon-emitter-v1/13072410

Franczak, M. & O. Táíwò 2022. "Here's how to repay developing nations for colonialism – and fight the climate crisis". *The Guardian*, 14 January.

Frase, P. 2016. *Four Futures: Life After Capitalism*. London: Verso.

Fraser, N. 2021. "Climates of capital". *New Left Review* 127: 94–127.

Freedom to Invest 2023. *Signatories*. 9 March https://www.freedomtoinvest.org/signatories/

Friede, G., T. Busch & A. Bassen 2015. "ESG and financial performance: aggregated evidence from more than 2000 empirical studies". *Journal of Sustainable Finance & Investment* 5(4): 210–33.

Friedman, M. 1970. "A Friedman doctrine: the social responsibility of business is to increase its profits". *New York Times*, 13 September.

Gabbatiss, J. 2022. "Explainer: how can climate finance be increased from 'billions to trillions'?" *Carbon Brief*, 4 November. https://www.carbonbrief.org/explainer-how-can-climate-finance-be-increased-from-billions-to-trillions/

Gabor, D. 2021a. "Revolution without revolutionaries: interrogating the return of monetary financing". *Transformative Responses to the Crisis*, Finanzwende, Heinrich-Böll-Foundation.

Gabor, D. 2021b. "The Wall Street Consensus". *Development and Change* 52(3): 429–59.

Gabor, D. 2023. "The (European) Derisking State". UWE Bristol Working Paper.

Gabor, D. & C. Ban 2016. "Banking on bonds: the new links between states and markets". *Journal of Common Market Studies* 54(3): 617–35.

Gabor, D. & S. Brooks 2017. "The digital revolution in financial inclusion: international development in the fintech era". *New Political Economy* 22(4): 423–36.

Galvin, R. & N. Healy 2020. "The Green New Deal in the United States: what it is and how to pay for it". *Energy Research & Social Science* 67: 101529.

Garschagen, M. & D. Doshi 2022. "Does funds-based adaptation finance reach the most vulnerable countries?" *Global Environmental Change* 73:102450.

Gates, B. 2021. *How to Avoid a Climate Disaster: The Solutions We Have and the Breakthroughs We Need*. London: Penguin.

Geddes, A., T. Schmidt & B. Steffen 2018. "The multiple roles of state investment banks in low-carbon energy finance: an analysis of Australia, the UK and Germany". *Energy Policy* 115: 158–70.

Generation Investment Management 2012. *Sustainable Capitalism*. https://www.genfound.org/media/1375/pdf-generation-sustainable-capitalism-v1.pdf

Generation Investment Management 2021. *Generation IM Global Equity Quarterly Investor Letter*. https://www.generationim.com/media/1797/generation-im-global-equity-q4-2020-investor-letter-1.pdf

GFANZ 2022a. *Financial Institution Net-Zero Transition Plans: Fundamentals, Recommendations, and Guidance*. Glasgow Financial Alliance for Net Zero. https://assets.bbhub.io/company/sites/63/2022/09/Recommendations-and-Guidance-on-Financial-Institution-Net-zero-Transition-Plans-November-2022.pdf

GFANZ 2022b. "GFANZ forms working group to support mobilization of private capital for the Indonesian Just Energy Transition Partnership (JETP)". Glasgow Financial Alliance for Net Zero, 15 November. https://www.gfanzero.com/press/gfanz-forms-working-group-to-support-mobilization-of-private-capital-for-the-indonesian-jetp/

Ghosh, D., G. Bryant & P. Pillai 2022. "Who wins and who loses from renewable energy transition? Large-scale solar, land, and livelihood in Karnataka, India". *Globalizations*, online early: 1–16.

Gibson-Graham, J. K. 2008. "Diverse economies: performative practices for 'other worlds'". *Progress in Human Geography* 32(5): 613–32.

Gifford, L. & C. Knudson 2020. "Climate finance justice: international perspectives on climate policy, social justice, and capital". *Climatic Change* 161(2): 243–9.

Go Fossil Free / 350.org 2021. *Divestment Commitments*. https://gofossilfree.org/divestment/commitments/

GOGLA 2022. *Investment Data*. https://www.gogla.org/access-to-finance/investment-data

Goldstein, J. 2018. *Planetary Improvement: Cleantech Entrepreneurship and the Contradictions of Green Capitalism*. Cambridge, MA: MIT Press.

Goldstein, J. & D. Tyfield 2018. "Green Keynesianism: bringing the entrepreneurial state back in(to Question)?" *Science as Culture* 27(1): 74–97.

Goodman, J. & J. Anderson 2020. "From climate change to economic change? Reflections on 'feedback'". *Globalizations* 18(7): 1–12.

Graeber, D. 2011. *Debt: The First 5000 years*. London: Melville House.

Gray, I. 2021. "Hazardous simulations: pricing climate risk in US coastal insurance markets". *Economy and Society* 50(2): 196–223.

Green, J. 2021. "Anti-woke ETFs are pitching to conservatives mad at corporate America". Bloomberg.com, 12 November. https://www.bloomberg.com/news/articles/2021-11-12/maga-etf-anti-woke-investing-targets-trump-loving-conservative-traders

Green, J. 2021. "Does carbon pricing reduce emissions? A review of ex-post analyses". *Environmental Research Letters* 16(4): 043004.

Guermond, V. *et al.* 2022. "Microfinance, over-indebtedness and climate adaptation: new evidence from rural Cambodia". Royal Hollaway, University of London. https://static1.squarespace.com/static/62f2cf0e5c1d785dc4090f66/t/6327baac4be25f1d0d3ec013/1663548086338/Microfinance-over-indebtedness-and-climate-adaptation_English.pdf

Hallegatte, S., J. Rentschler & J. Rozenberg 2019. *Lifelines: The Resilient Infrastructure Opportunity*. World Bank.

Hannam, P. 2022. "Australians facing prohibitive insurance premiums after climate-related disasters". *The Guardian*, 11 November.

Harvey, F. 2023. "Banks still investing heavily in fossil fuels despite net zero pledges – study". *The Guardian*, 17 January.

Hawley, J. & A. Williams 2007. "Universal owners: challenges and opportunities". *Corporate Governance: An International Review* 15(3): 415–20.

Heede, R. 2013. "Tracing anthropogenic carbon dioxide and methane emissions to fossil fuel and cement producers, 1854–2010". Climatic Change 1–13.

Hervé-Mignucci, M. & X. Wang 2015. *Slowing the Growth of Coal Power Outside China: The Role of Chinese Finance*. Climate Policy Institute.

Hervé-Mignucci, M. *et al.* 2015. *Slowing the Growth of Coal Power in China: The Role of Finance in State-Owned Enterprises*. Climate Policy Institute.

Hickel, J. 2018. "The Nobel Prize for Climate Catastrophe". *Foreign Policy*, 6 December.

Hickel, J. 2020a. *Less is More: How Degrowth Will Save the World*. Cornerstone Digital.

Hickel, J. 2020b. "Quantifying national responsibility for climate breakdown: an equality-based attribution approach for carbon dioxide emissions in excess of the planetary boundary". *The Lancet Planetary Health* 4(9): e399–e404.

Hickel, J. & G. Kallis 2019. "Is green growth possible?" *New Political Economy* 25(4): 1–18.

Hilbrandt, H. & M. Grubbauer 2020. "Standards and SSOs in the contested widening and deepening of financial markets: the arrival of green municipal bonds in Mexico City". *Environment and Planning A: Economy and Space* 52(7): 1415–33.

Hockett, R. 2020. *Financing the Green New Deal: A Plan of Action and Renewal*. Cham, CH: Springer.

Hodgson, C. & D. Sheppard 2023. "EU carbon price tops €100 a tonne for first time". *Financial Times*, 21 February.

Hook, L. 2019. "Chevron and Occidental invest in CO_2 removal technology". *Financial Times*, 9 January.

Hornborg, A. 2017. "How to turn an ocean liner: a proposal for voluntary degrowth by redesigning money for sustainability, justice, and resilience". *Journal of Political Ecology* 24(1): Article 1.

Howard, P. & J. Schwartz 2016. "Think global: international reciprocity as justification for a global social cost of carbon". *Columbia Journal of Environmental Law* 42(Symposium Issue): 203–94.

Howson, P. 2021. "Distributed degrowth technology: challenges for blockchain beyond the green economy". *Ecological Economics* 184: 107020.

Huang, P. *et al.* 2016. "How China became a leader in solar PV: an innovation system analysis". *Renewable and Sustainable Energy Reviews* 64: 777–89.

Huber, M. 2013. *Lifeblood: Oil, Freedom, and the Forces of Capital.* Minneapolis, MN: University of Minnesota Press.

Huber, M. 2022. *Climate Change as Class War: Building Socialism on a Warming Planet.* London: Verso.

Hull, D. 2020. "Elon Musk has made millionaires out of his most loyal fans". Bloomberg. com, 18 December. https://www.bloomberg.com/news/articles/2020-12-18/ tesla-s-tsla-stock-price-an-army-of-millionaire-retail-traders-hold-on

Hull, D. & H. Recht 2018. "Tesla doesn't burn fuel, it burns cash". Bloomberg.com, 30 April. https://www.bloomberg.com/graphics/2018-tesla-burns-cash/

Hyland, A. 2022. "Billionaire Mike Cannon-Brookes banks on turning Australia green". *Sydney Morning Herald*, 25 February. https://www.smh.com.au/national/ billionaire-mike-cannon-brookes-banks-on-turning-australia-green-20220225-p59zlr.html

Independent Evaluation Group 2020. *Jakarta Urban Flood Mitigation Project* [Implementation Completion Report Review]. World Bank. https://documents1. worldbank.org/curated/en/645041582041426391/pdf/Indonesia-Jakarta-Urgent-Flood-Mitigation-Project.pdf

Indigenous Environmental Network 2019. *Talking Points on the AOC-Markey Green New Deal (GND) Resolution.* 8 February. https://www.ienearth.org/talking-points-on-the-aoc-markey-green-new-deal-gnd-resolution/

Ingham, G. 2008. *Capitalism: with a New Postscript on the Financial Crisis and Its Aftermath.* Cambridge: Polity.

Intergovernmental Panel on Climate Change 2022a. *Climate Change 2022: Mitigation of Climate Change. Contribution of Working Group III to the Sixth Assessment Report of the Intergovernmental Panel on Climate Change.* Cambridge: Cambridge University Press.

Intergovernmental Panel on Climate Change 2022b. "Technical summary". In *Climate Change 2022: Mitigation of Climate Change. Contribution of Working Group III to the Sixth Assessment Report of the Intergovernmental Panel on Climate Change.* Cambridge: Cambridge University Press.

International Energy Agency 2020. *World Energy Investment 2020.*

International Energy Agency 2022. *Special Report on Solar PV Global Supply Chains.*

International Monetary Fund 2019. *Fiscal Monitor: How to Mitigate Climate Change.* International Monetary Fund.

IPCC 2014. "Summary for policy makers". In *Climate Change 2014: Impacts, Adaptation, and Vulnerability. Contribution of the Working Group II to the Fifth Assessment Report of the Intergovernmental Panel on Climate Change*, 1–32. Cambridge: Cambridge University Press.

IRENA & CPI 2023. *Global Landscape of Renewable Energy Finance*. International Renewable Energy Agency.

Jenkins, J. et al. 2022. *Preliminary Report: The Climate and Energy Impacts of the Inflation Reduction Act of 2022*. REPEAT Project, Princeton University.

Jerez, B., I. Garcés & R. Torres 2021. "Lithium extractivism and water injustices in the Salar de Atacama, Chile: the colonial shadow of green electromobility". *Political Geography* 87: 102382.

Johnson, L. 2013. "Catastrophe bonds and financial risk: securing capital and rule through contingency". *Geoforum* 45(1): 30–40.

Johnson, L. 2014. "Geographies of securitized catastrophe risk and the implications of climate change". *Economic Geography* 90(2): 155–85.

Johnson, L. 2015. "Catastrophic fixes: cyclical devaluation and accumulation through climate change impacts – Leigh Johnson, 2015". *Environment and Planning A: Economy and Space* 47(12): 2503–21.

Johnson, L. 2021. "Rescaling index insurance for climate and development in Africa". *Economy and Society* 50(2): 248–74.

Jones, R. et al. 2020. "Treating ecological deficit with debt: the practical and political concerns with green bonds". *Geoforum* 114: 49–58.

Kallis, G. 2018. *Degrowth*. Newcastle upon Tyne: Agenda Publishing.

Keen, S. 2021. "The appallingly bad neoclassical economics of climate change". *Globalizations* 18(7): 1149–77.

Keith, D. 2013. *A Case for Climate Engineering*. Cambridge, MA: MIT Press.

Kennedy, S. 2018. "Indonesia's energy transition and its contradictions: emerging geographies of energy and finance". *Energy Research & Social Science* 41: 230–37.

Keynes, J. 2018. *The General Theory of Employment, Interest, and Money*. Cham, CH: Springer.

KfW 2022. "KfW Group sustainability mission statement and sustainability action areas". https://www.kfw.de/nachhaltigkeit/Dokumente/Nachhaltigkeit/Nachhaltigkeitsleitbild-en.pdf

Khan, M. 2021. "Brussels faces backlash over delay to decision on whether gas is green". *Financial Times*, 21 April.

Khan, M. & J. Roberts 2013. "Adaptation and international climate policy". *WIREs Climate Change* 4(3): 171–89.

Kirsch, A. et al. 2020. *Banking on Climate Change: Fossil Fuel Finance Report 2020*. Rainforest Action Network (RAN), BankTrack, Indigenous Environmental Network (IEN), Oil Change International, Reclaim Finance, and the Sierra Club.

Kirsch, A. et al. 2022. *Banking on Climate Chaos: Fossil Fuel Finance Report 2022*. Rainforest Action Network (RAN), BankTrack, Indigenous Environmental

Network (IEN), Oil Change International (OCI), Reclaim Finance, Sierra Club, and urgewald.

Klasa, A. 2022. "European asset managers blame regulatory confusion for downgrade of ESG funds". *Financial Times*, 22 November.

Klein, N. 2014. *This Changes Everything: Capitalism vs the Climate*. New York: Simon & Schuster.

Kling, G. *et al.* 2018. "Climate vulnerability and the cost of debt". SSRN Electronic Journal.

Knox-Hayes, J. 2016. *The Cultures of Markets: The Political Economy of Climate Governance*. Oxford: Oxford University Press.

Knuth, S. 2015. "Global finance and the land grab: mapping twenty-first century strategies". *Canadian Journal of Development Studies / Revue Canadienne d'études Du Développement* 36(2): 163–78.

Knuth, S. 2017. "Green devaluation: disruption, divestment, and decommodification for a green economy". *Capitalism Nature Socialism* 28(1): 98–117.

Knuth, S. 2018. "'Breakthroughs' for a green economy? Financialization and clean energy transition". *Energy Research & Social Science* 41: 220–29.

Knuth, S. 2021. "Rentiers of the low-carbon economy? Renewable energy's extractive fiscal geographies". *Environment and Planning A: Economy and Space*, online early.

Kölbel, J. *et al.* 2020. "Can sustainable investing save the world? Reviewing the mechanisms of investor impact". *Organization & Environment* 33(4): 554–74.

Konings, M. 2018a. "Capital and time: for a new critique of neoliberal reason". In *Capital and Time*. Redwood City, CA: Stanford University Press.

Konings, M. 2018b. "How finance is governed: reconnecting cultural and political economy". *Distinktion: Journal of Social Theory* 19(2): 135–51.

Konings, M. & L. Adkins 2022. "Re-thinking the liquid core of capitalism with Hyman Minsky". *Theory, Culture & Society* 39(5): 43–60.

Kormann, C. 2018. "How carbon trading became a way of life for California's Yurok tribe". *The New Yorker*. https://www.newyorker.com/news/dispatch/how-carbon-trading-became-a-way-of-life-for-californias-yurok-tribe

Krippner, G. 2005. "The financialization of the American economy". *Socio-Economic Review* 3(2): 173–208.

Krippner, G. 2007. "The making of US monetary policy: central bank transparency and the neoliberal dilemma". *Theory and Society* 36(6): 477–513.

Langley, P. 2015. *Liquidity Lost: The Governance of the Global Financial Crisis*. Oxford: Oxford University Press.

Langley, P. 2020. "The folds of social finance: making markets, remaking the social". *Environment and Planning A: Economy and Space* 52(1): 130–47.

Langley, P. *et al.* 2021. "Decarbonizing capital: investment, divestment and the qualification of carbon assets". *Economy and Society* 50(3): 494–516.

Langley, P. & J. Morris 2020. "Central banks: climate governors of last resort?" *Environment and Planning A: Economy and Space* 52(8): 1471–79.

Lederer, K. 2019. "Meet the leftish economist with a new story about capitalism". *New York Times*, 26 November.

Lee, D., S. Lee & V. Feng 2022. "Wealthiest green entrepreneurs lose $141 billion as market turns". Bloomberg.com, 9 June. https://www.bloomberg.com/news/features/2022-06-09/green-billionaires-in-china-lose-141-billion-as-market-turns

Leitner, H., E. Sheppard & E. Colven 2017. "Ecological security for whom: the politics of flood alleviation and urban environmental injustice in Jakarta, Indonesia". In U. Heise, J. Christensen & M. Niemann (eds), *Routledge Companion to the Environmental Humanities*, 194–205. Abingdon: Routledge.

Liberati, D. & G. Marinelli 2021. "Everything you always wanted to know about green bonds (but were afraid to ask)". Bank of Italy Occasional Paper, No. 654. https://doi.org/10.2139/ssrn.4032708

Liegey, V. & A. Nelson 2020. *Exploring Degrowth: A Critical Guide*. London: Pluto.

Ligaiula, P. 2022. "Pacific Resilience Fund a win-win option says PIFS deputy SG at debt for climate swaps". Pacific News Service, 17 March. https://pina.com.fj/2022/03/17/pacific-resilience-fund-a-win-win-option-says-pifs-deputy-sg-at-debt-for-climate-swaps/

Liu, H. 2021. "In-depth Q&A: will China's emissions trading scheme help tackle climate change?" Carbon Brief, 24 June. https://www.carbonbrief.org/in-depth-qa-will-chinas-emissions-trading-scheme-help-tackle-climate-change

Lohmann, L. 2011. "The endless algebra of climate markets". *Capitalism Nature Socialism* 22(4): 93–116.

Lovell, H., H. Bulkeley & D. Liverman 2009. "Carbon offsetting: sustaining consumption?" *Environment and Planning A: Economy and Space*, 41(10): 2357–79.

Lu, J. 2020. "A simple way to close the multi-trillion-dollar infrastructure financing gap". Getting Infrastructure Finance Right, 15 April. https://blogs.worldbank.org/ppps/simple-way-close-multi-trillion-dollar-infrastructure-financing-gap

Lucas, C. & K. Booth 2020. "Privatizing climate adaptation: how insurance weakens solidaristic and collective disaster recovery". *WIREs Climate Change* 11(6): e676.

Luke, N. & M. Huber 2022. "Introduction: uneven geographies of electricity capital". *Environment and Planning E: Nature and Space* 5(4): 1699–1715.

Luke, T. 2009. "A green new deal: why green, how new, and what is the deal?" *Critical Policy Studies* 3(1): 14–28.

MacDowell, N. *et al.* 2017. "The role of CO_2 capture and utilization in mitigating climate change". *Nature Climate Change* 7(4): Article 4.

MacKenzie, D. 2009. "Making things the same: gases, emission rights and the politics of carbon markets". *Accounting, Organizations and Society* 34(3–4): 440–55.

Majority Action 2020. *Climate in the Boardroom: How Asset Manager Voting Shaped Corporate Climate Action in 2020*. https://www.majorityaction.us/asset-manager-report-2020

Malm, A. 2020. "Planning the planet: geoengineering our way out of and back into a planned economy". In J. Sapinski, H. Buck & A. Malm (eds), *Has It Come to This? The Promises and Perils of Geoengineering on the Brink*, 143–62. New Brunswick, NJ: Rutgers University Press.

Mangat, R., S. Dalby & M. Paterson 2018. "Divestment discourse: war, justice, morality and money". *Environmental Politics* 27(2): 187–208.

Mann, G. 2010. "Hobbes' redoubt? Toward a geography of monetary policy". *Progress in Human Geography; London* 34(5): 601–625.

Mann, G. 2013. *Disassembly Required: A Field Guide to Actually Existing Capitalism.* Chico, CA: AK Press.

Mann, G. 2022. "Check your spillover" [Review of *The Spirit of Green: The Economics of Collisions and Contagions in a Crowded World* by W. D. Nordhaus]. *London Review of Books* 44(03).

Mann, G. & J. Wainwright 2018. *Climate Leviathan: A Political Theory of our Planetary Future.* London: Verso.

Manning, B. & K. Reed 2019. "Returning the Yurok Forest to the Yurok Tribe: California's first tribal carbon credit project". *Stanford Environmental Law Journal* 39(71): 71–124.

Market Forces 2021. *The Adani List.* https://www.marketforces.org.au/info/key-issues/theadanilist/

Marois, T. 2021. *Public Banks: Decarbonisation, Definancialisation and Democratisation.* Cambridge: Cambridge University Press.

Marsh, A. & S. Kishan 2021. "Engine No. 1's Exxon win provides boost for ESG advocates". Bloomberg.com, 27 May. https://www.bloomberg.com/news/articles/2021-05-27/engine-no-1-s-exxon-win-signals-turning-point-for-esg-investors

Martin, R. 2002. *Financialization of Daily Life.* Philadelphia, PA: Temple University Press.

Massola, J. 2018. "Big surge in opposition to Adani, new polling reveals". *Sydney Morning Herald*, 31 January. https://www.smh.com.au/politics/federal/big-surge-in-opposition-to-adani-new-polling-reveals-20180131-p4yz4o.html

Mastini, R., G. Kallis & J. Hickel 2021. "A Green New Deal without growth?" *Ecological Economics* 179: 106832.

Matthews, H. 2016. "Quantifying historical carbon and climate debts among nations" *Nature Climate Change* 6: 60–64.

Mawdsley, E. 2018. "Development geography II: financialization". *Progress in Human Geography* 42(2): 264–74.

Mazzucato, M. 2015. *The Entrepreneurial State: Debunking Public vs Private Sector Myths.* Revised edition. New York: Public Affairs.

Mazzucato, M. & C. Penna 2016. "Beyond market failures: the market creating and shaping roles of state investment banks". *Journal of Economic Policy Reform* 19(4): 305–26.

McGee, P. & M. Badkar 2021. "Tesla soars past $1tn in market value". *Financial Times*, 25 October. https://www.ft.com/content/4eb7504e-94ef-4f99-937d-807aa159b282

McGlade, C. & P. Ekins 2015. "The geographical distribution of fossil fuels unused when limiting global warming to 2°C". *Nature* 517(7533): 187–90.

McKibben, B. 2012. "Global warming's terrifying new math". *Rolling Stone*, 19 July. https://www.rollingstone.com/politics/politics-news/global-warmings-terrifying-new-math-188550/

McKibben, B. 2020. "Citing climate change, BlackRock will start moving away from fossil fuels". *The New Yorker*, 16 January. https://www.newyorker.com/news/daily-comment/citing-climate-change-blackrock-will-start-moving-away-from-fossil-fuels

Meckling, J. 2011. *Carbon Coalitions: Business, Climate Politics and the Rise of Emissions Trading*. Cambridge, MA: MIT Press.

Mehrling, P. 2011. *The New Lombard Street: How the Fed Became the Dealer of Last Resort*. Princeton, NJ: Princeton University Press.

Mider, Z. & J. Quigley 2020. "Disney spent millions to save a rainforest. Why are people there so mad?" Bloomberg Green, 9 June. https://www.bloomberg.com/graphics/2020-disney-peru-deforestation/

Mildenberger, M. *et al.* 2022. "Limited impacts of carbon tax rebate programmes on public support for carbon pricing". *Nature Climate Change* 12(2), Article 2.

Milieudefensie et al. vs Royal Dutch Shell PLC 2021. C/09/571932 / HA ZA 19-379 (engelse versie). The Hague District Court 26 May 2021.

Millington, B. 2021. "NAB offers up \$565m loan to world's biggest coal port – and green groups are cheering". *ABC News*, 4 May. https://www.abc.net.au/news/2021-05-04/nab-to-fund-port-of-newcastle-under-strict-onditions/100114844

Minsky, H. 1980. "Capitalist financial processes and the instability of capitalism". *Journal of Economic Issues* 14(2): 505–23.

Minsky, H. 2015. *Can It Happen Again? Essays on Instability and Finance*. Abingdon: Routledge.

Mirowski, P. 2009. "Postface: defining neoliberalism". In P. Mirowski & D. Plehwe (eds), *The Road from Mont Pèlerin*, 417–56. Cambridge, MA: Harvard University Press.

Moloney, T. & D. Hull 2023. "Elon Musk may never be the world's richest person again". Bloomberg.com, 11 January. https://www.bloomberg.com/graphics/2023-elon-musk-might-never-be-worlds-richest-person-again/

Moore, J. (ed.) 2016. *Anthropocene or Capitalocene? Nature, History, and the Crisis of Capitalism*. Binghampton, NY: PM Press.

Morningstar 2021. *Sustainable Funds U.S. Landscape Report*.

Morningstar 2022. *Global Sustainable Fund Flows: Q3 2022 in Review*.

Morris, J. & H. Collins 2023. *(Mis)managing Macroprudential Expectations: How Central Banks Govern Financial and Climate Tail Risks*. Cheltenham: Elgar.

Müller, B., L. Johnson & D. Kreuer 2017. "Maladaptive outcomes of climate insurance in agriculture". *Global Environmental Change* 46: 23–33.

Mulvaney, D. 2019. *Solar Power: Innovation, Sustainability, and Environmental Justice*. Berkeley, CA: University of California Press.

Munro, P., V. Jacome & S. Samarakoon 2022. "Off-grid enterprise: a critical history of small-scale off-grid solar in Sub-Saharan Africa". In N. Ojong (ed.), *Renewable Energy Transformation or Energy Injustice: Off-Grid Solar Electrification in Africa*. Abingdon: Routledge.

Murphy, L. & N. Elima 2021. *In Broad Daylight: Uyghur Forced Labour and Global Solar Supply Chains* (China). Sheffield Hallam University.

Murray, S. 2021. "Measuring what matters: the scramble to set standards for sustainable business". *Financial Times*, 14 May.

Musthaq, F. 2021. "Unconventional central banking and the politics of liquidity". *Review of International Political Economy* 30(3): 1–26.

Nelson, A. & F. Schneider (eds) 2018. *Housing for Degrowth: Principles, Models, Challenges and Opportunities*. Abingdon: Routledge.

Nersisyan, Y. & L. Wray 2021. "Can we afford the Green New Deal?" *Journal of Post Keynesian Economics* 44(1): 68–88.

Newell, P. & D. Mulvaney 2013. "The political economy of the 'just transition'". *Geographical Journal* 179(2): 132–40.

Newell, P. & M. Paterson 2010. *Climate Capitalism: Global Warming and the Transformation of the Global Economy*. Cambridge: Cambridge University Press.

Nordhaus, W. 1991. "To slow or not to slow: the economics of the greenhouse effect". *Economic Journal* 101(407): 920–37.

Nordhaus, W. 2008. *A Question of Balance: Weighing the Options on Global Warming Policies*. New Haven, CT: Yale University Press.

Nordhaus, W. 2019. "Climate change: the ultimate challenge for economics". *American Economic Review* 109(6): 1991–2014.

Norton, L. 2022. "This is why Tesla's ESG rating isn't great". Morningstar, 22 May.

Ocasio-Cortez, A. 2019. *Text – H.Res.109 – 116th Congress (2019–2020): Recognizing the duty of the Federal Government to create a Green New Deal*. (2019/2020) [Legislation]. 2 December.

O'Connell, D. 2013. "Early re-payment of Tesla's ATVM loan". 7 March. https://www.tesla.com/en_JO/blog/early-repayment-tesla%E2%80%99s-atvm-loan

O'Connor, J. 1998. *Natural Causes: Essays in Ecological Marxism*. New York: Guilford Press.

OECD 2017a. "Green Investment Banks: innovative public financial institutions scaling-up private, low-carbon investment policy reform". OECD Environment Policy Paper, No. 6.

OECD 2017b. *Roadmap to Infrastructure as an Asset Class*. https://www.oecd.org/g20/roadmap_to_infrastructure_as_an_asset_class_argentina_presidency_1_0.pdf

OECD 2022a. *Climate Finance Provided and Mobilised by Developed Countries in 2016–2020: Insights from Disaggregated Analysis*. OECD Publishing. https://doi.org/10.1787/286dae5d-en.

OECD 2022b. *Pricing Greenhouse Gas Emissions: Turning Climate Targets into Climate Action*. OECD. https://www.oecd-ilibrary.org/taxation/pricing-greenhouse-gas-emissions_e9778969-en

OECD 2022c. *Climate-Related Development Finance Provider Perspective 2020*. Tableau Software, May, https://public.tableau.com/views/Climate-Related DevelopmentFinanceProvider2020/CRDFDP?%3Alanguage=en-US&publish= yes&%3Adisplay_count=n&%3Aorigin=viz_share_link&%3AshowViz Home=no#1

OECD 2022d. *Climate-Related Development Finance Recipient Perspective 2020*. Tableau Software, May, https://public.tableau.com/views/Climate-Related DevelopmentFinanceRecipient2020/CRDFRP?:language=en-US&publish= yes&:display_count=n&:origin=viz_share_link&:showVizHome=no#1

OECD 2022e. "Support for fossil fuels almost doubled in 2021, slowing progress toward international climate goals, according to new analysis from OECD and IEA". OECD, 29 August 2022. https://www.oecd.org/newsroom/support-for-fossil-fuels-almost-doubled-in-2021-slowing-progress-toward-international-climate-goals-according-to-new-analysis-from-oecd-and-iea.htm

OECD 2023. "Towards orderly green transition: investment requirements and managing risks to capital flows", https://www.oecd.org/investment/investment-policy/towards-orderly-green-transition.pdf

Office of Clean Energy Demonstrations 2022. *Guidance for Creating a Community Benefits Plan for Regional Direct Air Capture Hubs.* https://www.energy.gov/sites/default/files/2023-01/Community%20Benefits%20Plan%20Guidance%20DE-FOA-0002735.pdf

Okereke, C. 2015. "Opinion: the road to Paris – can we navigate the pot holes to a global deal in December?!" Walker Institute, 19 June. https://blogs.reading.ac.uk/walker-institute-climate-news/2015/06/19/the-road-to-paris-can-we-navigate-the-pot-holes-to-a-global-deal-in-december/

O'Mahony, P. 2019. "Are you sure you're investing ethically?" *Irish Times*, 10 December.

Oreskes, N. & E. Conway 2010. *Merchants of Doubt: How a Handful of Scientists Obscured the Truth on Issues from Tobacco Smoke to Global Warming.* London: Bloomsbury.

Osborne, T. 2015. "Tradeoffs in carbon commodification: a political ecology of common property forest governance". *Geoforum*, 67(Supp. C): 64–77.

Ouma, S. 2020. *Farming as Financial Asset: Global Finance and the Making of Institutional Landscapes.* Newcastle upon Tyne: Agenda Publishing.

Ouma, S., L. Johnson & P. Bigger 2018. "Rethinking the financialization of 'nature'". *Environment and Planning A: Economy and Space* 50(3): 500–11.

Overly, S. 2017. "This government loan program helped Tesla at a critical time. Trump wants to cut it". *Washington Post*, 16 March.

Özden-Schilling, C. 2021. *The Current Economy: Electricity Markets and Techno-Economics.* Redwood City, CA: Stanford University Press.

Özgöde, O. 2021. "The emergence of systemic risk: the Federal Reserve, bailouts, and monetary government at the limits". *Socio-Economic Review* 20(4): 2041–71.

Panitch, L. & S. Gindin 2012. *The Making of Global Capitalism: The Political Economy of American Empire.* London: Verso.

Parfitt, C. 2020. "ESG integration treats ethics as risk, but whose ethics and whose risk? Responsible investment in the context of precarity and risk-shifting". *Critical Sociology* 46(4–5): 573–87.

Parfitt, C. 2022. "A foundation for 'ethical capital': the Sustainability Accounting Standards Board and integrated reporting". *Critical Perspectives on Accounting* 102477.

Parfitt, C. 2024. *False Profits of Ethical Capital: Finance, Labour and the Politics of Risk.* Manchester: Manchester University Press.

Parfitt, C. & G. Bryant 2021. "Derivative socionatures: abstract risk and financial materiality in ESG integration". Environment and Planning E: Nature and Space, online early.

Patel, R. & J. Moore 2017. *A History of the World in Seven Cheap Things: A Guide to Capitalism, Nature and the Future of the Planet*. Berkeley, CA: University of California Press.

Pearse, R. 2017. *Pricing Carbon in Australia: Contestation, the State and Market Failure*. Abingdon: Routledge.

Pearse, R. & S. Böhm 2014. "Ten reasons why carbon markets will not bring about radical emissions reduction". *Carbon Management* 5(4): 325–37.

Pearse, R. & G. Bryant 2022. "Labour in transition: a value-theoretical approach to renewable energy labour". *Environment and Planning E: Nature and Space* 5(4): 1872–94.

Peck, J. 2012. "Austerity urbanism". *City* 16(6): 626–55.

Peck, J. & A. Tickell 2002. "Neoliberalizing space". *Antipode* 34(3): 380–404.

Pendleton, D. 2021. "Elon Musk tops list of 15 richest green billionaires". Bloomberg.com, 12 November. https://www.bloomberg.com/features/2021-green-billionaires/

Perry, K. 2020. "Realising climate reparations: towards a global climate stabilization fund and resilience fund programme for loss and damage in marginalised and former colonised societies". SSRN Scholarly Paper No. 3561121.

Pettifor, A. 2019. *The Case for the Green New Deal*. London: Verso.

Pickering, J. & C. Barry 2012. "On the concept of climate debt: its moral and political value". *Critical Review of International Social and Political Philosophy* 15(5): 667–85.

PIFS 2021. *Prospectus: Pacific Resilience Facility. Building Community Resilience in Extraordinary Times*. Pacific Island Forum Secretariat. https://www.forumsec.org/wp-content/uploads/2021/03/PRF-Prospectus.pdf

Pigou, A. 1932. *The Economics of Welfare*. Fourth edition. London: Macmillan.

Pindyck, R. 2013. "Climate change policy: what do the models tell us? NBER Working Paper No. 19244. https://doi.org/10.3386/w19244

Platt, E. 2021. "Berkshire succession: Greg Abel confirmed as Warren Buffett's heir apparent". *Financial Times*, 3 May.

Prudham, S. 2009. "Pimping climate change: Richard Branson, global warming, and the performance of green capitalism". *Environment and Planning A: Economy and Space* 41(7): 1594–613.

Purdom, S. & K. Zhou 2022. *A New Frontier for Drawing Carbon Down*. Climate Tech VC. 16 April. https://climatetechvc.substack.com/p/-a-new-frontier-for-drawing-carbon

PwC 2021. *State of Climate Tech 2021: Scaling Breakthroughs for Net Zero*.

Quinson, T. 2021. "SEC targets greenwashers to bring law and order to ESG". Bloomberg.com, 21 April. https://www.bloomberg.com/news/articles/2021-04-21/sec-targets-greenwashers-to-bring-law-and-order-to-esg-green-insight

Qureshi, Z. 2022. "Pakistan shouldn't get 'aid' after its devastating flood. It is owed climate reparations". *The Diplomat*, 29 September. https://thediplomat.com/2022/09/pakistan-shouldnt-get-aid-after-its-devastating-flood-it-is-owed-climate-reparations/

Ramachandran, V. & J. Masood 2019. "Are the Pacific islands insurable? Challenges and opportunities for disaster risk finance". Center for Global Development Working Paper 516.

Rathi, A. 2022. "Transcript zero episode 7: would you buy 'net-zero oil'?" Bloomberg. com, 27 October. https://www.bloomberg.com/news/articles/2022-10-27/transcript-zero-episode-7-would-you-buy-net-zero-oil

Rathi, A., N. White & D. Green 2022. "Big companies claim 'carbon neutrality' using junk carbon offsets". Bloomberg.com, 21 November. https://www.bloomberg.com/graphics/2022-carbon-offsets-renewable-energy/

REN21 2020. *Renewables 2020: Global Status Report*. REN21 Secretariat.

Rickards, L. *et al.* 2014. "Opening and closing the future: climate change, adaptation, and scenario planning". *Environment and Planning C: Government and Policy* 32(4): 587–602.

Riofrancos, T. 2022. "The security–sustainability nexus: lithium onshoring in the global north". Global Environmental Politics 1–22.

Robins, N., S. Dikau & U. Volz 2021. "Net-zero central banking: a new phase in greening the financial system". Grantham Research Institute on Climate Change and the Environment and Centre for Climate Change Economics and Policy, London School of Economics, and Centre for Sustainable Finance, SOAS, University of London.

Robinson, K. 2020. "Slowing climate change with sewage treatment for the skies". Bloomberg.com, 13 December. https://www.bloomberg.com/news/articles/2020-12-13/kim-stanley-robinson-direct-air-capture-is-a-public-good-for-climate-era

Robinson, K. 2020. *The Ministry for the Future*. London: Orbit.

Ropes & Gray 2023. *Navigating State Regulation of ESG Investments*. https://www.ropesgray.com/en/navigating-state-regulation-of-esg

Ross, A. 2013. "Climate debt denial". *Dissent* 60(3): 33–7.

Ross, A. 2020. *Investing to Save the Planet: How Your Money Can Make a Difference*. London: Penguin Business.

Sanderson, H. & M. Forsythe 2013. *China's Superbank: Debt, Oil and Influence – How China Development Bank is Rewriting the Rules of Finance*. Chichester: Wiley.

Schipper, E. 2006. "Conceptual history of adaptation in the UNFCCC process". *Review of European Community & International Environmental Law* 15(1): 82–92.

Schlosberg, D. 2012. "Climate justice and capabilities: a framework for adaptation policy". *Ethics & International Affairs* 26(4): 445–61.

Schlosberg, D. & L. Collins 2014. "From environmental to climate justice: climate change and the discourse of environmental justice". *WIREs Climate Change* 5(3): 359–74.

Schmelzer, M., A. Vetter & A. Vansintjan 2022. *The Future is Degrowth: A Guide to a World Beyond Capitalism*. London: Verso.

Schroeder, H. 2010. "The history of international climate change politics: three decades of progress, process and procrastination". In M. Boykoff (ed.), *The Politics of Climate Change: A Survey*, 26–41. Abingdon: Routledge.

Setzer, J. & C. Higham 2022. *Global Trends in Climate Change Litigation: 2022 Snapshot*. Grantham Research Institute on Climate Change and the Environment and Centre for Climate Change Economics and Policy, London School of Economics.

Shankleman, J. & J. Ainger 2021. "Greta Thunberg attacks CO_2 offset projects as 'greenwash' at COP26". Bloomberg.com, 3 November. https://www.bloomberg.com/news/articles/2021-11-03/thunberg-attacks-offsets-as-greenwash-as-anger-builds-at-cop26

ShareAction 2020. "Voting matters 2020: are asset managers using their proxy votes for action on climate and social issues?" https://shareaction.org/wp-content/uploads/2020/11/Voting-Matters-2020.pdf

Shelanski, H. 2013. "Refining estimates of the social cost of carbon". Whitehouse.gov., 1 November. https://obamawhitehouse.archives.gov/blog/2013/11/01/refining-estimates-social-cost-carbon

Silver, J. & L. Campbell 2018. "Conservation, development and the blue frontier: the Republic of Seychelles' debt restructuring for marine conservation and climate adaptation program". *International Social Science Journal* 68(229–30): 241–56.

SIMA 2022. *Energy Access Relief Fund (EARF)*. Social Investment Managers and Advisors. https://simafunds.com/fund-management/earf/

Smialek, J. 2023. "Powell says Fed will not be a 'climate policymaker'". *New York Times*, 10 January. https://www.nytimes.com/2023/01/10/business/economy/powell-fed-climate.html

Smith, K. 2007. *The Carbon Neutral Myth: Offset Indulgences for the Climate Sins*. Carbon Trade Watch and Transnational Institute.

Soanes, M. *et al.* 2021. "Follow the money: tracking least developed countries' adaptation finance to the local level". IIED. https://www.iied.org/sites/default/files/pdfs/2021-07/20326iied.pdf

Spash, C. 2007. "The economics of climate change impacts la Stern: novel and nuanced or rhetorically restricted?" *Ecological Economics* 63: 706–13.

Spies-Butcher, B. & G. Bryant 2023. "The history and future of the tax state: possibilities for a new fiscal politics beyond neoliberalism". *Critical Perspectives on Accounting*, 102596.

Stanford, J. 2015. *Economics for Everyone: A Short Guide to the Economics of Capitalism*. Second edition. London: Pluto.

Steffen, W. *et al.* 2015. "The trajectory of the Anthropocene: the Great Acceleration". *The Anthropocene Review* 2(1): 81–98.

Stern, N. 2007. *The Economics of Climate Change: The Stern Review*. Cambridge: Cambridge University Press.

Stern, N., J. Stiglitz & C. Taylor 2022. "The economics of immense risk, urgent action and radical change: towards new approaches to the economics of climate change". *Journal of Economic Methodology* 29(3): 181–216.

Sturman, A. & N. Heenan 2021. "Introduction: configuring the green new deal". *Economic and Labour Relations Review* 32(2): 149–54.

Sultana, F. 2022. "Critical climate justice". *Geographical Journal* 188(1): 118–24.

Sun, Y. & M. Burton 2020. "'Please mine more nickel,' Musk urges as Tesla boosts production". Reuters, 23 July.

Sun, Y., C. Leng & B. Goh 2019. "Exclusive: Tesla to take new $1.4 billion loan from Chinese banks for Shanghai factory – sources". Reuters, 23 December. https://www.reuters.com/article/us-tesla-china-loan-exclusive-idUSKBN1YR0U0

Sunak, R. 2021. *Remit for the Monetary Policy Committee (MPC)*. 3 March. https://assets.publishing.service.gov.uk/government/uploads/system/uploads/attachment_data/file/965782/2021_MPC_remit_FINAL_1_March_.pdf

Swiss Re Institute 2021. "Global insured catastrophe losses rise to USD 112 billion in 2021, the fourth highest on record, Swiss Re Institute estimates". https://www.swissre.com/media/press-release/nr-20211214-sigma-full-year-2021-preliminary-natcat-loss-estimates.html

Szerszynski, B. *et al.* 2013. "Why solar radiation management geoengineering and democracy won't mix". *Environment and Planning A: Economy and Space* 45(12): 2809–16.

Táíwò, O. 2022. *Reconsidering Reparations*. Oxford: Oxford University Press.

Táíwò, O. & P. Bigger 2021. *Debt Justice for Climate Reparations*. The Climate and Community Project. https://www.climateandcommunity.org/debt-justice-for-climate-reparations

Tapp, R. 2019. "Layers of finance: historic tax credits and the fiscal geographies of urban redevelopment". *Geoforum* 105: 13–22.

Taylor, N. 2023. "'Making financial sense of the future': actuaries and the management of climate-related financial risk". *New Political Economy* 28(1): 57–75.

Taylor, Z. 2020. "The real estate risk fix: residential insurance-linked securitization in the Florida metropolis". *Environment and Planning A: Economy and Space* 52(6): 1131–49.

TCFD 2017. *Final Report: Recommendations of the Task Force on Climate-Related Financial Disclosures*. Task Force on Climate-Related Financial Disclosures.

Tesla Inc. 2021. *Annual Report 2020*. https://ir.tesla.com/_flysystem/s3/sec/000156459021004599/tsla-10k_20201231-gen.pdf

Tett, G. 2022. "ESG exposed in a world of changing priorities". *Financial Times*, 3 June.

Texas Comptroller of Public Accounts 2022. "Texas Comptroller Glenn Hegar announces list of financial companies that boycott energy companies". 24 August. https://comptroller.texas.gov/about/media-center/news/20220824-texas-comptroller-glenn-hegar-announces-list-of-financial-companies-that-boycott-energy-companies-1661267815099

The Red Nation 2021. *The Red Deal: Indigenous Action to Save Our Earth*. Common Notions.

Thomas, A., O. Serdeczny & P. Pringle 2020. "Loss and damage research for the global stocktake". *Nature Climate Change* 10(8): 700.

Thomas, A. & E. Theokritoff 2021. "Debt-for-climate swaps for small islands". *Nature Climate Change* 11(11): Article 11.

Thomas, K. & K. Rhiney 2022. "Liberalism's limits for climate justice". Annual Meeting of the Association of American Geographers, online.

Tooze, A. 2018. *Crashed: How a Decade of Financial Crises Changed the World.* New York: Viking.

Tvinnereim, E. & M. Mehling 2018. "Carbon pricing and deep decarbonisation". *Energy Policy* 121: 185–9.

UC Center for Climate Justice 2022. *UC-initiated Indigenous-led Climate Project.* UC Center for Climate Justice. https://centerclimatejustice.universityofcalifornia.edu/projects/research/

UK Government & Steering Committee Members 2021. "Taskforce on Access to Climate Finance: revised concept note". UK Government and UN Climate Change Conference UK 2021. https://ukcop26.org/wp-content/uploads/2021/09/Taskforce-on-Access-to-Climate-Finance-Revised-Concept-Note.pdf

UNEP 2022. *Adaptation Gap Report 2022.* United Nations Environment Programme. http://www.unep.org/resources/adaptation-gap-report-2022

UNEP DTU 2018. *CDM Pipeline*, 1 March. http://www.cdmpipeline.org/publications/CDMPipeline.xlsm

Union of Concerned Scientists 2017. *What is Climate Engineering?* 6 November. https://www.ucsusa.org/resources/what-climate-engineering

V20 2022. Climate Vulnerable Economies Loss Report: Economic Losses Attributable to Climate Change in V20 Economies Over the Last Two Decades. Climate Vulnerable Forum. https://www.v-20.org/wp-content/uploads/2022/06/Climate-Vulnerable-Economies-Loss-Report_June-14_compressed-1.pdf

Vahn, G. & C. Lee 2022. "South Korea aims to gradually increase net-zero oil portion in US crude imports". 25 March. https://www.spglobal.com/commodityinsights/en/market-insights/latest-news/oil/032522-south-korea-aims-to-gradually-increase-net-zero-oil-portion-in-us-crude-imports

van't Klooster, J. & C. Fontan 2020. "The myth of market neutrality: a comparative study of the European Central Bank's and the Swiss National Bank's corporate security purchases". *New Political Economy* 25(6): 865–79.

Vargas, J. 2023. "Vargas, Casten launch sustainable investment caucus". US Congressman Juan Vargas of California's 52nd District, 25 January. https://vargas.house.gov/media/press-releases/vargas-casten-launchsustainable-investment-caucus

Vogel, S. 2018. *Freer Markets, More Rules: Regulatory Reform in Advanced Industrial Countries.* Ithaca, NY: Cornell University Press.

Volz, U. 2022. "The debt and climate crises are escalating – it is time to tackle both". Brookings, 8 July. https://www.brookings.edu/blog/future-development/2022/07/08/the-debt-and-climate-crises-are-escalating-it-is-time-to-tackle-both/

Volz, U. *et al.* 2020. "Debt relief for a green and inclusive recovery: a proposal". Heinrich Böll Foundation; Center for Sustainable Finance, SOAS, University of London; Global Development Policy Center, Boston University.

Wagner, G. *et al.* 2021. "Eight priorities for calculating the social cost of carbon". *Nature* 590(7847): 548–50.

Wagner, G. & M. Weitzman 2016. *Climate Shock: The Economic Consequences of a Hotter Planet.* Princeton, NJ: Princeton University Press.

Waldron, D. & A. Swinderen 2018. "Remote lockouts: the dark side of pay-as-you-go solar?" CGAP, May. https://www.cgap.org/blog/remote-lockouts-dark-side-pay-you-go-solar

Walker, O. 2018. "Al Gore: sustainability is history's biggest investment opportunity". *Financial Times*, 29 April.

Wang, P. *et al*. 2019. "Estimates of the social cost of carbon: a review based on meta-analysis". *Journal of Cleaner Production* 209: 1494–507.

Watt, R. 2021. "The fantasy of carbon offsetting". *Environmental Politics* 30(7): 1069–88.

Webber, S. 2016. "Climate change adaptation as a growing development priority: towards critical adaptation scholarship". *Geography Compass* 10(10): 401–13.

Webber, S. *et al*. 2022. "Financing reparative climate infrastructures: capital switching, repair, and decommodification". *Antipode* 54(3): 934–58.

Weber, I. 2021. *How China Escaped Shock Therapy: The Market Reform Debate*. Abingdon: Routledge.

Weber, I. & H. Qi 2022. "The state-constituted market economy: a conceptual framework for China's state–market relations". Economics Department Working Paper series. University of Massachusetts Amherst.

Weidmann, J. 2020. "Bundesbank chief: how central banks should address climate change". *Financial Times*, 19 November.

Weikmans, R. & J. Roberts 2019. "The international climate finance accounting muddle: is there hope on the horizon?" *Climate and Development* 11(2): 97–111.

Weikmans, R. *et al*. 2017. "Assessing the credibility of how climate adaptation aid projects are categorised". *Development in Practice* 27(4): 458–71.

Wemanya, A. *et al*. 2022. "Implementation of the Just Energy Transition Partnership in South Africa: lessons learnt for civil society organisations". Power Shift Africa, GermanWatch. https://www.germanwatch.org/sites/default/files/g7-g20_track-2_just_energy_africa_policy_brief_rev-1_met_1.pdf

Westfall, C. 2015. "Pacific catastrophe reinsurance pool mulls new 'tools' after country drops out". *Risk Market News*, 18 February. https://www.riskmarketnews.com/pacific-catastrophe-reinsurance-pool-mulls-new-tools-country-drops/

White, N. 2022. "Debt-for-nature swaps gain traction among developing countries". Bloomberg, 7 November. https://www.bloomberg.com/news/articles/2022-11-07/debt-for-nature-swaps-offer-option-for-developing-countries

White, N. 2023. "Adani shock rips through ESG funds as strategy fails test". Bloomberg.com, 13 February. https://www.bloomberg.com/news/articles/2023-02-13/adani-shock-rips-through-esg-funds-as-strategy-fails-latest-test

Wigglesworth, R. 2021. "The 'Tesla-financial complex': how carmaker gained influence over the markets". *Financial Times*, 23 November.

Williams, J., C. Robinson & S. Bouzarovski 2020. "China's Belt and Road Initiative and the emerging geographies of global urbanisation". *Geographical Journal* 186(1): 128–40.

Wilson, I. 2016. "Making enemies out of friends!". New Mandala, 2 November. https://www.newmandala.org/making-enemies-friends/

World Bank 2015. *Investing in Urban Resilience: Protecting and Promoting Development in a Changing World*. Washington, DC: World Bank.

World Bank 2019. *The World Bank Group Action Plan on Climate Change Adaptation and Resilience*. Washington, DC: World Bank.

World Bank 2021. *COVID-19 Energy Access Relief Fund Project Information Document* [PID]. Washington, DC: World Bank.

World Bank 2022. *State and Trends of Carbon Pricing 2022*. Washington, DC: World Bank.

World Bank, International Energy Agency, International Renewable Energy Agency, United Nations & World Health Organization 2022. *The Energy Progress Report 2022: Tracking SDG 7*. Washington, DC: World Bank.

Xue, Y. 2022. "China to relaunch voluntary emissions reduction plan. Here is why it is important". *South China Morning Post*, 31 January.

Yearwood, L. & B. McKibben 2020. "Opinion: want to do something about climate change? Follow the money". *New York Times*, 11 January.

Yusoff, K. 2013. "The geoengine: geoengineering and the geopolitics of planetary modification". *Environment and Planning A: Economy and Space* 45(12): 2799–808.

Zenghelis, D. & N. Stern 2016. "The importance of looking forward to manage risks: submission to the Task Force on Climate-Related Financial Disclosures". London School of Economics policy paper. https://www.lse.ac.uk/granthaminstitute/wp-content/uploads/2016/06/Zenghelis-and-Stern-policy-paper-June-2016.pdf

Zhang, S., P. Andrews-Speed & M. Ji 2014. "The erratic path of the low-carbon transition in China: evolution of solar PV policy". *Energy Policy* 67: 903–12.

Zhao, X., C. Wilson & B. Caldecott 2021. "The energy transition and changing financing costs". Oxford Sustainable Finance Programme. https://www.smithschool.ox.ac.uk/research/sustainable-finance/publications/The-energy-transition-and-changing-financing-costs.pdf

Zollmann, J. *et al.* 2017. "Escaping darkness: understanding consumer value in PAYGo solar". CGAP Access to Finance Forum, No. 13. https://www.cgap.org/sites/default/files/researches/documents/Forum-Escaping-Darkness-Dec-2017.pdf

INDEX